THE SINKING MIDDLE CLASS

THE SINKING MIDDLE CLASS

A POLITICAL HISTORY

DAVID ROEDIGER

To Paul --
Freedom now,

O/R

OR Books

New York · London

All rights information: rights@orbooks.com
Visit our website at www.orbooks.com
First printing 2020

Published by OR Books, New York and London

Library of Congress Cataloging-in-Publication Data: A catalog record for this book is available from the Library of Congress.

Typeset by Lapiz Digital. Printed by Bookmobile, USA, and CPI, UK.

paperback ISBN 978-1-68219-302-0 • ebook ISBN 978-1-68219-242-9

"And then perhaps this misery of class-prejudice will fade away, and we of the sinking middle class—the private schoolmaster, the half-starved free-lance journalist, the colonel's spinster daughter, . . . the jobless Cambridge graduate, the ship's officer without a ship, the clerks, the civil servants, the commercial travelers, and the thrice-bankrupt drapers in the country towns—may sink without further struggles into the working class where we belong, and probably when we get there it will not be so dreadful as we feared, for, after all, we have nothing to lose but our aitches."

—George Orwell, journalist and socialist

CONTENTS

Preface and Acknowledgments   1

One: Political Languages of Class in the Time
       of Endless Elections: An Introduction   7

Two: Macomb-Overs: Stanley Greenberg, the
       Middle Class, and Making Progressive
       Politics a White Place   26

Three: The Pretenses of a Middle-Class United States   85

Four: How the Left Has Lived With the Problem of
       the Middle Class   139

Five: Falling, Misery, and the Impossibilities of
       Middle-Class Life   177

Afterword: The Newest Rage? Listening to the
       White Working Class Joins Saving the
       Middle Class   224

Index   255

PREFACE AND ACKNOWLEDGMENTS

My childhood taught me that the middle class could be both a site of extreme misery and the location for labor militancy. That upbringing made it logical that I would write this book, questioning as it does the idea that the middle class ought to be saved and proposing that the practice of separating it, as a category, from the working class should be abandoned.

My grandfather had a "good working-class job," a concept that has decreasing meaning to young people. He worked hard in a quarry in a strongly unionized area. Three of my uncles had similar industrial jobs, in printing, electrical work, and pipefitting.

My dad bucked that trend. Clever and good with numbers, he took a white collar job at the quarry after navy service in World War II. Being employed in the office meant he was not in the union. He kept the books in the company's headquarters, right next to where limestone was crushed. He shared office space with the quarry's owner and his son, the quarry's heir apparent. In the next room several other clerks and technical workers toiled. The owners came and went at will; my dad clocked in and out. The owners showily kept copies of *Playboy* on their desks. My dad increasingly smuggled in whiskey bottles, having just enough un-bossed time, and for a while enough wits, to drink while doing a thankless, demanding job scrutinized by two bosses, each not ten yards away. That setup helped to kill him before age fifty. The owners dressed expensively in what would later be called business casual attire. My dad literally wore white collars, spending a fair amount to signal success. He was upwardly mobile. Nevertheless, materially, and most of the time spiritually, he fared far less well than his relatives in the skilled trades.

My mom, orphaned by age five, lost her mother during the birth of her twin brothers, and her father—together with his substantial income as a unionized railroad worker—in a work accident. Raised by a grandmother and two aunts, she came from a family that rose to the middle class and declined materially. One aunt processed accounts for a coal company; the other was a longtime telephone operator, a job eventually unionized and waged rather than salaried, but nevertheless carrying requirements of education and diction that placed it in a contradictory class location. Those mentors made sure that my mom studied for two years in a teacher's college before she reached nineteen. She had taught grade school for a quarter century before she managed to graduate from college, taking a course whenever she could. She made even less money than my dad. The professional teacher's organization that she joined saw teaching as a respectable middle-class profession. It arrayed itself against unions and strikes, until nearby work stoppages by militant unions attracted imitators. By mid-career—she taught forty-nine years—my mother was a local union and strike leader. It was only then that she secured something like a middle-class income.

I began thinking about this project more than a decade ago and contracted with OR Books for it shortly thereafter. Several new books of mine have appeared since then, while this one languished. In part, this reflects the fact that I increasingly find short books harder to write. Moreover, some of my other work was tied to anniversaries—for example, the sesquicentennial of emancipation in the United States—and I consequently gave them priority. But, as time passed, I also realized that the ground of US politics and society was shifting, and the design of this book needed to change as well. What had begun as a book interrogating the idea of "saving the middle class" increasingly required paying attention to how the center and right in both major parties couched appeals to the "white working class." Through long delays, my excellent editor at OR, Colin Robinson, remained encouraging while also leaving room for the time needed to rethink matters. This book would not exist without him.

Time to write has been generously provided by the University of Illinois Program for Research in the Humanities Fellowship, the Center on Democracy in a Multiracial Society Fellowship at the same university, the Distinguished Visiting Fellow Award at the Center on Sustainable Futures at the University of South Carolina, and generous course releases and research funds provided in connection with the Foundation Distinguished Professorship at the University of Kansas. Shorter-term fellowships at Queen Mary University in London, Hobart and William Smith Colleges, the University of Iowa, and New York University's Department of Social and Cultural Analysis also allowed me to share and develop ideas. At the University of Illinois, the Working Class History Group provided sustained opportunities to hear and share ideas, as has the Place, Race, and Space Seminar at the Hall Center for the Humanities at the University of Kansas. Librarians at the University of Illinois, University of Kansas, and at the Bentley Library at the University of Michigan were especially helpful.

Particularly formative discussions of work going into this book took place at the Million Artists Group in St.

Paul's East Side Freedom Library; at the Colloquium on "Whiteness: The Meaning of a Racial, Social, and Legal Construct" at Emory University's James Weldon Johnson Institute and the Carter Presidential Library; at the John Hope Franklin Institute at Duke University; at Brown University in public conversation with Tricia Rose; at the Kansas City Mid-America Arts Alliance; at the Du Bois Sesquicentennial Seminar at the University of Texas; at the Fairfield University American Studies Annual Lecture; at the Walter Rodney Lecture at Atlanta University; at the California American Studies Conference at Long Beach State University; at the St. Louis University American Studies Lecture; at the Swedish Association of American Studies in Stockholm; at the conferences of the Working Class Studies Association; at the Race, Whiteness, and Indigeneity Conference of the National Indigenous Research and Knowledges Network in Surfers Paradise, Queensland, Australia; at the Historical Materialism conferences in New York, Toronto, and London; and at the Rethinking White Societies Conference at the University of the Free State, Bloemfontein, South Africa.

While not drawing directly on my existing work, this book benefits greatly from editorial and blogger feedback from pieces appearing in the *Los Angeles Review of Books*, *Verso Blog*, *Critical Race and Whiteness Studies* (Australia), the *American Philosophical Association Newsletter on*

Philosophy and the Black Experience, Counterpunch, Journal of American Ethnic History, Cultural Critique, and *Historical Materialism.*

Among many colleagues and friends contributing ideas and critiques, special thanks go to Tim Engles, Ludwin Molina, Shawn Alexander, Roderick Ferguson, May Fu, Rebecca Hill, Robert Warrior, Andrew Zimmerman, John Abromeit, Brendan Roediger, Minkah Makalani, Donovan Roediger, Zachary Sell, Sterling Stuckey, Neil Roos, John Beck, Tom Klug, Graham Cassano, and Peter Linebaugh. Hannah Bailey and Zach Madison provided excellent research assistance. I chaired the American Studies Department at the University of Kansas while writing and could not have so easily done both without the work of Terri Rockhold. The influence of my colleague, partner, and sometimes co-author, Elizabeth Esch, is present throughout.

One

POLITICAL LANGUAGES OF CLASS IN THE TIME OF ENDLESS ELECTIONS: AN INTRODUCTION

> By the late 1990s, I sat through numerous sessions where well-known national pollsters instructed labor leaders to replace the word *working class* with *middle class* . . .
>
> —Jane McAlevey, organizer

I regretted the words as they left my mouth. The occasion, perhaps fifteen years ago, was a friendly gathering of scholars, students, union leaders, and union members. My prepared remarks were unexceptionable and warm. Somehow in delivering them, an extemporaneous reflection came out. I observed, perhaps a little scornfully, that while much writing on labor remained full of references to the working class, union appeals increasingly spoke of their constituency as the middle class. This seemed worth discussion, but the tone was too harsh for an aside. Some fidgeted. No one took the point up in the subsequent exchanges. Just when I was settling into regret, a labor journalist approached and told me something that made me feel raising the issue was worthwhile after all. She edited the publications of a state federation of labor whose style sheet—decidedly not reflecting her views—so mandated the use of "middle class" over "working class" that search-and-replace technology came into play.

Over the last thirty years, this book argues, self-serving, vague, and often empty political rhetoric regarding "saving the middle class" has provided the language for rightward political motion finding its way even into unions. Put forward first by the Democrats, it has debased how we understand social divisions in the United States and sidelined meaningful discussions of justice in terms of both class and race. In the last decade, the rise of an allied language tying political possibilities to the "white working class" has done much the same work in telling us why dramatic social change is impossible given the supposed, and supposedly understandable, defensiveness of a group named by a collective noun hardly better defined than the "middle class."

To insist on these points implies no golden age that we should yearn to recapture. The languages of mainstream electoral politics have offered only very loosely drawn conceptions of class, and still less that is useful on race and class at their intersection. The people, the yeomen, Americans, free laborers, the progressives, the forgotten men, and the Silent Majority, busily realizing Manifest Destinies, making New Deals and traversing New Frontiers—all left much unspecified in the interests of putting together winning coalitions. However, they did so in eras when electoral politics did not so thoroughly define the universe of all things political and preoccupy everyday life for so many—while fully alienating an equally massive number who often conclude that they couldn't care less about that thing called politics. Prior elections gave those in the United States a language vaguely defining and liquidating class every four years, not every day of the year. The story of the great modern Democratic conjuring trick of making the unspecified but clearly white middle class define the limits of possibility along austere neoliberal lines thus allows us to consider how the media and the candidates make such class terminology both a series of platitudes and a seemingly exciting insider's argot underpinning liberal warnings against going too far.

The New(s) Toy: Political Sound Bites of Class

"What characterizes consumer society is the universality of the news item," the theorist Jean Baudrillard wrote half a century ago. "All political, historical, and cultural information is received in the same—at once anodyne and miraculous—form of the news item."[1] The US writer Waldo Frank had anticipated Baudrillard by four decades, writing in *The Re-Discovery of America* that "THE NEWS IS A TOY"—that is, a seemingly wonderful novelty and one immediately requiring replacement by a new wonder.[2] To update this wisdom for the contemporary United States we would need to add that the "news item" is overwhelmingly the sound bite of alleged political news, and that "anodyne" must now be in boldface. Drowning in political news items, especially on television and in social media, we nevertheless have generated only the barest beginnings of a renewed radical political thought, almost all of it confined to electoral politics and to supporting candidates continuing a veneration of the middle class and, less volubly, discoursing on the need to pay attention to the "white working class."

The ease with which we assume that being interested in politics means being interested in election news contributes to the huge advantages in defining the commonsense of class and race held by those who follow the electoral

1   Jean Baudrillard, *The Consumer Society: Myths and Structures* (London: SAGE Publications, 1998), 33. For the chapter's epigraph, see Jane McAlevey, *No Shortcuts: Organizing for Power in the New Gilded Age* (New York: Oxford University Press, 2016), xvii; for the book's epigraph, see George Orwell, *The Road to Wigan Pier* (New York: Harcourt, Brace and Company, 1938), 263-64.

2   Waldo Frank, *The Re-Discovery of America* (New York: Duell, Sloan, and Pearce, 1947, originally 1929), 116ff.

cycle and its logic religiously. Elections now rarely seem anything but imminent and historic. We heard in 2018 of the most important election of our lifetime. As soon as it was over candidates announced for the infinitely more important 2020 presidential vote. Neither is the creep toward an omnipresent election cycle driven only by candidates, cable news, and the desperate need to raise money to campaign. Many of us *desire* those electoral news items, desperately wanting to be seen as the first to know them, and count that as being engaged in politics. People ask me if I heard what Chris Matthews or Rachel Maddow said last night and I can't always say "Of course not."

Against all the chatter, it is hard to understand the wisdom of the political scientist and class warrior Adolph Reed, Jr., who writes, "Elections are much more likely to be effective as vehicles for consolidating victories won on the plane of social movement organizing than as short-cuts or catalysts to jumpstart movements."[3] Reed's point here is overwhelmed by the self-perpetuating tendency to register the enthusiastic traffic in electoral news as itself a sign of a quickening of political action. Looking to 2020, the venerable left activists Carl Davidson and Bill Fletcher, Jr., warn sternly that the left must learn yet again

---

3   Reed, Jr., "Vote for the Lying Neoliberal Warmonger: It's Important." *Common Dreams*, August 18, 2016, at https://www.commondreams.org/views/2016/08/18/vote-lying-neoliberal-warmonger-its-important.

that "Electoral politics not a sideshow." The problem that Davidson and Fletcher, Jr. identify with centering elections is not that they are endless but that they end.[4]

Delivered in sound bites and tethered to candidates all about saving the middle class or listening to the white working class, most talk about national elections proves a poor vehicle for learning about social divisions. Neither does it energize imagination of what it might be possible to accomplish at the level of the community or workplace. Two decades ago, the logic ran that electing the Democrats came first, and was only then followed by card-check and other labor law reforms, and then organizing. Now you hear that it would be good to have a stronger labor movement membership in the service of electing Democrats as the end goal. Pulling activists from organizing campaigns to electoral ones usually goes unremarked and such reallocation may seem more exciting to the activists who are moved.

The very way that we see the working class narrows when electoral victory is the watchword. We struggle to remember those who choose not to vote, or who are prevented from doing so, as recently arrived and/or undocumented, as felons, as workers frequently moving around—that is, a substantial majority of poor and working

---

4   Davidson and Fletcher, Jr., "A Left Strategy for the 2020 Elections and Beyond," *Truthout* (April 21, 2019) at https://truthout.org/articles/aleft-strategy-for-the-2020-elections-and-beyond/.

people in the United States—when the assumption is that politics largely equals voting and talking about elections. In that sense the very composition of the working class is obscured, not only by politicians shoehorning so many working people into a simplified middle-class category, but also because those most urgently needing to organize live outside electoral politics. We lavish attention on the split, close in the recent past, between the Republican and Democratic votes of working-class whites, searching for deep meaning in small fluctuations while a larger share of this group does not vote. In pursuing electoral analyses, even radicals follow the example of TV pundits in relying on the most quickly available voting data to construct simplistic definitions of class that have little to do with social relations. Thus income—above or below $50,000 a year— or education—college or not—somehow define a class relationship.[5]

Donald Trump has helped assure that passionate embraces of electoral politics and its attendant drumbeat of saving the middle class seem urgent and meaningful. It is so hard to argue that he is just a garden-variety

5   For relatively sophisticated examples, see Nicholas Carnes and Noam Lupu, "It's Time to Bust the Myth: Most Trump Voters Were Not Working Class," *Washington Post,* June 5, 2017, https://www.washingtonpost.com/ news/monkey-cage/wp/2017/06/05/its-time-to-bust-the-myth-most- trump-voters-were-not-working-class/?utm_term=.81b1b0800a69   and Kim Moody, "Who Put Trump in the White House?" *Against the Current,* 186 (January-February, 2017), https://solidarity-us.org/atc/186/p4859/.

representative of one wing of the elite that there are, inevitably and not wrongly, even self-proclaimed anarchists who campaign against Trump.[6] Whether it is that he presents a definable fascist threat, that he winks at knowing that he provides a pole around which a growing alt-right and white nationalist movement accretes, or that he is just a loose racist talker emboldening other racists, a sexual predator, a packer of courts with reactionary judges, a jailer of children, and/or an authoritarian eager to suspend civil liberties, Trump so alarms us that politics as usual on the liberal side seems compelling even if we'd never otherwise speak of the middle class as the key to forward motion.

In the interminable run-up to the 2016 presidential election, my revolutionary friend, the late historian Noel Ignatiev, offered a fresh framing of the venerable left stances regarding elections—those being don't vote, vote for the less alarming major party, vote for a third, fourth or fifth party, or vote for such a small party only in states where the major party winner is a foregone conclusion. Ignatiev did not rehearse those choices. Instead, he challenged prospective voters to imagine that making

6   See Chris Crass, "Beyond Voting: Anarchist Organizing, Electoral Politics, and Developing Strategy for Liberation," *Colours of Resistance Archive* (originally 2004), http://www.coloursofresistance.org/508/beyond-voting-anarchist-organizing-electoral-politics-and-developing-strategy-for-liberation/ on twenty-first century anarchism and voting.

an electoral choice might be the least important political activity out there for them in the year and more of primaries and general elections to come. He allowed that he was himself a non-voter.[7] But he was now staking out a different position. However much people decided to mail in ballots, go to the polls, and even participate in campaigns, their priorities might usefully remain on the larger mix of political work that they were doing: aiding refugees and other border crossers, organizing, teaching, learning, supporting strikes, and getting people out of jail. Such a view deserves consideration not only in the interests of making the definition of politics broad, but also of tempering the illusions about class that elections enjoin.

Reverence for the electoral cannot change via eloquence, citations, whines, nor even frontal attack. Indeed, this book does not pretend to strike a decisive blow against the hegemony of the electoral. Instead it asks us to be aware of the costs to clear-thinking about class and race that viewing politics through electoral majorities creates. It seeks to renew left critiques of the middle class as a social formation itself wildly varied in class terms, as a site of misery, and as needing the presence of working-class movements (including movements of working-class people who also call themselves middle class) to save itself.

7   Noel Ignatiev, "To Those Who Believe in Voting," *Counterpunch*, May 12, 2015, https://www.counterpunch.org/2015/05/12/to-those-who-believe-in-voting/.

The Book and Its Chapters

Being late and wrong often works out fine. For all of the 2010s and a little before, I have nominally been working on this book. I first planned for it to appear in 2012 to coincide with a presidential election that I knew would be all about who could most loudly convince voters that he or she defended the middle class. When it became more urgent to instead finish a book pegged to the sesquicentennial of the self-emancipation of U.S. slaves—in the end four other books elbowed this one aside—there seemed little to fret about. Preoccupation with the fate of the middle class had only grown in recent experience. Even as I learned about complications and countertrends, there seemed little doubt that 2016's election would again follow hollow defenses of a middle class defined in such distended ways that it took in almost everybody.

But real life carried things in a different direction, with the term "middle class" for a moment less zealously claimed in presidential politics. The 2016 campaign's big winner, Donald Trump, preens as perhaps the modern political leader least interested in claiming affinity with the middle class and commonality with its experiences. While capable of uttering the phrases "middle class" and even "working class" at opportune times, he never tries to keep himself from bragging of his 1 percent status. Overemphasizing his self-made success and deemphasizing his debts, he seldom asks that we see him as anything but rich, if also allegedly close to rough-and-tumble construction workers. Hillary Clinton did hint at having experienced economic anxieties, both in her youth and somehow in the Clinton White House, but she proved far less able than her husband to speak as even an ersatz champion of the middle class. Bill Clinton had advanced the deft appeals to "middle-class dreams," described in the chapter that follows, by standing ever ready to hear white suburban angst regarding affirmative action, welfare, and crime, fashioning flirtations with racism and vague appeals to "economic" issues as a populism of society's white middle. Hillary Clinton had moved on from that.[8]

The avowedly socialist candidate, senator Bernie Sanders, most insistently positioned himself as the candidate of, and in some measure from, the middle class. Just as the recent campaigns against anti-union legislation in Michigan and Indiana conducted themselves as defenses of the middle class, with perhaps an added nod to defending "working families," the Democratic Party's left defended the middle class as it attempted to contest inequality. To complete the confusion, opinion polls showed

8   See http://money.com/money/4449015/hillary-clinton-economic-plan-middle-class-donald-trump/ for efforts to establish her middle class credentials; see also https://news.vice.com/en_us/article/zm7d85/hillary-clinton-told-wall-street-shes-kind-of-far-removed-from-the-middle-class and especially https://wikileaks.org/podesta-emails/emailid/3282.

more and more people identifying no longer as middle class but as working class—by some accounts the greatest percentage in recent U.S. history. This change, registering decline of "middle class" living standards and broader resentments, seemed a dream come true for radicals like myself. The problem was that those newly identifying as workers sometimes moved to the right when doing so, becoming Trump supporters and rallying around the idea that immigrants, not corporations, had pushed them downward. Such developments demand a book that raises questions about both listening to the white working class and saving the middle class.[9]

The chapters and arc of this short book are easily sketched. Four chapters and an afterword follow this introduction. Each is meant to be short enough to read in three or four coffee breaks. Chapter 2 introduces an unprepossessing figure who nevertheless is sometimes touted, not implausibly, as the central "progressive" figure of the last three dozen years. It sets his genius and his stark limits in the county that made him known and sought after. The man is Stanley Greenberg, a former more or less Marxist academic who became a central and centrist

9   See Bernie Sanders, *The Speech: On Corporate Greed and the Decline of Our Middle Class* (New York: Bold Type Books, 2015); for 2020, Sanders seems hopeful that the odd sound bite "The Middle Class Has a Right to Exist" might catch on. See his remarks under that title in the *Daily Mail*, February 23, 2019, https://www.dailymail.co.uk/video/news/video-1279006/Bernie-Sanders-Middle-Class-right-exist.html.

Democratic pollster and consultant, especially around the
1992 election. The place is Macomb County, Michigan, a
site of former strength of the most conservative region of
the United Auto Workers (UAW). That suburban Detroit
county had been the most Democratic one in the nation
in 1960. However, its residents had soon broken from such
a tradition, acting instead on an attraction to the proto-
alt-right and alt-white candidacy of George Wallace and
hatred for the peace and multiculturalist candidacy of
George McGovern.

In the '80s, the UAW hired Greenberg, who was
transitioning from university teaching and radical political
science to consulting, to figure out what had gone wrong and
how to bring what was being called the Reagan Democrat
back into the fold. Greenberg eventually polled the nearly
all-white county and returned frequently, indeed through
the 2016 presidential election. Especially after Bill Clinton
discovered and embraced his work, Greenberg promoted
Macomb County—seen from its white houses and not
its factories—as the key to election victories. Central to
his success was ambiguity. Macomb's voters were seen as
white and workers on the one hand, ennobled by their
labor and rightly concerned with straitening economic
circumstances. They were to be paid attention on the other
hand as a suburban white middle class, not as trade union-
ists. There being few economic fixes or even meager labor

law reforms on offer, the listening that Greenberg urged seized on racially coded issues: neighborhood schools, taxes, crime, and welfare, the last two of which the Clinton administration did deliver on with a vengeance. The sad genius of Greenberg and Clinton was to be able to promise to save the middle class—Greenberg's signature book on Macomb County was *Middle Class Dreams*—while placing a specifically white space at the center of what they called progressive politics. Macomb County and its unions would have to accept economic decline and ultimately the North American Free Trade Agreement in order to be saved from integration and social spending. Black voters would need to abjure far-reaching demands and accept defeats because keeping Macomb County Democratic had become a top progressive priority. Sliding from white working-class to middle-class appeals became a feature of various returns to Macomb County, right through the 2018 elections.

The third, fourth, and fifth chapters modestly propose that we not save the middle class. They regard the middle class as a problem, indeed a congeries of miseries not defined by a specifiable class location. Chapter 3 contests the idea that the United States is a middle-class nation, either now or over long stretches of its history. The term itself found little use until the last ninety years, and not commonly until the Cold War. Electorally, an obsession with courting the middle class appeared later still, from the 1990s onward at the national level. The strata we might retrospectively call the middle class of the nineteenth century (farmers, free professionals, and shopkeepers) differed utterly from those of twentieth (clerks, salespeople, employed professionals, and managers). The earlier un-bossed middle class seems a font of manly independence, distinctive by world historical standards. Ideologues can therefore invoke this mostly disappeared set of independent proprietors as the keys to the idea of American exceptionalism, a shining entrepreneurial example to the rest of humanity. In this way, the small sliver of entrepreneurs shapes imaginations of the middle class, as well as policy, obscuring the reality that most of the middle class works—and not at all independently. Indeed, they are the workers most overseen by supervisors and observed by customers, the employees whose personalities first became fully for sale. Moreover, in the present the United States is, by overdeveloped world standards, not at all a relatively equal society in which a fair share of work and income go to those in the middle.

Chapter 4 captures the sometimes conflicted, hamstrung, and supercilious—but also careful, impassioned, and humane—ways that the left has apprehended the middle class. The chapter makes no extravagant claims for radical tradition's interventions regarding the middle class, except in comparison to alternative approaches. It starts from

Marx's Marxism, noting his impatience with and political distrust of the middle class, except insofar as it was poised to slip into the working class and to be attracted by the labor movement's dynamism. Marx mostly had in mind a nineteenth-century middle class of small property holders and independent professionals, but in later writings he came to briefly glimpse a "new middle class" of paid functionaries of capital—managers, clerks, sales staff, accountants, and other workers around offices. His tendency to define the latter groups as doing "unproductive" work, and to describe them using the same terms as the propertied middle class—seen as the enemy of emancipation—imparted confusion and a certain enduring brittleness to left accounts of the middle class. However, twentieth-century Marxists also inherited a fierce need to study and understand the "problem" of the middle class. Beginning from material conditions, they most clearly saw how numerous workers with white collars had become. Especially in Germany (Emil Lederer and the Frankfurt School's efforts to understand the middle class and fascism) and the United States (Lewis Corey, C. Wright Mills, Barbara Ehrenreich, and Erik Olin Wright), the left wrestled with its inherited texts and incredible real-life complexities to produce remarkable insights. In particular, the differences between the "old" self-employed middle class and the "new" salaried one received the most productive attention from radical intellectuals, who also took the study of the middle class into the realm of psychology.

The fifth chapter acknowledges that older emphases on the falling of the middle class are important but insists that it is also the daily misery, and increasingly the sheer impossibility, of middle-class life that ought to command our attention. Quotidian miseries of those surviving in the middle class greatly complicate any political appeals to be their saviors. Middle-class people stood and stand in various relations to the production process, and the material experiences uniting them—debt, anxiety, segregation, and personality salesmanship—are hardly worth saving. The so-called decline of the middle class involves falling, to be sure, but also living in an untenable position before falling, peculiarly alienated at work, indebted and seeking satisfaction in joyless consumption. Equally, the great radical critics of middle-class life writing fiction, Herman Melville and Theodore Dreiser for example, saw middle-class existence as a soul-killing problem and site of precarity for those living the dream.

An afterword laments the recent resort to explaining Trump's election as the fault of the "white working class," who had been the middle class when it suited Democratic strategists. Believing that our present crisis is to be remedied by listening to white workers represents as dead an end as does seeking to save the middle class. Rhetorically both race-conscious and class-conscious, it adapts to an electoralism that, like Greenberg's middle-class dreams, disallows substantive policy discussion on those issues. Greenberg himself has recently cast matters more explicitly in terms of "white" and "worker." The most celebrated advocate of the idea that Trump won because Democratic elites lost touch with the "white working class," law professor Joan Williams, wants a new Bill Clinton specifically able to hear but not substantively speak for the interests of that group.[10] Like Greenberg in the 1990s, she sees the issues involved as ones on which the supposed conservatism of white workers, especially regarding immigration, must be respectfully heard and mentions unions hardly at all.

The afterword considers the work of Williams along with a number of recent political interventions concerning the white workers and the white working class. It asks how their auto-ethnographic and ethnographic gaze manages to see such white workers from a distance as alternately terrifying and understandable—a close match for the expectations of their readers and a foundation for the continuation of politics as usual. The concluding pages also

10 See David R. Roediger, "Who's Afraid of the White Working Class," *Los Angeles Review of Books*, May 17, 2017, https://lareviewofbooks.org/article/ whos-afraid-of-the-white-working-class-on-joan-c-williamss-white-working-class-overcoming-class-cluelessness-in-america/; and Joan C. Williams, *White Working Class: Overcoming Class Cluelessness in America* (Cambridge: Harvard Business Review Press, 2017).

query whether there is any "white working class," arguing instead that white is bound to get the emphasis when that usage is invoked. It looks back at histories of pairing white and worker, finding that the policy outcomes of such pairings have been retrograde ones regarding crime, incarceration, integration, welfare, and affirmative action, and have not led to the winning of class demands.

A preemptive word or two is perhaps in order. The book argues as strongly as I know how that we ought neither to save the middle class nor to pay attention to the white working class. It courts iconoclasm in those regards but it does not mean to embrace callousness. Certainly many white working people—I grew up with and go home to them—are afraid. They fear "falling" out of the middle class, falling ill in a society that sneers at safety nets, and falling behind on payments. They fear being "replaced" by immigrants and becoming "strangers in their own land" as some informants recently conveyed to the ethnographer Arlie Russell Hochschild.[11] But the land is not "their own," and neither a commitment to saving an indefensible system nor the premising of white workers' human claims on their epidermis will make any of us free or even secure.

---

11 Barbara Ehrenreich, *Fear of Falling: The Inner Life of the American Middle Class* (New York: Pantheon, 1989); Arlie Russell Hochschild, *Strangers in Their Own Land: Anger and Mourning on the American Right* (New York: New Press, 2016).

Two

MACOMB-OVERS: STANLEY GREENBERG, THE MIDDLE CLASS, AND MAKING PROGRESSIVE POLITICS A WHITE PLACE

> Is it possible politicians are turning to pollsters, consultants, and spin doctors not to better align themselves with shifting public sentiment but to . . . manage it?
>
> —Stanley Greenberg, pollster

We sometimes name "ages" of history after their reputedly towering figures: the Age of Jefferson, of Jackson, or of Lincoln. When the era itself was revolutionary or genocidal such naming surely misses forces from below and slights history's victims, but it has a kind of logic. It matches the outsized great man to the portentous historical moment. When the moment or the movement that is being described remains uncertain in its hold on history, identifying an age with its "great man" is considerably chancier.

It may be that the smaller, more underwhelming secondary leader better captures the stalemates and underlines the missing grandeur of such flatter eras. This chapter warms up with a brief account of how the sometimes plodding and ultimately tragic career of Herbert Hoover circuitously established him as the representative figure of his Progressive Era, even though the label scarcely fit him by his later life. That vignette prepares us to discuss the arguably "leading progressive" of our time, the Democratic pollster Stanley Greenberg, and his role in developing a logic of stalemate in which neither people of color nor working people generally have been able to make significant claims on the US state over the last three decades. Known intimately to political junkies and hardly at all to the general public, Greenberg developed skills, connections, and ideas over a varied career that enabled him to deploy the categories "middle class" and "white working class" interchangeably and with potent effect. More famous than his own name is that of Macomb County, Michigan, the almost all-white, mostly working-class area he established as the supposed "bellwether" of Democratic electoral success. From polling there, Greenberg has made an enduring case that disastrous Republican electoral victories could be fended off only by keeping demands for racial and gender justice meager. Such caution was required so as not to alienate working class whites whose worsening economic plight could not be much addressed but who could be listened to in their conservative views on race, tradition, and culture.

In 1975 the iconoclastic historian Joan Hoff Wilson attempted what might be read as a rehabilitation of Hoover. She subtitled her biography of him *Forgotten Progressive*. Allowing that few thought much or highly of the thirty-first president anymore, Hoff Wilson showed why that was both true and a little unfortunate. In her understatedly dramatic telling, Hoover's rise to becoming one of a handful of iconic progressive U.S. leaders in the 1920s was far less about him than his moment and world. Growing up in small town Iowa, he was "in no way memorable as a child" and "no less awkward as an adult." Orphaned by age nine, Hoover shuttled from relative to Quaker relative. His mother's itinerant Quaker preaching and a host of experiences with that religion in the Midwest and then the Far West left Bert, as he was called, eager to jettison religious strictures against smoking and drinking, naked ambition, and self-promotion. But Quaker ideals of order, moderation, and communities of interest remained.[1] Nothing in Hoover's academic record suggested he would attend an elite university. In fact, when he applied, Stanford was neither elite nor even a university. Instead, it was a

---

1   Joan Hoff Wilson, *Herbert Hoover: Forgotten Progressive* (Long Grove, IL: Waveland Press, 1992, originally 1975), 3 and 4-10. The chapter's epigraph is from Stanley B. Greenberg, *Dispatches from the War Room: In the Trenches with Five Extraordinary Leaders* (New York: St. Martin's Press, 2009), 5.

start-up that desperately needed students and therefore conditionally admitted Hoover to its inaugural 1891 class after he first failed the entrance exam. At Stanford he cared about student government but from behind the scenes, where his odd mannerisms were less on display. Still lackluster as a student, he developed interests in both business and mine engineering and did impress mentors, especially on the geology faculty.[2]

Most of Hoff Wilson's story concerns the rise of Hoover in international business and, more improbably, as a national hero and an exemplar of US progressive values. Hoover built a lucrative transnational engineering career based on improving the productivity of mines and miners. Especially influential, though far from universally successful, in South African, Chinese, and Australian ventures, he gained a reputation for engineering, managerial, and racial knowledge. Hoover won praise as the "world's highest-paid employee," an exalted title within the growing managerial stratum that helped birth a new middle class.[3] He got far more than rich. Globetrotting, entertaining with his feminist wife Lou Hoover, and holding out the promise that technical solutions and growth could eliminate conflict without

2   Hoff Wilson, *Herbert Hoover*, 10-12.

3   Elizabeth Esch and David Roediger, *The Production of Difference: Race and the Management of Labor in U.S. History* (Oxford University Press, 2012), 116-22; Hoff Wilson, *Hoover*, esp. 31-53.

addressing inequality, made him a celebrity and a symbol
for a progressive nation. When he coordinated relief efforts
during and after the First World War, Hoover became a
political figure whom progressives in both parties courted.
His main credential—a devotion to making all things effi-
cient and systematic—made him unknowable in terms of
party politics but emblematic of progressive and corporate impulses in both of them. As secretary of commerce in
the early 1920s, Hoover emerged as a Republican, but not
a conservative. He brought together industry leaders, and
sometimes labor and consumer groups, into countless conferences designed to plan production and profit efficiently,
without direct state coercion. His solid victory in the 1928
presidential election marked the triumph of a certain kind
of progressivism.[4] It soon all collapsed. In the face of the
stock market crash and a deepening depression, the meetings that looked like the epitome of progressive action in the
mid-'20s symbolized the ineffectual and uncaring image of
Hoover by the early '30s. By the time he was trounced in the
1932 presidential election, Hoover had taken a place on the
right as the center shifted left.[5]

I of course have no interest in shoring up the reputation of Herbert Hoover. Nor perhaps did Hoff Wilson aim to

---

4   Hoff Wilson, *Hoover*, 54-121; Joseph Kip Kosek, "Henry Ford for President!"
    History News Network, https://historynewsnetwork.org/article/138750.

5   Hoff Wilson, *Hoover*, 122-282.

do so as much as she wanted to remind readers of the ties of progressivism to corporate efficiency, business interests, and global expansion. However, Hoover's story does underline how the term "progressive"—like the "middle class" label given to the group sometimes said to provide the social base for progressive politics—is plastic enough to assume shifting shapes.

Stanley Greenberg is our era's emblematic, unprepossessing progressive, typifying a time of diminished political possibilities. The Greenberg moment ripened in the post–civil rights era when, radicals had long assumed, all sorts of political possibilities would open up based on African American votes and the defeat of that bulwark of reaction, the white Southern Democrat. Greenberg occupies the position of leading progressive by claiming mastery over understanding the categories of race and labor.

Greenberg theorized a middle class roughly interchangeable with an alleged white working class—their votes available for the mining in countless electoral campaigns. In the process, he made a suburban, almost entirely white Michigan county seem to be the key to all "progressive" possibility. His work in Macomb County turned on evoking an ignored middle class, assumptively white, when the need was to pretend that center-right Democratic appeals transcended identity politics. He identified a "white working class" rarely, when the desire was to talk about class without wrestling with what concretely would unite workers across color lines. So successful has the project of Greenberg and other Democratic centrists been that we have hardly appreciated the amount of ideological work that has gone into disciplining both the civil rights and labor movements to accept austerity and rollbacks while Democratics still campaign on the basis of racial justice and concern for a middle or white working class. Finally, Greenberg's incredible career resonates with Hoover's in that he is perhaps soon to be unrecognizable as a progressive as politics shifts to the center-left and he turns further to the right.

Class, Race, and Memory in the Making of a Progressive

George Stephanopoulos, who as communications director shared with Greenberg the "war room" in William Jefferson Clinton's 1992 presidential campaign, later praised his fellow warrior in these words: "No single strategist has done more to lay the foundation for modern progressive politics." Others echo such hosannas and the detailed oral histories Greenberg has given describe a life spent preparing to grasp the "leading progressive" mantle.[6] Because of his rise to the presidency, we know lots about Hoover's life via the

---

6   "About the Founders," *Democracy Corps*, undated, http://www.democracycorps. com/the-founders/.

often stern reminiscences of family, teachers, and friends and the digging of historians. Greenberg's story is overwhelmingly of his own invention. It is told especially in two wide-ranging, strategically self-deprecating, and wildly self-congratulatory histories produced for the Presidential Oral Histories Project of the University of Virginia's Miller Center. Small, frothy interviews and articles such as "Why Are You So Smart, Stan Greenberg?" add spice."[7]

Even across these asymmetries, similarities of the backgrounds of Hoover and Greenberg emerge. So do differences based on personal histories and on the changing character of what it takes to be a leading progressive, especially where claims to knowledge of race and class matter. Greenberg's early years position him to accept both that the Black freedom struggle held the moral high ground in US politics and that appealing to center-right white working-class voters led to Democratic Party success. So much is that the case for his recollections of his pre-college years that we might wonder if the child was the father of the man or vice versa. Greenberg grew up, he insisted, "in the city," and specifically in "a relatively poor neighborhood, an all-black

---

7   Noah Davis, "Why Are You So Smart, Stan Greenberg?" *Pacific Standard*, June 13, 2013, https://psmag.com/news/why-are-you-so-smart-stan-greenberg-61117. The main oral histories are "Stanley Greenberg (2005), Pollster," January 27, 2005, https://millercenter.org/the-presidency/presidential-oral-histories/stanley-greenberg-oral-history-2005-pollster and "Stanley Greenberg (2007), Pollster," October 11, 2007, https://millercenter.org/the-presidency/presidential-oral-histories/stanley-greenberg-oral-history-2007-pollster.

neighborhood" in Washington D.C. where, nonetheless, his orthodox Jewish extended family could easily walk to the synagogue.[8] He resembled Hoover both in being raised in a strong and somewhat isolated religious community and in being mostly indifferent to K-12 education.

Greenberg recalled making grade-school friends across the color line. "All of my friends were black," he maintained. This was somehow true despite so much of his family's social life centering on the synagogue, despite local public education being segregated in his primary school years, and despite his family quickly moving to a D.C. area he remembers as "mostly Jewish." After the *Brown v. Board of Education* desegregation decision he joined white classmates who took public transportation to a junior high that nominally "integrated" but kept whole classrooms Black and others white. He remembered white school crossing guards being menaced by Black young people but being himself protected from trouble by African American friends from the old neighborhood. His family soon removed to nearby Silver Spring, Maryland, where his dad worked as an engineer at the American Instrument Company. According to his oral history, a high school American Studies class then quickened his interest in both school and injustice. A school trip through the

---

8   "Stanley Greenberg (2005), Pollster," January 27, 2005, unpaginated.

Jim Crow South deepened these impulses. Greenberg was also in the orbit of a Jewish social justice group for a time until his family forbade it, fearing possible Communist presence might run afoul of requirements relating to government contracts on which his father worked. Greenberg expressed sympathy for a union at the firm where his dad worked and where he had a summer job, again meeting decisive family disapproval. According to his oral reminiscences, he went back into the city to help organize the great 1963 pro–civil rights March on Washington.[9]

There is every reason to approach Greenberg's recollections with caution in terms of fact and spin. My colleagues who lived in African American Washington, D.C. when Greenberg did, or who have studied that city's history, raise red flags about many of the details, from "all-black neighborhood" forward. Moreover, as they point out, the racial adventure story he offers obscures a much more standard one: his family lived in the city while schools were segregated, moved first within the city, and then suburbanized. The Greenbergs' intense commitment to orthodox Jewish faith added complexity, but not necessarily in the direction of rich interracial experience. Silver Spring is today an exciting, diverse community. It wasn't then. The unincorporated suburb expanded in the 1920s

9   Ibid.

and after with housing based on racially restrictive cove-
nants, some of which used language preventing transfer of
property to races "whose death rate is higher than that of
the white race." As the historian of race and space David
Rotenstein has written, "Silver Spring was a strictly segregated Southern town that vigorously resisted integration
well into the 1960s."[10] Greenberg reminisced ambiguously
that he "was very much in a racial culture" growing up, but
the one concrete example of white racism that he mus-
tered concerned working class whites at the factory where
he had a summer job—"people from Appalachia," specifically West Virginia.[11]

Likewise spun is the class position of Greenberg's own
family. They are variously placed among D.C.'s "poor" residents, among the "working class," and among the "lower
middle class" Jewish community to which both his mother
and his father provided religious leadership. Partly this
reflects that the father's job lay in what the late Marxist
sociologist Erik Olin Wright called "contradictory locations within class relations."[12] Not a college graduate but

10 Ibid and Rotenstein, "Silver Spring, Maryland Has Whitewashed Its Past,"
    History News Network, October 15, 2016, https://historynewsnetwork.org/
    article/163914. Thanks to the great historian John Bracey for discussions
    of race, neighborhood, and schools in Washington, D.C., in the 1950s and
    early '60s.

11 "Stanley Greenberg (2005), Pollster," unpaginated.

12 Erik Olin Wright, "Class Boundaries in Advanced Capitalist Societies,"
    New Left Review, 98 (July-August, 1976), 26 and 3-41. For Wright the

with post–high school education in engineering, his father combined ability, white advantage, and experience as a worker at Westinghouse to find a good professional job at American Instrument after failing as a small businessman. The Greenbergs both were and weren't like the Macomb County, Michigan, residents whom Stanley would later bring into the national spotlight. His family lived seemingly outside of US racial structures, finding their politics in synagogues rather than in polling places or social movements.[13] Sympathizing with Macomb County's suburban workers was nominally available as a result of his own suburban upbringing, but his capacity for understanding them owed more to academic study and political experience than acknowledged personal affinity. His focus on historical materialist ideas about class might have led to a more precise understanding of his family but, though it provided progressive credentials and ties to labor organizations that made his work in Macomb County possible, his interest in Marxism was not sustained.

contradiction is not simply that the father moved from entrepreneurship to waged and salaried labor or that he was in a skilled professional job without a college degree. The engineer's bossed but necessarily somewhat autonomous job itself contained contradictions for Wright.

13 "Stanley Greenberg (2005), Pollster," unpaginated.

The Young Progressive and His Conservative Mentors

Due regards to high school American Studies, but credit for the flowering of Stanley Greenberg as an intellectual and a political actor belongs to Ohio's Miami University. Credit also goes to Yale and Harvard, where he encountered both conservative mentors and a left insisting on a frank confrontation with class in ways that would later allow him to make sweeping claims to know just what white workers were (in)capable of. He followed his more athletic, charismatic, scholarly, and tall older brother, Edward, to Miami. Both found their ways to political science, first as undergraduates, then as doctoral students, then as professors.[14] Although he would later credit Robert F. Kennedy's hopes for interracial organization of the poor as decisive in his political evolution, at other junctures he referred to an earlier attraction of John F. Kennedy. In any case, Greenberg was a Young Democrat from his undergraduate days at Miami, where he was also a leader in student government. As the anti-war movement grew, he concentrated his campus politics on questions of the university assuming parental responsibilities dictating student housing choices, especially by keeping women students out of off-campus apartment housing. His political science internships focused on the Democratic Party and electoral campaigns. In 1964, as a Democratic intern, he

14   Ibid. and Davis, "Why Are You So Smart, Stan Greenberg?" unpaginated.

wrote a memo supporting the war on Vietnam, though he soon came to question that support.[15]

Insofar as Greenberg arrived at his doctoral program at Harvard as a self-described "mainstream Democrat," it is noteworthy that he came, over the next twenty years, to produce significant radical political science scholarship. He moved in this direction in nothing like a straight line. In 1964, with friend-of-friend access to Lyndon Johnson's family, he attended the Democratic National Convention as a most enthusiastic Johnson supporter. He remembers sympathies with the Mississippi Freedom Democratic delegation picketing the convention over Jim Crow voting and becoming a protester who nevertheless then went inside to enthuse over Johnson. The same willingness to split differences cheerfully characterized his graduate student experience as well. Moving left, including on the war, and taken especially with Bobby Kennedy's vision of what Greenberg thought of as Black and "ethnic Catholic" unity, he nonetheless worked at Harvard with James Q. Wilson as his doctoral supervisor. The arch-conservative Edward Banfield, Wilson's own mentor, helps round out his dissertation committee. Wilson was for the moment still a Democrat, and his work on amateur versus professional political participation made him a logical adviser for

15 "Stanley Greenberg (2005), Pollster," unpaginated; Greenberg, "Unlearning the Lessons," unpaginated.

Greenberg. The latter had secured a paid consultancy evaluating the effect of the Great Society Office of Economic Opportunity (OEO) anti-poverty programs—his qualification being that he conducted a modest mail survey as part of his senior thesis at Miami. The research examined political participation by the poor in a hundred cities. Greenberg drew on the data in his doctoral dissertation.[16]

By 1974, Greenberg's doctoral work had become his first book, *Politics and Poverty: Modernization and Response in Five Poor Neighborhoods*. He was a young faculty member at Yale; OEO wobbled on its last legs with Banfield serving as consultant to the Nixon administration during the dismantling of the agency; James Q. Wilson had joined Banfield as an intellectual darling of the right. Banfield's excruciating earlier book, *The Moral Basis of a Backward Society* encapsulated its pessimistic and victim-blaming argument in its very title. By the mid-'70s, Wilson had concluded that policing and prison, not welfare, were what the state most urgently needed to provide to the poor. Indeed, Wilson is credited with inspiring "broken windows policing." He produced the huge and extravagantly subtitled *Crime and Human Nature: The Definitive Study of the Causes*

16 James Q. Wilson, "A Life in the Public Interest," *Wall Street Journal*, *September 21, 2009*; James Q. Wilson, *The Amateur Democrat: Club Politics in Three Cities* (University of Chicago Press, 1962); Greenberg, "Unlearning the Lessons," unpaginated; "Stanley Greenberg (2005), Pollster," unpaginated; Jim Crumer, "Banfield's Back," *Harvard Crimson*, August 1, 1975.

of Crime in 1985 in concert with the white supremacist psychologist Richard Herrnstein. Not surprisingly, the left sharply attacked both of Greenberg's mentors.[17]

Politics and Poverty effectively established limited distance between Greenberg's views and those of powerful, but in liberal circles increasingly infamous, teachers. He proceeded with great empirical detail, fashioning limited alternatives to the grim views of the poor as the ineffectual, apolitical, and dysfunctional people who populated the works of Wilson and Banfield. Developing and using extensive data, especially on attitudinal matters, he argued for there not being any one story but lots of particular and local ones. In addition to his own mentors, the influential and controversial 1965 report by Daniel Patrick Moynihan on the African American family had argued that oppression and deprivation left the poor unable to act on their own behalf. Greenberg concluded that this was sometimes more true—"hillbillies" were portrayed as bereft of cultural resources for problem-solving—and sometimes less true. Banfield had grouped all of humanity

---

17   James Q. Wilson and George L. Kelling, "Broken Windows: The Police and Neighborhood Safety," *The Atlantic*, March, 1982, https://www.theatlantic.com/magazine/archive/1982/03/broken-windows/304465/; Wilson and Herrnstein, *Crime and Human Nature: The Definitive Study of the Causes of Crime* (New York: Simon and Schuster, 1985). For reception, see Robert A. Beauregard, *Voices of Decline: The Postwar Fate of U.S. Cities* (New York: Routledge, 2002), 159-76. See also William Muraskin's rollicking review essay "The Moral Basis of a Backward Sociologist: Edward Banfield, the Italians, and the Italian-Americans," *American Journal of Sociology*, 74 (May, 1974): 1484-1496.

deemed "not lower class" as "normal," with the poor so in
search of speedy gratification as to be deemed "pathologi-
cal."[18] Only some of the poor fit that description, Greenberg
countered. In most of the places studied, Greenberg found
political networks operating. Goals continued to be artic-
ulated, even amidst misery, and an orientation toward the
future survived. Mexicans, he thought, kept hope alive on
far different grounds than did the "alienated," and in some
places violence-accepting Blacks, such as those on the east
side of Detroit. Where women and family were concerned,
Greenberg was far more reticent, eschewing any mention
of Moynihan's contention that a "tangle of pathology"
characterized Black family life. Greenberg later regarded
such a view as not wrong but one-sided. It failed to balance
"culture" and "economics" as factors of equal power."[19]

 Greenberg's limited challenge to received wisdom
left much of the approach of his mentors intact. Those

18 Banfield as quoted in Chaim Isaac Waxman, *The Stigma of Poverty: A
Critique of Poverty Theories and Policies* (New York: Pergamon Press, 1983),
13; Greenberg, *Politics and Poverty: Modernization and Response in Five Poor
Neighborhoods* (New York: John Wiley and Sons, 1974), esp. 75-103.

19 Stanley Greenberg, "Unlearning the Lessons of Hillbilly Elegy," *American
Prospect Longform* (January 8, 2019), https://prospect.org/article/unlearn-
ing-lessons-hillbilly-elegy; Greenberg, "From Crisis to Working Majority,"
The American Prospect, Fall 1991, https://prospect.org/article/crisis-work-
ing-majority; Greenberg, *Politics and Poverty*, 49 ("resignation") and passim.
It is of course not the case that Appalachian migrants were incapable of political organization. See, for example, Kathy Kahn, *Hillbilly Women: Struggle
and Survival in Southern Appalachia* (New York: Avon, 1973); Amy Sonnie
and James Tracy, *Hillbilly Nationalists, Urban Race Rebels and Black Power:
Community Organizing in Radical Times* (New York: Melville House, 2011).

strands were taken up at later junctures, especially in commentaries that entertained as reasonable the Macomb County residents' pathologizing of nearby Black Detroit. Indeed even at the level of defense of anti-poverty initiatives, *Politics and Poverty* proved agnostic, not least when it quoted community organizer Saul Alinsky's not-quite-clear but apparently irresistible remark on the "pornography" of anti-poverty initiatives.[20] The book's five case studies promised rich local texture based in part on political economy and the San Jose/Chicano report delivered on that promise. But the examples are so plainly focused on studying narrowly "racial" cases (Appalachian white, Northern African American, Southern African American, and Chicano) that reductive readings were unavoidable.[21]

In a recent review essay, Greenberg put on display some of *Politics and Poverty*'s enduring problems. The essay took on J.D. Vance's blockbuster exercise in victim-blaming, *Hillbilly Elegy*. Greenberg quickly conceded that Vance was right about the pathologies of the "hillbillies," citing his own, now very old, book. The Appalachian migrant community that he had studied in Hamilton,

---

20 Stanley Greenberg (2005), Pollster," unpaginated; Greenberg, *Politics and Poverty*, esp. 169-70, including the Alinsky quotation, and passim.

21 The exception is that Greenberg did establish differences, very loosely based on political economy, among Black neighborhoods in Chicago and Detroit. See Greenberg, *Politics and Poverty*, 75-6 for the quote and esp. 53-72.

Ohio, suffered from "fatalism, personal impotence, limited time perspective, disorganization and apathy that combine to suppress any collective political urge." Their beliefs and participation did not rise above a "politics of resignation." Greenberg levelled this indictment against "hillbillies" across time and space. Vance's disdain for Appalachian culture was "painfully accurate," his review maintained. But, Greenberg added, there was no reason to use that dysfunction to cast suspicion on similar failings of the "white working class" on the whole, which he sees as proud, political, and planful, at least until jobs are lost. Greenberg's recent recollections of *Politics and Poverty* themselves describe not so much a rich variety of different cities but a handful of racial/regional types of responses, which distinctly can be ranked in terms of efficacy and modernity.[22]

Strangely, at the beginning and end of *Politics and Poverty*, a very different book attempts to emerge. The start features the possibility of the rise of "radical political man," acting to respond to the indignities of dispossession and exploitation. The language is often stirring, though the hardest-hitting passages are in the voice of a vaguely identified someone who "expects, or at least hopes for, a

---

22 All the quotes come from Greenberg, "Unlearning the Lessons," save the passage ending in "collective political urge" and "politics of resignation," which are from Greenberg, *Politics and Poverty*, 75-76 and 49, respectively.

radical response to oppression," rather than squarely in Greenberg's voice. "Radical political man" is only momentarily imagined as a rational and modern political actor in the book. The radical is "apt to endorse bizarre forms of political expression, such as sit-ins or marches." In less than a page, radical political man is ushered offstage, and "liberal political man" takes over. The latter knows misery but responds "pragmatically," taking what is on offer from the political system. He—I follow Greenberg's relentlessly gendered language here—"views the ballot box with some reverence" and deplores those seen as "disruptive." Radical political man is absent for upwards of two hundred pages. However, in spots there are brief evocations of radical ideas, or at least quotations from Marx on alienation and class consciousness. Such passages sit oddly against the book's decidedly non-Marxist reliance on the category of the "lower class" to structure its arguments.[23]

Such brief Marxist quotations surely do not prepare the reader for the book's astounding, ultra-left conclusion, in which Greenberg confesses a desire to have been able to write a volume discovering radical political men. The brief conclusion to the book begins by offering a Goldilocks problem to the reader. For the migrating "lower" classes that the book studies, three twentieth-century "scenarios"

---

23 Greenberg, *Politics and Poverty*, 2 ("bizarre forms"), 3 (quotes on "liberal political man"), 75-103 (on the "lower class"), 108-09, and 195-200.

were possible. They could have remained "indifferent and uninvolved" where politics was concerned; they could have "become power brokers . . . tinkering and bargaining for their share"; or, they could have refused to "tinker" and instead entered a radical "confrontation with history."[24] The middle alternative, neither too hot nor too cold, was, according to Greenberg, the choice of those whom he had studied. Though posed as a continuum of possibilities, In reality, Greenberg offered in these scenarios a Manichean choice. In a way that structured the very design of the book, he pitted the feckless mass mired in a culture of poverty against the liberal political man. Arguing instead for differences among groups and for an exceptional, dysfunctional case among Appalachian whites, Greenberg hesitantly portrayed the poor as rational and modern political actors.

Early and late in the book, however, he adds brief material on a second stark opposition, between the liberal poor whom he documented and the radical poor whom he alternately caricatured and longed for. By the last two pages, the longing becomes overwhelming. Greenberg very frankly worries that the "limits of explanation" in his project might outstrip its accomplishments. "Our work has not been trivial [nor] without possible consequence," he wrote

24 Ibid, 206–07.

with sudden modesty, but it left much "unexplained," especially regarding the disparities between communities and the under-theorized connection between belief and action. Tied to electoral politics, his own investigations had been insufficiently "demanding of history" because they were too tethered to examining options reflecting the thin possibilities on offer in US politics and in US political science. Perhaps, Greenberg mused, the poor were favorably disposed toward the "formation of cabals, correspondence societies . . . conspiracies" and the seizure of factories—or they would have been if not for the "failure of revolutionary politics." He concluded that the problem lay in his studying places and times in which the range of political differences that his surveys captured was so small. That range, he reckoned, stretched from one to three instead of—as he wished—from one to ten.[25] In New Haven, Connecticut, and then in South Africa, he would soon find expanded ranges of possibility. Greenberg held on to those dreams of possibility briefly before leaving academic Marxism for political consulting, in which the range was again narrow and, by the time the road reached Macomb County, Michigan, had dropped down into negative numbers.

Whether writing a liberal book within a conservative framework or adding a minor revolutionary chord wishing

---

25 Ibid., 206-29, with quotations at 226 ("limits," "cabals," and "trivial"), 228 ("demanding"), and 229.

that infinitely more were possible, Greenberg produced a strikingly judgmental book, even when absolving some of the communities studied. In comparing Black sites of research, the question of willingness to use "violence" is especially crudely drawn. This imperial and empirical tone, suggesting a secret knowledge among liberals of the limits of what was feasible, would prove a great asset in his work for the Democratic Party in Macomb. By then this self-assurance had bonded with confidence born of a brush with left political forces committed to a belief that they could know "the left wing of the possible."[26]

Another Progressivism: Academic Marxism, the South African Revolution, and the Democratic Party

Greenberg sped through his doctoral research at Harvard, and as the '70s began, he moved with his first wife and their twins to New Haven, where he took up a tenure-track job at Yale. The city and the campus were intensely politicized spaces. 1970 saw the trial and fiercely fought defense campaign of Black Panthers charged with the murder of a

---

26 Emphasis on "the left wing of the possible" is most associated with the work of the far leftist turned reformist socialist Democrat Michael Harrington, especially through the 1960s, '70s, and '80s. during that time, as journalist Victor Navasky wrote, Harrington's fuller goal became to discover "the left wing of the possible within the Democratic Party." See Navasky, "The Left Wing of the Possible," *New York Times*, May 28, 2000. On violence, see Greenberg, *Politics and Poverty*, esp. 13-14, 63-77, 106-16, 160-72, and 202-11.

suspected police informer. In 1972, Greenberg coordinated
New Haven activities in George McGovern's spectacularly
unsuccessful left liberal Democratic presidential campaign. Attempting to negotiate the "high barrier between
academia and politics," he seemed to be on a trajectory
leading to increasingly radical political conclusions that
might end in advocacy of socialism, especially in his
work in South Africa.[27] It took him instead to center-right
Democratic Party politics and the discovery of the (white)
middle class in Macomb County. Insofar as we can briefly
suspend our knowledge of that destination, we might
more fully appreciate Greenberg's journey, which was not
his journey alone.

New Haven hosted a strong labor movement centered
on strikes and organizing on the Yale campus and beyond.
So much was labor part of local life and politics that when
the legendary local organizer Vince Sirabella ran an insur-
gent campaign for mayor in the early '70s—Greenberg
later called it, with some overstatement, a "Labor Socialist
challenge to the machine"—Yale law student Bill Clinton
headed Sirabella's voter registration committee. A small
Communist Party remained active in the city's Democratic
Party politics and in labor struggles under a "progressive"
banner. Also active in the Sirabella campaign was Rosa

---

27   "Stanley Greenberg (2005), Pollster," unpaginated; Greenberg, *Dispatches from the War Room*, 118-19.

DeLauro, who would soon become Greenberg's second wife and the longtime Democratic US representative for New Haven and its surrounding areas. Through DeLauro and on his own, Greenberg became active in labor causes, befriending the dynamic young radical hotel and restaurant organizer John Wilhelm, with whom he co-taught classes at Yale. The organizing campaign for Local 34 at Yale was run in part out of the basement of Greenberg's house.[28]

Greenberg's fellowship in South Africa in 1973 coincided with major strikes, especially while he was based in Durban. His second book project, a broad comparative study of race, class, and politics in the United States, Northern Ireland, Israel, and South Africa, was taken over in its largest and best sections by the South African story. The Marxist analysis that would frame *Race and State in Capitalist Development: Comparative Perspectives*, published in 1980, reflected close contact with and deep admiration for the Congress of South African Trade Unions, radical pro-labor intellectuals, and movements in which Communists played pivotal roles. The book exemplified a mature grasp of political economy based on a sharp understanding of land and power. It quoted Marx

---

28 "Stanley Greenberg (2005), Pollster," unpaginated for the quote; for the context, Julius Getman, *Restoring the Power of Unions: It Takes a Movement* (New Haven: Yale University Press, 2010); Zach Schwartz-Weinstein, "On Bill and Hillary's First Date in 1971, They Crossed a Picket Line," *In These Times*, February 9, 2016, http://inthesetimes.com/working/entry/18841/hillary_rodham_bill_clinton_and_the_1971_yale_strike.

and Marxist classics—by Lenin and, especially, the Italian Communist Antonio Gramsci—both to settle questions and to talk back to the texts. His taking up of challenges regarding how to think through categories of class and the state alongside those of race contributed much. "The problem of persistent racial conflict and domination," the earliest pages averred, "is at the center of this research." Back at Yale, Greenberg began offering classes on "Marxian Political Economy and the Social Sciences" and on "Race and Ethnic Conflict in Southern Africa." Looking back three decades later, Greenberg derided *Race and State in Capitalist Development,* by far his best book, for its "inelegant" title and "indecipherable" content. How he got to that judgment and how he embraced Macomb County are halves of the same walnut.[29]

Two setbacks in life sped Greenberg's move to a far more centrist course. The first came when the "high barrier" separating academia from politics "took a knock." He was denied tenure at Yale. His later interviews claim that he was "pretty indifferent" to the decision. However, they also betray how much trouble Greenberg has had in letting go of discussing it, and justifiably so. The decision came from the newly appointed Yale president, A. Bartlett Giamatti,

---

29 Greenberg, *Race and State in Capitalist Development: Comparative Perspectives* (New Haven: Yale University Press, 1980), ix-x, 73-74, 115, 116-18, and passim.

who proved over time to be an adversary of both Local 34 and of divestment of Yale from investments in South Africa. Greenberg's recollections emphasize the technical violations in the tenure process, errors which he thought laid the basis for a lawsuit even as he moved in a different direction. He arranged to head a Rockefeller Foundation initiative on human rights in South Africa, but while celebrating the publication of *Race and State in Capitalist Development* in a private home, he was spied upon and overheard saying that international investment did not mitigate the evils of apartheid. The South African state blocked his Rockefeller work and also attacked his Ford Foundation relationships. Ultimately, there were negotiations, and Greenberg was able to stay on at Yale for another decade in a variety of Ford Foundation-funded research on South Africa and in adjunct positions in American Studies and African American Studies. But for a critical time in 1980, Yale and apartheid had each in its own way assured that he would have time on his hands and reason to think of a new career. [30]

As Greenberg faced these two career difficulties, DeLauro was managing the campaign of Christopher Dodd, the mainstream Democratic congressman seeking

---

30 "Stanley Greenberg (2005), Pollster," unpaginated; Greenberg, *Dispatches from the War Room*, 19; Robert T. McFadden, "Giamatti, Scholar and Baseball Chief, Dies at 51," *New York Times*, October 2, 1989, https://www.nytimes.com/1989/09/02/obituaries/giamatti-scholar-and-baseball-chief-dies-at-51.html.

a Connecticut US Senate seat. Greenberg wrote a memo that impressed Dodd, who fired his existing pollster. Dodd preferred Greenberg, who came with the added benefit that he worked "for free." Recalling that he'd "never done any polling in a political campaign," Greenberg back-handedly credited his apartheid victimizers for his new career, soon to be centered on saving the middle class. "But for the intelligence service for the South African government who bugged my presentation," Greenberg wrote, he might have remained an activist academic researcher.[31] He did for a time remain one, but in South Africa, where the Black trade union movement continued to inspire him, where he had a role in fighting for curbs on US corporate investments in the apartheid state, and where he continued to defend a broadly Marxist analysis. As late as 1987, when he published *Legitimating the Illegitimate: State, Markets, and Resistance in South Africa*, he issued a rousing call for a new society grounded in the activities and imaginations of those in the townships.[32] In the United States, however, Greenberg had by then succeeded mightily as a pollster and consultant. Joseph Lieberman, running for the US Senate from Connecticut from the right of his

31 "Stanley Greenberg (2005), Pollster," unpaginated.

32 Greenberg, *Legitimating the Illegitimate: State, Markets, and Resistance in South Africa* (Berkeley: University of California, 1987), 201; Greenberg, *Dispatches from the War Room*, 16, 115, and 447.

Republican opponent, would soon be his most famous client. Greenberg's changing fortunes stemmed very much from his discovery of Macomb County, Michigan, in 1985.[33]

Greenberg, Macomb County, and the Erasure of Race and (Anything Except Middle) Class

According to his own reminiscences, Stanley Greenberg went to Macomb County after the comprehensive Republican victories in the 1984 presidential election. He discovered the wayward Republican-voting Reagan Democrat, listened to him (it was usually a him), and, over fierce opposition, persuaded the Democrats by 1992 to attract the Reagan Democrat back into the progressive fold. Collected in his 1995 book *Middle Class Dreams* (*MCD*), his section on Bill Clinton in *Dispatches from the War Room*, and in the documentary film *The War Room*, Greenberg's stories of Macomb County mix personal triumph and national salvation promiscuously.[34] However, read with a healthy dose of skepticism, the stories become different and more compelling. They illuminate how issues of race, class, and power came to be effaced even by those most

33 "Stanley Greenberg (2005), Pollster," unpaginated.

34 Greenberg, *Dispatches from the War Room*, passim; Stanley B. Greenberg, *Middle Class Dreams: The New American Majority* (New York: Times Books, 1996, originally 1995); *The War Room*, directed by Chris Hegedus and D.A. Pennebaker, appeared from October Films in 1993.

claiming credit for discussing them electorally in the neo-liberal United States.

Greenberg did not by himself discover the Democratic strategy that made Macomb County the dead center of how the party could enduringly finesse race and class issues—just as Hoover did not invent the combination of technical knowledge, claims to expertise in managing colonized and racialized workers, and infusions of capital that made him famous. Like so many geniuses, Hoover and Greenberg reassembled and marketed. The latter, for example, did not coin the term "Reagan Democrat"[35]—it had been used in the 1970s—but did popularize it as the descriptor of the working class, trade union, white, beleaguered, ignored, presumptively male figure who turned from New Deal loyalties to vote for Ronald Reagan in the 1980 and 1984 elections. Writers had come to address working class conservatism long before Greenberg. Pete Hamill, the talented journalist of the underdog, had been warning of the volatility and alienation of the "white lower middle class," as the title of his most famous article on the subject put it in 1969, although the cover of the issue of *New*

35 "Reagan Democrat," *Oxford Dictionaries* (accessed March 25, 2019), https://en.oxforddictionaries.com/definition/us/reagan_democrat; Michael Rogin, "Politics, Emotion, and the Wallace Vote," *British Journal of Sociology*, 20 (March, 1969): 27-49; Pete Hamill, "The Revolt of the White Lower Middle Class," *New York*, April 14, 1969, http://nymag.com/news/features/46801/; see also Joseph Kraft, "The Revolt of the Lower Middle Class," *San Francisco Examiner*, June 15, 1968.

York containing the piece portentously changed its title to "Rising Anger of the White Working Class." The George Wallace candidacies of 1964, 1968, and 1972 surfaced the volatility in working-class whites' voting patterns, seen in the returns themselves and, even more clearly, in how the returns were oversimplified.

Nor were changes in Macomb County flying under the radar before Greenberg's arrival. In the 1972 Democratic primary, Wallace won with a larger vote total than McGovern achieved in the general election, with both elections occurring during a bitter period of organized and disorganized racism in response to busing designed to integrate schools.[36] In 1980, the left newsmagazine *In These Times* had received articles from their political reporter regarding the conservatism of Macomb County workers. When Michigan overwhelmingly voted for Reagan again in 1984, both the United Auto Workers regional leadership and the head of the state Democratic Party regarded Macomb County as diagnostic of their crisis. It was for that very reason that union leadership agreed to join a Democratic Party request to invite and fund a Greenberg visit in 1985 to figure out what had gone so very wrong.[37]

36 David Riddle, "Race and Reaction in Warren, Michigan, 1971 to 1974: 'Bradley v. Milliken' and the Cross-District Busing Controversy," *Michigan Historical Review* 26, Fall 2000, 1–49.

37 Zack Stanton, "The Bellwether County That Explains Eminem and Kid Rock," *Politico Magazine*, October 11, 2017, https://www.politico.com/

Also already in place, though often now associated with Greenberg's rise, was the technique of the "focus group" poll, one gathering groups of people associated demographically and often interviewing them collectively for an extended period, an expensive practice that had previously been used more by Republicans.[38]

The most tantalizing phrase in Greenberg's best-known writing on Macomb County, the 1995 book *Middle Class Dreams* (*MCD*), describes the county as "an exaggeration, a caricature of America." The phrasing offered a clever hedge in that it made the location seem hyper-representative of the nation and fully strange at the same time. Credentialing the county in that way relied on the view that it "so thoroughly identified with the currents that swept the nation . . . following the Second World War." That is, its residents were "just working Americans who made their way to the suburbs," a migration apparently all about American Dreaming and not about race. Macomb County certainly was not representative. It was too Catholic and too unionized to be typical as a suburb, and at that time too prosperous. Despite the accelerating

magazine/story/2017/10/11/eminem-kid-rock-macomb-county-politics-215700. On the 1980 stories, see "John Judis to David Roediger," email in Roediger's possession (December 10, 2019).

38 On prior focus groups on the Republican side see "Stanley Greenberg (2005), Pollster," unpaginated; John Judis, "Exposing the Opposition in 2016 May Be the Best Strategy," *The Democratic Strategist*, June 5, 2015, https://thedemocraticstrategist.org/2015/06/exposing_the_opposition_in_201/.

decline of the auto industry, its average income exceeded by half again the average for the nation. It also had too many boat owners, a category in which the county was said to have led the nation. The county's population moved from about 406,000 in 1960 to over 717,000 in 1990. This boom reflected the emptying out of white Detroit as a result of the 1967 rebellion, of integration of schools, of fear of crime, and of Black political power, not to mention the relocation of jobs. The idea that Macomb County went from being the most Democratic suburban county in the 1960s to one of the least Democratic in the 1980s, as inhabitants shifted views in light of the Democrats' racial liberalism and tax policies, is not quite accurate. Many of Macomb's families in the 1980s were not there in the 1960s. Macomb's overwhelming whiteness made it unrepresentative of the United States and still less of the Democratic electorate, regardless of how many times Greenberg stated that "these were America's workers."[39]

To cast Macomb County as an exaggeratedly "American" place involved impressive ideological work, based on the assumption that white identity politics in the United States need not speak its name. Such manipulation effaces both race and class. The land and history of Macomb County itself carried profound racial baggage.

---

39   Greenberg, *Middle Class Dreams*, 26, 27, 19, and 23-54 passim; "Macomb Voters Turn from Dems," *Detroit Free Press*, October 6, 1985.

Home to the Ojibwe long before colonial settlement, the
county took its name from that of the scion of the largest
slaveholding family in Michigan and one instrumental in
maneuvering much Detroit land from indigenous control.[40] The term "middle class" served particularly to allow
a predominantly white county to stand in for all counties, even in analyzing an election in which Jesse Jackson's
Rainbow Coalition challenge to party leadership was the
most noteworthy Democratic development. Consigned
to a footnote in *Middle Class Dreams* (*MDC*) is the fact
that, according to what Greenberg considered the best
study at the time, about 45 percent of the United States
regarded itself as middle class, and the same percentage
claimed working-class status. The book's title focused on
the former term because more of those polled in Macomb
County chose it. Moreover, according to Greenberg, the
term "middle class" ought to extend to include those who
called themselves working class, because being middle
class was an aspiration even for those of modest means. It
is worth recalling that the title of Greenberg's book gives
us "middle-class" as a collective adjective, not a collective
noun, so that the dreams matter more than actual class
position. In the long main chapter on Macomb County in

---

40 See Tiya Alicia Miles, *The Dawn of Detroit: A Chronicle of Slavery and
    Freedom in the City of the Straits* (New York: New Press, 2017), 74-79, 102-
    03, 132, and 298, n. 96 on the Macombs, Detroit, and Macomb County.

MCD, "middle class" recurs upwards of three dozen times and "working class" surfaces not at all, though "blue collar" stands in a handful of times.[41]

At the time of his 1985 Macomb County studies, Greenberg regarded himself as uncommonly able and willing to address both class and race, and those studies are now recalled as milestones in studying "white working class" voters. His mission, or selling point, focused on educating Democratic leaders who were supposedly held back by being able to talk about race but not class. The class dimension seemed a fit one for someone who was still active on the left in South Africa and who described himself as coming to his study of Macomb "from the left in my own thinking." As late as 2009, Greenberg was describing the initiative he and Clinton undertook as "thinking through how [to] reconnect with the working class." His brief in addressing Democratic officials was to say that without a viable (white) working class base, no effective Democratic Party was possible. He also prided himself on being a fearless reporter of the depth of racism in Macomb County. One informant there told a focus group that had been given quotations from Robert Kennedy that Kennedy's liberalism made his assassination less than regrettable: "No wonder they killed him." But so committed was Greenberg to

---

41 Greenberg, *Middle Class Dreams*, 322 for the 45 percent figures. See also 36-38 and 23-54 passim.

"listening to Macomb" that there was little counsel beyond registering such views, which he both branded as "venomous" and regarded as worth heeding. Indeed, the whole section in *MCD* on "White Victims, Black Privilege" made it hard to determine where reportage ended and endorsement began. Here was a case where Greenberg's left liberal credentials helped to reassure that no malice could be meant.[42]

Accounts of Greenberg's arrival in Macomb stress the drama of the coming of an unconventional figure, making for an odd encounter between pollster and polled. He was a "short, dark-haired Ivy League professor," Jewish, liberal, and in some accounts Marxist as well. They were white, allegedly bigger than average due to hard blue-collar work, Catholic, high-school educated, and conservative, if complicated. His advantage in securing trust, on his own account, lay in a willingness to hear them and an unwillingness to condescend. He would hear their truth, though inevitably and designedly a partial and at times prefabricated truth. The very invitation for him to study Macomb County grew out of a sense that Democrats needed to shift away from racial justice and feminist issues. The United

---

42 "Hannity vs. Limbaugh Attack Mastermind," *Fox News*, March 26, 2009 https://www.foxnews.com/story/hannity-vs-limbaugh-attack-mastermind; Greenberg, *Dispatches from the War Room*, 19 ("venomous"); Greenberg, *Middle Class Dreams*, 32-34 ("listening to Macomb"), 39, and 40-2.

Automobile Workers hosts were the leaders of Region One, a bastion of conservative Democratic politics and of opposition to reforms within the union.[43]

Left-then-right-wing journalist Christopher Hitchens's searing and superb 1999 account of (Bill) Clintonism, *No One Left to Lie To*, offered the provocation that "[t]he polling business gives the patricians an idea of what the mob is thinking and of how that thinking might be 'shaped.'" It produced, he said, "capsules of 'message' to be prescribed for variant constituencies." Residents of Macomb County contributed to their own capsules through focus group answers. But the contents of the capsules were much compounded by Greenberg himself, especially in his constituting of the groups and choice of settings in which they met. The original 40 subjects—those to whom the Democratic Party most urgently had to listen—were 75 percent male and the rest "housewives." They were all white and all Reagan-voters in 1984. The focus groups met in Macomb County private rooms, mostly in sex-segregated groups of ten for about two hours. No one in the initial four groups was less than thirty years old. Within these chosen settings—and among the residents of Macomb generally, Greenberg implied—great admiration for Reagan as a man

43 Nancy L. Cohen. *Delirium: How the Sexual Counterrevolution Is Polarizing America* (Berkeley: Counterpoint, 2012), 92 ("short"); Greenberg, *Middle Class Dreams*, 29.

who stood up for himself and for the "average American white guy" outweighed economic grievances. Nearby Detroit stood in for all that threatened good lives. In a fascinating formulation, Greenberg distilled the views of the focus group as defining class through race: "Not being black was what constituted being middle class; not living with blacks was what made a neighborhood a decent place to live." Integrated and historically class-conscious workplace and trade union settings did not figure in the study.[44]

The report's conclusions regarding the unvarnished racism of "blue-collar" and unionized workers overshot the evidence by far. Indeed, as Michael Rogin showed, similarly glib analyses of the George Wallace vote had set the pattern of accenting the racism of his blue-collar supporters while missing that of white suburban professionals. The so-called "Southern Strategy" of both Democrats and Republicans was never purely about courting the white vote across class lines in the rural South. It also set up shop in suburbs of the North and West, offering whites reassurance that they were not under threat. The symbol of metropolitan racism became

44 Christopher Hitchens, *No One Left to Lie To: The Triangulations of William Jefferson Clinton* (New York: Verso, 1991), 17-18; Cohen, *Delirium*, 92 and 93-100; Greenberg, *Middle Class Dreams*, 325-26, n.14 and 44-9. For Reagan and masculinity in the focus groups, see also "Stanley Greenberg Oral History (2007), Pollster," unpaginated; Stanley B. Greenberg, *The Two Americas: Our Current Political Deadlock and How to Break It* (New York: Thomas Dunne Books, 1984), 235-37; see Richard David Riddle, "The Rise of the Reagan Democrat in Warren, Michigan, 1964-1984" (PhD dissertation, Wayne State University, 1998), 251-80.

the white working man needing to be soothed. In fact, even in Macomb County, the working class and self-identified middle classes were increasingly white-collar workers and skilled tradespeople in auto. Half or more of the voters were women. A 40 percent "union household" rate meant quite less than that in terms of union density on a per capita basis. From 1979 to 1989, the more unionized manufacturing sector in Macomb lost nearly one job in ten, while service, health care, and retail jobs all increased astronomically. Macomb County voters were brought together as whites and reduced to the skewed samples Greenberg polled to get the unrelieved picture that he discovered and solicited.[45]

Nothing in the setup of the research and little in *MCD* reflected the integrated workplaces and unions in which many in Macomb also existed. Nothing interrupted the free exchanges of whitelore that the settings fostered. The UAW auspices under which the initial polling proceeded generated little for unions policy-wise. Some union leaders had reason to fear "McGoverniks" in politics, and Black caucuses and other leftist challenges in their organizations, more than they valued state action to improve labor's position. Labor law reform and broader questions about what it would have taken to revitalize unions received scant attention. The major class issue hesitantly discussed, especially

---

45 Rogin, "Politics, Emotion, and the Wallace Vote," 27-49; Riddle, "The Rise of the Reagan Democrat in Warren," 290 and 315-16.

in the years after 1985, was the relationship between trade and jobs. However, the support for the North American Free Trade Agreement and other trade deals emerged as settled Democratic policy, largely impervious to focus group polling. Any listening to the "white working class" necessarily attended to their laments as whites, not as working-class people, which in any case would have required tough give-and-take across color lines. The choice of middle class, and not white working class, in the title of *MCD* perhaps made the absence of the unionized worker and his class interests a little less jarring.[46]

The line between a middle-class focus group and a whites-only encounter group proved very thin. Listening to Macomb County had to be severely attenuated when it came to issues on which the Democrats would be hurt or divided by a full airing. Inattention to organized labor was only one such spectacular instance. In Greenberg's writing on Macomb County for public consumption, abortion featured hardly at all, although it was a big part of the area's politics and did figure in Greenberg's 1985 unpublished reports on the county. So did the deep gendered

46 Cohen, *Delirium*, 93 ("McGoverniks") is also excellent at establishing the point that unionized autoworkers were not in fact among the most reactionary people in the United States. For some of the possible logic of the union leaders, see Daniel Galvin, "Resilience in the Rust Belt: Michigan Democrats and the UAW," Institute for Policy Research: Northwestern University, December, 2012, https://www.ipr.northwestern.edu/publications/docs/workingpapers/2013/IPR-WP-13-04.pdf.

crises of time and money in a county losing a sixth of its family income from 1960 to 1990, even as three times as many women entered the labor force. Such matters largely vanished, however, in Greenberg's published writings, where race crowded them out. His most famous polling, for Bill Clinton in 1992, came when it was possible to debate the chance of a "peace dividend" following the fall of the Soviet Union. However much Greenberg strained to listen to "blue-collar" grievances on taxes, and despite doing some polling on military issues, Greenberg left little space for informants to connect spending on war to their tax burdens, as they might have in an integrated, union-based focus group or in a county in which tank production figured less in patterns of working-class employment than it did in Macomb.[47]

Twenty years after the initial polling in Macomb County, its role in Greenberg's rise still seemed so profound that he remembered that period using present-tense verbs in rapid-fire reminiscences. From 1985 through 1994, he later recalled, "I have this odd politics because I come from

47 Riddle, "The Rise of the Reagan Democrat in Warren," 104-79, 251-65, 288, 293-94, and 300-14; Cf. The Analysis Group [Greenberg], *Recapturing Democratic Majorities: Housewives and Their Men* (New Haven: The Analysis Group, 1985), 16, 17-18 (for some expressed opposition to arms spending in the focus groups), 58, and passim; Greenberg, *Report on Democratic Defectors, Prepared for the Michigan House Democratic Campaign* (New Haven: The Analysis Group, 1985), 31-32. On the real but limited cross-racial class politics in plants, especially in the '70s, see Riddle, "The Rise of the Reagan Democrat in Warren," 251-89.

the Left in my own thinking." The phrasing captures much. We are invited to either render "thinking" as meaning in his political analysis or in his self-imagining. Both were true, especially if we consider that he was still a political presence in revolutionary South Africa in the mid-'80s, where the political spectrum stretched much further. In the United States, the oddness of his position rested on the fact that he mainly worked for the Democratic Leadership Council (DLC), which expressed a rightward pull rapidly becoming what he called "the main intellectual and political force for changing the Democratic Party." Although he and his co-thinkers would mostly come to claim that the pull was toward the "new" and not to the right or even to the center, Greenberg said of a potentially uneasy relationship with the DLC that they were "comfortable with that because we have a similar kind of interest in trying to reach the same kind of voters."[48]

In his own telling, Greenberg had few other choices but the DLC. The Michigan Democrats quickly arranged for him to present his Macomb County research conclusions to a national meeting of state party chairs, where he found the audience cold, especially to the fact that he "focused very much on the race issues and values in that discussion"

---

48 "Stanley Greenberg (2005), Pollster," unpaginated; Stanley Greenberg, "The Mythology of Centrism," *The American Prospect*, September-October, 1997, https://prospect.org/article/mythology-centrism.

raising painful differences with the anti-racist Rainbow Coalition. The DLC's interest in Greenberg was exceptional and sustained after he showed results in Lieberman's right-of-the-Republican Senate campaign. It was Lieberman's national center-right appeal that made Greenberg a figure in presidential politics, long before he was in the Clinton campaign's "war room" in 1992. In the 1988 presidential election, the issue of race remained Greenberg's wheelhouse. The George H.W. Bush campaign mounted attack ads using the image of Black inmate Willie Horton, who re-offended while on a weekend furlough approved by Democratic candidate Michael Dukakis, to appeal to white fear. Leaders called upon Greenberg in devising a strategy to disarm the "race issue."[49] He broadened his portfolio in 1990 by urging the need for Democrats to undertake a "middle-class" or "working middle class" project.[50]

The Macomb County Studies did not circulate publicly, save for material Greenberg published in *The American Prospect* in 1991 that drew on them and summaries included in *MCD* in 1995. Instead, he anonymized the county's identity, calling it Greene County, and then sent reports to those whom he hoped might find it, and him, useful. He functioned, he later told interviewers, as

---

49 "Stanley Greenberg (2005), Pollster," unpaginated.

50 Stanley Greenberg, "Reconstructing a Democratic Vision," *The American Prospect*, Spring, 1990, https://prospect.org/article/reconstructing-democratic-vision.

a "pamphleteer" to a target audience. The psychoanalytical reading of the renaming—Greenberg was claiming the county as his own—is appealing. But it is also worth mentioning that Greene County, Alabama, had twenty years before been central to the story of how and where the electric words "Black Power" entered the US political lexicon. Greenberg's "Greene County" announced, at the peak of Jesse Jackson's political appeal, limits on how the Democratic Party could respond to Black demands.[51]

The full 1985 reports generated by Greenberg and his Analysis Group in Macomb County remain hard to get. A brief comparison of them to *Middle Class Dreams* is valuable. Both *Report on Democratic Defectors* and *Recapturing Democratic Majorities: Housewives and Their Men* reside in the University of Michigan's Bentley Library. Greenberg, very prone to post his own work on the internet, seems to have not posted these. The former distills many quotations from informants in focus groups into a position paper. The second, zeroing in on "housewives" at the very time working wives and mothers became increasingly important, is even more leading, featuring quotations that help to argue that relative openness to women's demands for justice on the job among the middle class presents opportunities for

51 Stanley Greenberg. "From Crisis to Working Majority," *The American Prospect*, Fall, 1991, https://prospect.org/article/crisis-working-majority. See also AAIHS Editors, "Rethinking H. Rap Brown and Black Power," *Black Perspectives*, September 29, 2018, https://www.aaihs.org/rethinking-h-rap-brown-and-black-power/.

Democrats. These original reports nicely establish how much the term "middle class poor" emerged in the focus groups, a fact noted only briefly in *MCD*. The unapologetic racism of focus group participants that made its way into *MCD* receives even more expression in the original reports. They also present even more starkly the problem of how to read the reportage of such vitriol. Reading the "Whites as Victims" section in *Report on Democratic Defectors* very much leaves open the question of whether it means to be reporting knowledge based on experience, one truth among many, or something to be combatted. A respect for white identity politics simmers, one in which what counts is the "feeling" of those claiming grievance when they display "vulnerability." At one point, informants comfortably suggest abolishing affirmative action for Blacks, but continuing it for women, who are somehow all-white in their view, which goes unchallenged in the reports.[52]

More unexpected is the rich, lengthy material in the original reports emerging from focus groups gathering trade union members. They urge a return to shop-floor militancy and union power, hearkening back to the time, twenty-plus years earlier, of frequently interracial wildcat strikes in the plants. Sober in their reflections on how

---

52 Greenberg, *Report on Democratic Defectors*, 3 ("vulnerability"), 17 ("victims"), 18-31 and passim; The Analysis Group [Greenberg], *Recapturing Democratic Majorities: Housewives and Their Men*, 3 and 6 ("middle class poor"), and passim.

capital flight, automation, and trade policy made militancy difficult, they nevertheless blame the Democrats and union leaders, not just structural forces in the economy. Reflecting "on a weak and divided labor movement and a self-confident management," one informant observed, "Democrats are the union and the Republicans are management." The report read such a remark as evidence that the Democrats need more "John Wayne" leadership, not that they needed to support union power. Whether in deference to the union leadership, the Democratic leadership, or tensions between union and non-union members of the middle class, such material was sidelined when *MCD* appeared a decade later.[53]

When Greenberg recollects that he "came from the left," it is tempting to reply that he then headed elsewhere. Such repartee oversimplifies and misses the realities conditioning austerity-minded neoliberal Democrats. The emphasis of much of left liberalism on what the labor writer Harold Meyerson called (in a review essay partly on Greenberg's *MCD*) a "deracialized, more class-based liberalism" resonated with the least supple of Marxisms, with the white populism of the best-selling journalist Michael Lind, and,

53 Greenberg, *Report on Democratic Defectors*, 27 ("Republicans are management"), 29 ("John Wayne"), 38-47 and passim; The Analysis Group (Greenberg), *Recapturing Democratic Majorities: Housewives and Their Men*, 36, 38 and passim. On earlier militancy, which however coincided with conservative turns politically, see "The Rise of the Reagan Democrat in Warren," 251-94.

Greenberg hoped, with the voters of Macomb County. Greenberg and the DLC nevertheless retained spiffy "progressive" credentials. The think tank founded by the DLC in 1989 took the name Progressive Policy Institute. Two years later, Representative DeLauro, Greenberg's wife, became an early and leading figure in the Progressive Caucus in Congress. Greenberg's conclusion to *The New Majority*, a 1997 collection co-edited with Theda Skocpol, appeared under the title "Popularizing Progressive Politics." The trajectory of a "more class-based liberalism" has had little place for unions except as campaign contributors. Greenberg wrote in 2009 of his lack of enthusiasm for unions' ability to play a transformational role in the United States as based in part on his experiences with brave and radical unions of South African workers, whose demands he would only later seek to curb.[54]

Clinton, James Carville, Greenberg—all continued even amid disagreements to know each other and themselves as seekers of the left wing of the possible. They could dismiss critics righteously. In particular, the Macomb County Studies' brew of a raceless middle class

---

54 Greenberg, *Dispatches from the War Room*, 116 and, for an unhappy ending to that romance, 12-32 and chapter 4 of this volume; Greenberg, "Popularizing Progressive Politics" in Greenberg and Theda Skocpol, eds. *The New Majority: Toward a Popular Progressive Politics* (New Haven: Yale University Press, 1997), 279-98. Harold Meyerson, "Wither the Democrats," *The American Prospect*, March-April, 1996, https://prospect.org/article/wither-democrats. Unions, then in the midst of a brief period of reform, are still more strikingly absent from Greenberg's 2004 study, *The Two Americas*, than even from the union-supported *Middle Class Dreams*.

that everyone knew was white and an angry working class called white obviated the need for far-reaching visions of change. Health care reform perhaps took the Clinton forces closest to a class-based appeal, but the failed plan remained "moderate" and "market-oriented," as Greenberg himself acknowledged. Polling mattered, not the hard work of thinking through and organizing around what would bring working people, oppressed differently, together. For those other targets of the Democrats' Southern/suburban strategies—the suburban, white, well-to-do voters—there was little need to examine their own race and class advantage, and still less to critique the system structuring advantage and disadvantage.

When Bill Clinton announced his longshot candidacy in 1992 as a crusade for the "hard-working forgotten middle class," Greenberg and his ideas worked hard in the campaign. In the election, the amalgam of middle and working class, both reading white, delivered a much closer loss in Macomb County than McGovern or Walter Mondale had suffered. In June 1992, in what a *Chicago Tribune* columnist referred to as the "most important moment" in the campaign, Clinton visited a meeting of Jackson's Rainbow Coalition to pick a public fight. He attacked the rapper Sister Souljah for her expressed lack of surprise that whites would be victims of violence in the Los Angeles rebellions against police violence. Jackson had invited Souljah to perform, and this licensed Clinton to go after both of them. Clinton accused her of somehow being just like the white nationalist David Duke, reversed. Jackson responded, vigorously defending Souljah and wryly adding that he thought Clinton must have been speaking to an audience not in the room. That audience lived in Macomb County. Greenberg himself had suggested the confrontation with Jackson.[55]

In terms of the math Greenberg used to conclude *Politics and Poverty* just a decade earlier, his Macomb County Studies fashioned a political menu in which the choices ranged not from 1 to 10 but from 1.0 to 1.2—or more exactly, given the penchant for negativity, from -1 to 1. The Macomb County Studies defined what could not be fully heard by Democrats. That included the message of Jackson and the Rainbow Coalition, to the extent that they were pushing toward more forthright positions on racial justice and sometimes on class and trade issues as well. Positing and polling a (white) middle class whose racial interests need not be named and a white working class in need of recognition but not consistent mention would have a great future in tailoring electoral appeals to accepting austerity

---

55 "Bill Clinton Presidential Campaign Announcement," C-SPAN, October 3, 1991, https://www.c-span.org/video/?21803-1/governor-bill-clinton-d-ar-presidential-campaign-announcement; Hitchens, *No One Left to Lie To*, 33-4; Ishmael Reed, *Airing Dirty Laundry* (Reading, MA; Addison Wesley, 1993), 35; "Stanley Greenberg (2007), Pollster," unpaginated.

and capital flight. At a moment when vigorously supporting affirmative action, for example, would have to have
been paired with reforms targeted at all working people to
maintain a coalition, Macomb County perfectly explained
why it was best to do neither.[56]

The Hooverizing of Stan Greenberg?

Macomb County and the obsession with working-class
whites at their worst pulled Democrats to the right, as the
evolution of Greenberg's career has shown. Increasingly,
the progressive reputation of Greenberg seems so fragile
and beleaguered as to be fanciful. The changes in how he is
viewed by some liberals and the left have two causes. One
is the rightward motion of Greenberg himself. The other is
a possible change of political moments that requires more
substance regarding both race and class demands by those
wishing to stay in the admittedly capacious confines of
progressive politics.

The threat to Greenberg's reputation as a liberal and as
a person of the left stems from his business activities and
his political drift. It centers especially on his corporate and
political consulting activities, both internationally and

56 See David Roediger, "White Workers, New Democrats, and Affirmative
    Action" in Wahneema Lubiano, ed., *The House That Race Built* (New York:
    Random House, 1997), 48-65; Roediger, "The Racial Crisis of American
    Liberalism," *New Left Review*, 196 (November–December, 1992): 114-19, for
    cries in the wilderness at the time.

at home. For almost forty years, Greenberg has worked as a consultant, beginning in a basement room with a phone bank with range rarely reaching past Connecticut. Subsequent polling and image consulting partnerships proved to be much more lucrative and polished, culminating with Greenberg co-founding Greenberg Quinlan Rosner (GQR) Research, Inc., for which he serves as CEO. Democracy Corps, his non-profit venture with folksier-even-than-Bill-Clinton presidential adviser James Carville, allows for the Corps' activities to be framed as providing free services to worthy centrist and progressive Democrats. The paid political consulting is substantial. In the 2018 elections, for example, GQR received 6.75 million dollars in consulting and polling fees, with the Democratic Congressional Campaign Committee paying the largest share.[57] Greenberg's activities and the status of his wife as one of the wealthiest members of the US Congress make for a large family fortune. The scandals attending the discovery that Greenberg and DeLauro provided Rahm Emanuel with free housing over a period

57 See the 2018 data from Open Secrets at https://www.opensecrets.org/expends/vendor.php?year=2018&vendor=Greenberg+Quinlan+Rosner+Research; "Stanley Greenberg (2005), Pollster," January 27, 2005, https://millercenter.org/the-presidency/presidential-oral-histories/stanley-greenberg-oral-history-2005-pollster, unpaginated; Scott Beaulieu, "Senator Blumenthal Is One of 10 Richest in Congress" NBC Connecticut, August 23, 2011), https://www.nbcconnecticut.com/news/local/Sen-Blumenthal-is-One-of-the-Ten-Richest-in-Congress-128244983.html.

of years got traction in part because Emanuel was in powerful positions from which to help Greenberg secure Democratic polling jobs.[58]

Greenberg's consulting businesses soon reached in two directions. Both lent credence to charges that he had moved to the right. The first was corporate consulting, which involved clients against whom social movements arrayed themselves. These included Monsanto, British Petroleum (later BP), Boeing, and United Healthcare—a veritable who's who of environmental catastrophes, anti-labor practices, consumer complaints, and health and safety violations. The most damaging of the firm's consultancies engineered the greenwashing of BP as a friend of the environment following the deadly Gulf of Mexico Deepwater Horizon oil spill of 2010. Another instance came in 2009, when a bill was introduced by Representative DeLauro that was seen as very favorable to Monsanto by opponents of genetically modified seeds. Critics jumped on the possible connection of Greenberg's consultancy for Monsanto with the bill's content, but Greenberg's supporters objected that his contract work with Monsanto

58 Ryan Lizza, "The Gatekeeper: Rahm Emanuel on the Job," *The New Yorker*, February 21, 2009, https://www.newyorker.com/magazine/2009/03/02/the-gatekeeper; Owen Thomas, "Rahn Emanuel Bunked for Free in Pollster's Apartment," *Gawker*, February 5, 2009, https://gawker.com/5147456/rahm-emanuel-bunked-for-free-in-pollsters-basement.

was limited and had lapsed.[59] Such reassurances prevailed but they glossed over the role that informal ties between big businesses, political parties, and the state play as movers and shakers change roles. Greenberg increasingly functioned as what historian Thomas McCormick has brilliantly called an "in-and-outer," collapsing and transgressing boundaries between political power and corporate power. His role in this regard becomes clearer still when we consider his paid work for politicians beyond the United States.[60] That work too has increased doubts about Greenberg's continuing role as a progressive.

The irony in the steady rightward trajectory of Greenberg internationally is worth lingering over. At first, he was arguably more progressive internationally than at home. In 1994, internationalist work burnished Greenberg's reputation among left liberals, because he advised Nelson Mandela during the defeat of apartheid and the beginnings of African National Congress (ANC) rule in South Africa. His later reflections rightly regarded

---

59 Aimee Levitt, "Dick Durbin and Monsanto: An Unholy Alliance that Will Put an End to Agricultural Freedom?" *Riverfront Times*, August 31, 2010, https://www.riverfronttimes.com/foodblog/2010/08/31/dick-durbin-and-monsanto-an-unholy-alliance-that-will-put-an-end-to-agricultural-freedom.

60 Thomas J. McCormick, *America's Half-Century: United States Foreign Policy in the Cold War and After* (Baltimore: Johns Hopkins University Press, 1989), esp. 12-16.

that experience as his greatest moment.[61] Other consultancies necessarily paled in comparison, but at first
would have seemed almost as understandable to left liberals in the United States as supporting the ANC. Tony
Blair was hopefully poised to rescue Britain from the
conservative onslaught of Thatcherism, and his curbing
trade union power in the Labour Party roughly mirrored
the turn to a focus on the middle class among liberals in
the United States. Supporting the Partido Revolucionario
Institucional (PRI) in Mexico in 2000 aligned Greenberg
with the continuation of a hopelessly corrupt regime and
the continuation of one-party rule. However, such work
supported those making a failed pledge to keep a kind of
Mexican Thatcherism at bay. Greenberg's 2001 interven-
tion in Austrian politics opposed a far-right anti-Semite.[62]
Those who were progressive-except-for-Palestine and
those hoping for a little progressivism within Israel might
have applauded Greenberg's contribution of expertise to

---

61 Ron Brownstein, "The American Operatives Behind Mandela's
Presidential Campaign," *The Atlantic*, December 12, 2013, https://www.
theatlantic.com/politics/archive/2013/12/the-american-campaign-opera-
tives-behind-mandelas-presidential-campaign/439116/.

62 Dennis W. Johnson, *Democracy for Hire: A History of American Political
Consulting* (New York: Oxford University Press, 2017), 385; Roger Cohen,
"Haider the Rightist Is Firing Up Vienna's Election with Slurs," *New York
Times*, March 12, 2001, https://www.nytimes.com/2001/03/12/world/haid-
er-the-rightist-is-firing-up-vienna-s-election-with-slurs.html.

Israeli Labor candidate Ehud Barak's 1999 electoral victory, in what the *New Yorker* called a "stunning upset."[63]

As the 2000s wore on, regarding Greenberg's international activities as progressive became trickier business. Campaigning for Barak, he remembered in 2009, had "allowed [him] to develop an instinctive identification with Israel." He soon polled not only for a center-left candidate in Israel but—via The Israel Project and under the slogan "We're fighting to win"—for Zionism itself.[64] His consulting in the 2002 Bolivian election opposed the indigenous leader and left icon Evo Morales. Portrayed in the film *Our Brand Is Crisis*, the activities of Carville and Greenberg came to symbolize the export southward of "dirty tricks" campaigning.[65] Greenberg opposed generally the leftward motion associated with Latin America's "pink tide," especially in Venezuela, where GQR faced charges of cooperation in the manip-

---

63 "About the Founders," unpaginated; and Shmuel Rosner, "Bibi's Blunders," *The New Republic*, December 23, 2008, https://newrepublic.com/article/63860/bibis-blunders.

64 Greenberg, *Dispatches from the War Room*, 347.

65 "Our Mission," *The Israel Project*, undated but accessed April 11, 2019, https://www.theisraelproject.org/mission; Sudhir Muralidhar, "The Making of El Presidente," *The American Prospect*, March 17, 2006, https://prospect.org/article/making-el-presidente; for an incredibly defensive account of the Bolivian election, the failed presidency of Gonzalo Sanchez de Lozada, the film, and the questionable notion that "elites" supported Evo Morales and were behind criticisms of the "pollster-consultant industrial complex," see Greenberg, *Dispatches from the War Room*, 392 and 348-91.

ulation of polling data in order to deepen gloom among Hugo Chavez supporters. When former New Left leader turned reform Democrat Tom Hayden broached possible division between Barack Obama and the Clintons over the 2009 coup in Honduras, he noted the role of Carville and Greenberg in broadly advancing anti-left free trade policies in much of Latin America.[66]

In South Africa Greenberg has recently supported the Democratic Alliance (DA), into which the main party of apartheid moved. Whatever sharp questions must be raised regarding ANC politics, this striking embrace of parochialism and reaction again called Greenberg's progressive credentials into question. The political activist and writer Melissa Levin, an admiring colleague of his in ANC campaigning, put it in just those terms. Levin was so insistently and happily a protégé of Greenberg in 2004 that she was called by her friends "Little Stan Greenberg." In 2013, she reacted to his changed allegiances in an article titled "Little Stan Greenberg Is Dead," in which she asked, "How on earth is the DA 'progressive'?"[67]

---

66 Justin Delacour, "Spinning 'Lies, Damn Lies, and Statistics' in Venezuela," *Venezuela Analysis*, July 31, 2004, https://venezuelanalysis.com/analysis/608; Tom Hayden, "Obama vs. Clinton on Honduras?" *Huffington Post*, May 26, 2011, https://www.huffpost.com/entry/obama-vs-clinton-on-hondu_b_231168.

67 Melissa Levin, "Little Stan Greenberg Is Dead," *Africa Is a Country*, August 5, 2013, https://africasacountry.com/2013/08/little-stan-greenberg-is-dead; Levin and Greenberg together wrote over sixty radio scripts for the ANC's

Greenberg's political-entrepreneurial peregrinations show how hard it is for centrist election strategies without firm commitments regarding race and class not to drift to the right. But more interesting is the possibility that constant focus on Macomb County is becoming less compelling as the electorate, and more importantly the society, changes. We might usefully begin with a recent remark from someone distinctly in Greenberg's world, the editor and pundit John Judis. Responding in an incredibly extended recent roundtable on the "white working class" in *The Democratic Strategist* to Greenberg's lead article, Judis first paid an obligatory tribute to Greenberg's accomplishments in Macomb in assessing what was now being called the "white working class's voting patterns." He added, "I worry it [continuing to emphasize the county] is becoming a cul-de-sac. Along with the blanket designation of minorities . . . as automatic Democrats, it has mainly served simply to provide calculations that either produce or deny a 'rising Democratic majority' and these exercises may provide less insight about the present or the future than they have in the past."[68]

successful presidential campaign in 1999. See Greenberg, *Dispatches from the War Room*, 175-76.

68 John Judis, "Exposing the Opposition in 2016 May Be the Best Strategy," *The Democratic Strategist*, June 5, 2015, https://thedemocraticstrategist. org/2015/06/exposing_the_opposition_in_201/.

Judis expressed a weariness with Greenberg's continued offering, thirty-five years on, of another encore at a one-trick pony's performance. But the awareness of how much Macomb County leads away from considerations of racialized populations also registers how clearly inadequate the "middle class" model is when elections are decided by turnout in Detroit, not just by how the vote splits in adjacent white counties. Without expressing sympathy for Hillary Clinton, it is useful to reconsider the much-wholesaled indictment that her disdain for frequent visits to Michigan, and specifically to Macomb County, cost the Democrats the 2016 election. The charge, a favorite of Greenberg, ignores the fact that she would have had to not just show up but also to say something. What she said for electoral consumption in Macomb County ran sharp risks of suppressing turnout in Detroit. A Sister Souljah moment of high demagoguery was not available to her, as much thanks to Black Lives Matter as to changes in the Democratic Party itself. Indeed, she paid in 2016 for the race-saturated pro-incarceration rhetoric—Black youth as "superpredators"—she and her husband had traded on in appealing to Macomb County's middle-class dreams in the 1990s.[69]

---

69 Heidi Gillstrom and others, "Clinton's 'Superpredators' Comment Most Damaging by Either Candidate," *The Hill*, September 30, 12016, https://the-hill.com/blogs/pundits-blog/crime/298693-hillary-clintons-superpredators-still-the-most-damaging-insult-by.

History regarding appeals to class set further limits on the possibility of a "Macomb redux" strategy and on any clear future role for Greenberg. Clinton barely won Macomb County in the 2016 Democratic primary. She bested Bernie Sanders, who won the statewide balloting, by 649 votes of about 100,000 cast. However, in the general election, she lost Macomb County to Trump—his campaign made recapturing the county a high priority— by over 48,000 votes of about 419,000 cast. Trump and Sanders could talk about class and jobs in ways unavailable to Clinton, especially given the aggressive promotion by the Clintons of free trade, an issue on which Greenberg has been all over place. Greenberg has kept wide distance between himself and Sanders, and is in a position, not unlike that of an aging Herbert Hoover, of being bypassed by the leftward movement, even if slight, around him. If that continues some of us will be tempted to process his isolation as comeuppance for an opportunist. A more useful stance might be to see Greenberg trapped in bigger dramas and in illusions regarding "saving the middle class" shared by much of electoral liberalism and some of the left.[70]

70 Thomas B. Edsall, "How Immigration Foiled Hillary," *New York Times*, October 5, 2017, https://www.nytimes.com/2017/10/05/opinion/clinton-trump-immigration.html; Greenberg and Nancy Zdunkewizc, "Macomb County in the Age of Trump," *Democracy Corps*, March 9, 2017, http://rooseveltinstitute.org/wp-content/uploads/2017/03/Dcor_Macomb_FG-Memo_3.9.2017_v8-2.pdf.

Three

THE PRETENSES OF A MIDDLE-CLASS UNITED STATES

"Like the Holy Ghost, the Middle Class relies on faith rather than empirical evidence of its seemingly immortal omnipresence."
—Bill Onasch, Kansas City labor activist

At the intersection of Google searching, journalism, and comedy lies a new but already boring form of social criticism. Search engines assemble sound bites in which every conservative talk show host, or everyone in the "liberal media," or every leading Republican politician, or every prominent Democrat says more or less the same hackneyed thing. The echoing comments, put together equally well by Rush Limbaugh's or Stephen Colbert's staff, both imply a conspiracy of "talking points" being foisted onto the public and an utter lack of substance and conviction in what is being parroted. No such montage would lead to more revealing and plentiful results than one constructed around a search for the phrases "defending the middle class" or "saving the middle class." That rallying cry crosses the partisan political divide. Democrats and Republicans vie for the lead in terms of promises to stand up for the putatively noble but chronically fragile middle strata of the class structure. Both parties praise the middle class as the broken heart of the nation and hold that only they can mend it.

The 2012 presidential elections typified the relentless appeals to the supposed center of the social structure. In February 2012, the political scientist Cal Jillson concluded that president Barack Obama had "settled on a message of middle-class support." Jillson correctly predicted that, knowing they "were on to something," the Obama strategists would be systematically pursuing the issue throughout the campaign. Obama, hardly silent regarding professing his love for the middle class before that point, redoubled his commitment by declaring himself a "warrior" for that group in pursuing reelection. Practically the first act of the Obama presidency's first term had been to set up the Middle Class Task Force, led by vice-president Joe Biden. Charged with getting "the backbone of this country up and running again"; the initiative identified a "strong middle class" with a "strong America." To speak even louder about those in the middle class in 2012, Obama was careful to insist, was not about "class warfare." Instead, it concerned the "nation's welfare." The "make or break moment for the middle class," Obama argued first at a small high school gym in Kansas and then to the nation, defined the stakes of the election. By July 2012, a typical short Obama campaign speech would feature more than a dozen invocations of the glorious, precarious "middle class."[1]

The Republicans faced the difficult fact that polls showed Obama clearly besting GOP candidate Mitt Romney in being trusted to look out for middle-class economic interests. Reporting on the number of Romney's lavish homes and estates did not help matters. Some Republicans responded by insisting that Obama's appeals to the middle class somehow constituted unfair instigation of class hatred, but Romney's decision was to match the Democrats' emphasis. He insisted that after almost a full term in office, with increasing misery among the middle class, the Obama administration could hardly claim to be effectively battling for forgotten Americans. Romney drew on "class" appeals similar to those of the Democrats while he declared initiatives like the Obama task force

1   Lucy Madison, "Obama: I'm a Warrior for the Middle Class," *CBS News*, September 22, 2011, http://www.cbsnews.com/news/obama-im-a-warrior-for-the-middle-class/; Amie Parnes, "For 2012, White House Casts President Obama as Warrior for the Middle Class," *The Hill*, December 29, 2011, http://the hill.com/home news/administration 20195-white house-casts-obama-as-warrior-for-the-middle-class; Jon Ward, "President Obama Outpacing Mitt Romney in Mentions of 'Middle Class,'" *Huffington Post*, July 16, 2012, http://www.huffingtonpost.com/2012/07/16/obama-romney-middle-class_n_1677043.html. The chapter's epigraph is from Bill Onasch, "No Middle Ground," *Labor Advocate Online*, January 1, 2012, http://www.kclabor.org/nomiddleground.htm.

to have been calamities that led to further erosion of middle-class standards. The two presidential campaigns even shared a definition of middle class: those making less than $250,000—sometimes Romney mentioned $300,000—a year, upwards of 96 percent of the population. The 96% was not so much a class as it was a nation. To wage political war on its behalf seemed good patriotic politics.[2] Those hovering between partisan cheerleading and political journalism spread the word, from Lou Dobbs's slightly earlier *War on the Middle Class* on the right, to Stanley Greenberg and James Carville's almost parodic *It's The Middle Class, Stupid*, on the left.[3]

Here was a "middle" that includes pretty much everybody, leaving out only a relative handful of the fabulously rich and, if taken literally, nobody who is poor. Obama deftly liquidated the issue of how a country with such astronomical rates of poverty could be almost all middle class. He defined the middle class as "not only folks who are currently

2   Dylan Matthews, "What Is the Middle Class?" *Washington Post Wonkblog*, September 16, 2012, http://www.washingtonpost.com/blogs/wonkblog/wp/2012/09/16/what-is-the-middle-class/; Middle Class Task Force, "A Strong Middle Class Equals a Strong America," Middle Class Task Force website, January 30, 2009, http://www.whitehouse.gov/blog_post/Todaysevent; Kim Velsey, "How Many Houses Does Mitt Have?: A Helpful Guide to Romney's Landholdings," *Observer*, August 14, 2012, https://observer.com/2012/08/how-many-houses-does-mitt-have-a-helpful-guide-to-romneys-landholdings/.

3   Lou Dobbs, *War on the Middle Class* (New York: Penguin, 2007); Stanley Greenberg and James Carville, *It's The Middle Class, Stupid* (New York: Plume, 2013).

[in] the middle class, but also people who aspire to be in the middle class." Thus, he continued, "We're not forgetting the poor." At the same time, political rhetoric about the losses of the middle class tempted the rival camps to offer more precise, if contradictory, definitions. Indeed, Obama's chief economist held in January 2012 that the middle class was no longer a majority in the United States. It had dwindled, the adviser said, from 50 percent of the population to 42 percent over the last four decades, though some surveys placed the figure of those self-identifying as still middle class at double that. Romney's camp predictably emphasized that much of any decline had occurred under Obama.[4] Both campaigns ultimately settled on the below $250,000 income figure as a way of defining the middle class, placing all but a few Americans in it. An appeal to the middle class worked, wrote political scientist Mark Sweet, because "most people describe themselves as middle class." The political wisdom that winning the middle-class vote predicted electoral victories could hardly have failed so long as almost all the electorate could be wrangled into that group.[5]

4   Middle Class Task Force, "A Strong Middle Class Equals a Strong America"; Hope Yen, "What Does It Mean to Be 'Middle Class'?" *Christian Science Monitor*, July 18, 2012, http://www.csmonitor.com/USA/Latest-News-Wires/2012/0718/What-does-it-mean-to-be-middle-class; David Rohde, "The American Working Class Is Shrinking," *Reuters* (U.S. edition), January 13, 2012, http://blogs.reuters.com/david-rohde/2012/01/13/white-house-the-american-middle-class-is-shrinking/.

5   Yen, "What Does It Mean to Be 'Middle Class'?"

But the fiction that such slight-of-hand constituted political analysis—or even, given Obama's clever play on class war in taking up the "warrior for the middle class" mantle, materialist analysis—suffered from its being about equally accessible to both parties. It left the task of assembling a coalition of far more particularized voters than the 96 percent as before. The 2012 campaign captured in miniature a compelling and confounding array of contemporary realities and illusions about the middle class. The questions of whether a "class" can encompass virtually the whole of society, of whether it can persistently be described as the moral center of a society and nevertheless as hopelessly adrift, and of whether it can be defined sociologically by its own aspirations and illusions came squarely before us even before 2012 and remain today.

Meanwhile, Citigroup analysts, thinking in 2011 about investments rather than elections, dismissed the idea of a middle-class society altogether. As political journalist Don Peck put it in asking, "Can the Middle Class Be Saved?" their study found that "America was composed of two distinct groups: the rich and the rest. For the purposes of investment decisions, the second group didn't matter; tracking its spending habits or worrying over its savings rate was a waste of time. All the action in the American economy was at the top: the richest 1 percent of households earned as much each year as the bottom 60 percent put together;

they possessed as much wealth as the bottom 90 percent." Noting that the concentration consistently increased, they "coined a term for this state of affairs: *plutonomy*."[6]

Even as it registers changes, the handy to-the-center-and-right emphasis on the middle class persists in politics. Nevertheless ten months before the 2016 election, the labor writer and political analyst Harold Meyerson predicted that we would shortly see a presidential campaign that was not centered on winning the middle class. He added, incorrectly, that this would be unprecedented, as no national elections had centered the middle class before the 1990s. With pollsters as his sources, Meyerson held that the middle class has been so devastated under political leaders all claiming to champion its interests that only a dwindling percentage of voters identified with the label. Shifts in such a direction certainly did occur just before the 2016 election, when Pew Charitable Trust research found the difference in numbers between those choosing "middle class" and "lower class" from the menu of identities to be insignificant.[7] For a time both Clinton and

6 Peck, "Can the Middle Class Be Saved?" *The Atlantic*, September, 2011, https://www.theatlantic.com/magazine/archive/2011/09/can-the-middle-class-be-saved/308600/.

7 Pew Charitable Trust Fact Tank, "Socioeconomic Class," Pew Charitable Trust website, December 17, 2014, https://www.pewresearch.org/topics/socioeconomic-class/2014/.

Trump hesitated to specify the middle class as their prize constituency and guiding star.

Nevertheless, Meyerson's prediction did not materialize. Ironically it was the avowedly socialist candidate, Bernie Sanders, who most insistently positioned himself as the candidate of, and in some measure from, the middle class. Just as the recent campaigns against anti-union legislation in Michigan and Indiana described themselves as defenses of the middle class, with perhaps a nod, too, toward defending "working families," the Sanders campaign attempted to appeal to the middle class in contesting inequality. His campaign's bible, *The Speech: On Corporate Greed and the Decline of Our Middle Class*, authored by Sanders, earned sufficient royalties that, in the 2020 campaign, he has been attacked as a millionaire with lapsed credentials to speak for the middle class.[8] Sanders and Clinton followed Obama and Romney in ballparking "below $250,000" annual family income as the benchmark of middle-class membership, though limiting its use to details of tax policy.[9]

8   Bernie Sanders, "The War on the Middle Class," *Boston Globe*, June 12, 2015, https://www.bostonglobe.com/opinion/2015/06/12/bernie-sanders-the-war-middle-class/hAJUTAjWgupBLx4zAMh7nN/story.html; Sanders, *The Speech: On Corporate Greed and the Decline of Our Middle Class* (New York: Nation Books, 2015).

9   CNN Wire, "Is $250,000 Middle Class? Hillary Clinton and Bernie Sanders Think So," reposted at *Fox 8*, February 18, 2016, https://myfox8.com/2016/02/18/is-250000-middle-class-hillary-clinton-and-bernie-sanders-think-so/.

Both Clinton and Trump picked up "saving the middle class" in a more desultory way, but significantly. The former sometimes conveyed both the grandeur and peril of middle-class life in pledging to (re)create a "healthy middle class" and invoked the term especially in more populist moments of her campaign. The fiercest assertions of a populist middle-class message in Clinton's campaign came from Sanders himself. After losing the nomination, he stumped on Clinton's behalf, including in Michigan venues her campaign ignored. "What this campaign is about," he told a crowded rally for her at the United Automobile Workers hall in Dearborn, "is the survival of the middle class." Trump campaigned on the idea of a "middle class tax cut," while lacing the term "working families"—one that for me conjured up child labor when spoken by him—into his tax reform rhetoric. It was a campaign of awkward silences on class generally. Trump presented himself as a modern political leader uniquely unmoved by pretending affinity with the middle class. He bragged repeatedly of his 1 percent status. Overemphasizing his self-made success and deemphasizing his debts, he courted being seen as filthy rich. Hillary Clinton meanwhile only rarely rehearsed economic worries she experienced growing up. Pundits nevertheless clearly saw the race as one for the votes of a declining middle class.[10]

In the early run-up to 2020, Joe Biden vaulted to front-runner status by persistently recycling Obama's "warrior for the middle class" rhetoric. Elizabeth Warren's campaign trail book, *This Fight Is Our Fight: The Battle to Save America's Middle Class*, is her third book with "middle class" in either its title or subtitle. Meanwhile Trump gets to, or perhaps has to, campaign on his middle-class tax cut, however skewed to the rich it turned out to be.[11] Popular media, meanwhile, feed obsessions with the salvation of the middle class,

---

10   "Hillary Clinton: Imperative to Bring Back a Healthy Middle Class," *Breaking CNBC*, March 4, 2016, https://www.cnbc.com/video/2016/03/04/hillary-clinton-imperative-to-bring-back-healthy-middle-class-.html; Kathleen Gray, "Bernie Sanders: Campaign Is about Survival of the Middle Class," *Detroit Free Press*, October 6, 2016, https://www.freep.com/story/news/politics/2016/10/06/bernie-sanders-election-survival-middle-class/91666238/; Amy Chozick, "Stress over Family Finances Propelled Hillary Clinton into Corporate World," *New York Times*, August 10, 2016, https://www.nytimes.com/2016/08/11/us/politics/hillary-clinton-money.html.

11   Tim Hains, "Trump TV Ad Highlights Middle Class Tax Cut Proposals," *RealClear Politics*, October 6, 2016, https://www.realclearpolitics.com/video/2016/10/06/trump_tv_ad_highlights_middle_class_tax_cut_plans.html; Dan Balz, "Charting Trump's Rise through the Decline of the Middle Class," *Washington Post*, December 12, 2015, https://www.washingtonpost.com/politics/charting-trumps-rise-in-the-decline-of-the-middle-class/2015/12/12/0f5df1d8-a037-11e5-8728-1af6af208198_story.html; Kevin Liptak, "With 2016 Speculation Mounting Biden Brings Populist Fire to Florida," *CNN Politics*, September 2, 2015, https://www.cnn.com/2015/09/02/politics/biden-florida-president-campaign/index.html; Elizabeth Warren, *This Fight Is Our Fight: The Battle to Save America's Middle Class* (New York: Metropolitan Books, 2017).

suggesting that women, Starbucks, and the wisdom of bowling-alone-critic Robert Putnam just might get it done.[12]

A fair question remains: So what? Some will say that the United States simply is and always has been a nation filled with people who unswervingly identify as middle class and that even if they are wrong objectively to do so, politicians need to meet them around their senses of self. Others might allow that the middle class is ill-defined and fractured, but hold that if appealing to it strengthens the chances even a little of electing a middle-of-the-road Democrat in the mold of Hillary Clinton over someone worse, the ambiguities are worth it. Among the young and not-so-young are many who think that the Democratic Party is about to be transformed into a vehicle for winning democratic socialism around Sanders, a presidential candidate who champions middle-class demands in a way that suggests he thinks they can be made to equal approximately "universal" entitlements.

In keeping with the tone set out in this book's introduction, the goal here is not to try to dissuade those eager to make such tradeoffs but rather to remind ourselves that there are arenas of struggle and visions of what is possible other than electoral ones. Appeals to the middle class serve

---

12 Marc Parry, "Can Robert Putnam Save the American Dream?" *Chronicle of Higher Education*, March 27, 2015, https://www.chronicle.com/article/Can-Robert-Putnam-Save-the/228443; Amanda Ripley, "Can Starbucks Save the Middle Class," *The Atlantic*, May, 2015, 60-72; Mandi Woodruff, "Why Women Just Might Save the Middle Class," *Yahoo Finance*, April 8, 2014, https://www.wsj.com/articles/the-middle-class-squeeze-1443194736.

us poorly in forwarding the former and in dreaming the latter. The argument consists of three parts. The first, set out in this chapter, is that the United States, in important ways, is not a middle-class country, past or present, and to see it as such inevitably draws us into an "American exceptionalist" mythology—one that sees the United States as both the most free country and the one best serving ordinary people. This assumption has long been dear to elites, who have helped to inflate the middle-class category. The second and third, pursued in succeeding chapters, focus on the content of a long radical, and even liberal, tradition of analyzing the middle class as a problem and showing that there are reasons why reactionaries often fare well in courting the middle class and the left historically does not. These chapters argue that we ought not throw that body of thought away lightly. Strands of older and new insights allow us to understand the middle class in the United States as not simply formed in either relative advantage or in fear of downward mobility but as miserable even while able to claim middle-class status.

Undefinable and Tending to the Right

The lament that official society makes it hard to identify as anything but middle class is a common one among radicals. Being a middle-class society is often enough said to be uniquely American and even what makes the

United States unique. It is easy to suppose that if such notions were abandoned we would be much closer to the sober analysis necessary to assert meaningful egalitarian goals. Almost every spring for the past thirty-five years for example, I have taught a survey class to almost seven hundred state university students. In each case, when lecturing on the history of the middle class, I have asked, "How many of you are middle class?" Immediately almost every student listening has raised a hand. Of the fifteen thousand or so respondents over the years, perhaps fifty have answered my further question: "So who is not middle class?" The outliers sometimes said they were working class, more often poor. One student held improbably that he was already a member of the "ruling class," causing others in the University of Minnesota auditorium to ask what he was doing there. At first I thought I could convince, or remind, lots of students that they came from working-class families and would tellingly hint that many of the middle-class jobs they thought they would soon occupy were disappearing. Given the few hours that they heard my lectures, that was mostly an idle wish in the context of flagship state university classrooms, themselves incubators of the idea that middle-class aspirations made student debt seem supportable. The legendary Dadaist Julien Torma once aphorized that "Hunger justifies the middle classes." We might now want to add,

"So does student debt."[13] And yet among the hundreds of graduate students whom I have also taught, pursuing degrees in mostly leftish disciplines and not discernibly different from undergraduates in terms of socio-economic background, a majority make at least some claim to working-class identities and often share a lofty disdain for the middle class. Context matters.

The vexing questions of the size and the composition of the middle class are so variously posed and answered as to make the category a blunt tool for political analysis. In the section above we encountered the discrepant figures of 42 and 96 percent of the US population fitting within the middle class. Those estimates are offered by presidential advisers paid to know. *CNN Business* recently built a series around the question "What Is Middle Class, Anyway?" It offered five headings as possible ways to figure out an answer: income, wealth, consumption, aspiration, and demographics, the last based on a complex matrix, even flow chart, developed recently by staff at the St. Louis Federal Reserve Bank. The text under each heading suggests several more approaches. The article counts between 20 and 60 percent of the people as middle class, avoiding

---

13 Terry Hale and others, trans. and eds, *4 Dada Suicides: Selected Texts of Arthur Cravan, Jacques Rigaut, Julien Torma, and Jacques Vache* (London: Atlas Books, 1995), 165.

the astronomical numbers more often given by not putting a figure to the "Aspirations" category.[14]

Problems of definition cannot fail to appear because the middle class is, at least as theorized to date, not really a class. The greatest US study of the middle class, C. Wright Mills's *White Collar*, tells us as much as early as its subtitle, which announces a study of the "middle classes," plural. Later in the book Mills describes the futility of expecting class-conscious mobilizations from the middle class by pointing out that the middle class is a jammed-together group, one "contradictory in its material interest" and even "dissimilar in ideological illusion." It gets created either in the imaginations of experts or those of men and women claiming membership.[15]

The foundational distinction, and confusion, in popular and scholarly attempts to define a middle class lies in whether the label is to be applied by sociologists and pollsters based on set criteria or whether it is a self-sticking one chosen by respondents based on their subjective consciousness of themselves and of the social structure. *CNN Business* had it both ways, holding that it was necessary to "read this" to learn if one is middle class, but also including

14 Tami Luhby and Tiffany Baker, "What Is Middle Class Anyway?" *CNN Business*, undated but 2016, https://money.cnn.com/infographic/economy/what-is-middle-class-anyway/index.html.

15 C. Wright Mills. *White Collar: The American Middle Classes* (New York: Oxford University Press, 1956, originally 1951), title page and 351-52.

a subjective category based on aspiration and presumably self-identification. Some recent schemes have identified certain quintiles, for example of income, wealth, or spending, as manifestly middle class. These tend to be the very middle, for example the quintiles straddling the median income. But others categorize wide sectors of society as poor or working class and look for the middle class nearer the top, for example between the fiftieth and ninetieth percentiles.[16]

Such mechanisms, because they hold the middle class as a constant percentage of the population, have the advantage of creating easy ways to compare the resources held by those in the middle of the hierarchy of wealth over time. They therefore underpin many of the recent laments for the "shrinking," "hollowing out," "vanishing," or even "lost" middle class, although in fact if the middle class declines in prosperity, the quintiles do not disappear at all; only its wealth does. Another twist also sets statistical parameters for middle-class membership not by proceeding from median income, but by reckoning that households making between two-thirds and twice the median income are middle class. This method allowed a splashy 2015 Pew Charitable Trust study to declare that the middle

---

16   Luhby and Baker, "What Is Middle Class Anyway?"; Nicolas Rapp and
     Matthew Heimer, "The Shrinking Middle Class: By the Numbers," *Fortune*,
     December 20, 2018, http://fortune.com/longform/shrinking-middle-
     class-math/; *Fortune* staff, "The Shrinking Middle Class," December 20,
     2018, http://fortune.com/longform/shrinking-middle-class/.

class had reached a "tipping point" on its way to becoming a minority. It dwindled from 61 percent in 1970 to 50 percent forty-five years later.[17]

The very studies reporting the crisis of the middle class amidst growing inequality also at times endorse the idea that in the United States, "If you think you're middle class, you are." Reliance on self-identification helps to generate huge majorities in the United States that are middle class, upwards of 70, 80, or even 95 percent. Those percentages make the middle class seem a shiny object to political strategists, the place to seek support from voters ranging "from a single, part-time bartender scratching by on $13,000 a year to a suburban power couple pulling in $230,000, or 90 percent of US households in all."[18]

The hottest controversies over the size of the middle class have come from the left, and especially from writer-activists in the developing field of working-class studies. In rejecting the idea that an overwhelming majority of Americans are members of the middle class, Michael Zweig,

17 See n. 12 above and Pew Research Center, "The American Middle Class Is Losing Ground," Pew Research Center website, December 9, 2015, https://www.pewsocialtrends.org/2015/12/09/the-american-middle-class-is-losing-ground/; Jim Tankersley, "Why America's Middle Class Is Lost," *Washington Post*, December 12, 2014, https://www.washingtonpost.com/sf/business/2014/12/12/why-americas-middle-class-is-lost/?utm_term=.1d1b2d495b9c. For a generative account of the structural matters underpinning such decline see Peter Temin, *The Vanishing Middle Class: Prejudice and Power in a Dual Economy* (Cambridge, MA: MIT Press, 2017).

18 *Fortune* staff, "The Shrinking Middle Class," unpaginated.

longtime professor of economics at the University of Stony Brook, and labor studies educator Jack Metzger offer critiques turning on how "middle class" is defined. They point out that surveys in which the term "working class" is absent from the choices offered to respondents artificially inflate the numbers of those choosing a middle-class self-identification. Zweig cites cases in which, in the absence of a working-class alternative, an overwhelming majority choose middle class. With a working-class category on offer, the proportion choosing to identify as middle class drops to less than half. In the recent past, such trends, documented by Zweig for two decades now, have accelerated. More recent studies show the middle class not only losing wealth but faith in its own status, and opting to identify in new ways.[19]

Zweig's 2000 book, straightforwardly titled *The Working Class Majority: America's Best-Kept Secret*, also parts company with the idea that class is simply a matter of self-identification. He argues that the relationship of most wage earners to an employer or manager puts them objectively in the working class, their responses to sociological surveys notwithstanding. Zweig is cautious about determining when declining conditions of work and pay push certain occupational groups into the working class.

19 Michael Zweig, *The Working Class Majority: America's Best-Kept Secret* (Ithaca: ILR Press, 2012, originally 2000), esp. 2-36; see also Unsigned, "Working Definitions," *Class Matters*, http://classmatters.org/working_definitions2.php; this distills Metzger's conclusions.

Only in his most recent writings do nurses and teachers register as proletarianized. Even reckoning so cautiously, Zweig concludes that objectively two-thirds of the labor force is working class and that subjectively up to half or more at times claim that status.[20] Meanwhile, the radical journalist Barbara Ehrenreich and social policy expert John Ehrenreich argue that even members of the professional-managerial class, which they alternately call the "professional middle class," have seen a degradation of work leaving many of them outside the middle class.[21]

The plea here is not just for more exactitude. Real life itself is complicated and inexact. Many of us know someone who once had a good, unionized job earning $35 an hour who now makes $11 as a "manager" in a box store. Or we befriend a farm family holding onto a small amount of valuable land by undertaking waged work providing health insurance. Nevertheless, notions concerning the outsized middle class, spread by many political campaigns, journalists, and even social scientists, ought to provoke challenges. Emphases on the importance of that group help to guarantee that politics is played on a terrain far more congenial to the right (and ultra-right) than to the left. This is true no matter how much

20 Zweig, *The Working Class Majority*, vii and 23-45.

21 Barbara Ehrenreich and John Ehrenreich, *Death of a Yuppie Dream: The Rise and Fall of the Professional-Managerial Class* (New York: Rosa Luxemburg Stiftung, 2013), 2-11.

some hope that the middle-class 96 percent, posited by the Republican and particularly by the Democratic Party, will magically transform into the class-conscious 99 percent hoped for by the Occupy movement. Social divides of real importance struggle to emerge when a social category is so distended and when the metaphor comes to seem real and to imply the basic goodness of the system.

Two examples illustrate the costs of the 96 percent metaphor. Where labor rights and the minimum wage are concerned, the 96 percent includes wage workers, their managers, and their employers. Not surprisingly, the glue binding possible coalitions together leaves labor law reform and the fight for a $15 minimum wage end-lessly deferred, and space is opened for vaguely drawn and authoritarian appeals that link prosperity with aus-terity, borders, and the rallying call of national greatness. Secondly, seeing matters through the frame of a nearly universal middle class especially obscures questions of race and class. If we measure the middle class via median wealth the problem emerges starkly. In 2013, for example, wealth of the white family at the exact statistical mid-dle of the US social structure was just north of $95,000, while the median Black household wealth was just over $11,000. Controlling for (middle) class by including educa-tion alongside race as a variable, the wealth differential for those with college degrees remained just short of 8:1, white over Black.[22] Many factors conspire to lead US citizens to think "white middle class" when they hear the words "middle class." Patterns of who has historically done hard manual labor and of relative access to education have left whites overrepresented in professional, white collar, and managerial labor.[23] Loose talk of saving the middle class obscures this past and present.

The Unites States as Not a Particularly Middle-Class Nation

Fortune magazine weighed in on the dire fate of the middle class in a 2018 spread titled "The Shrinking Middle Class." So stark was economic decline that being middle class had gone from seeming a rightful expectation to being a rare privilege. And yet amidst the gloom, reporters for the magazine briefly reminded readers that anyone could become middle class simply by deciding to do so. Moreover, they held that "The US is a middle class nation, founded on middle class ideals."[24] Such reassurances already sickened the

---

22 Janelle Jones, "The Racial Wealth Gap," Working Economics Blog of the Economic Policy Institute, February 13, 2017, https://www.epi.org/blog/the-racial-wealth-gap-how-african-americans-have-been-shortchanged-out-of-the-materials-to-build-wealth/.

23 Jerome P. Bjelopera, "White Collars and Blackface Race and Leisure among Clerical and Sales Workers in Early Twentieth-Century Philadelphia," *The Pennsylvania Magazine of History and Biography*, 126 (July, 2002): 471-90.

24 *Fortune* staff, "The Shrinking Middle Class," unpaginated; Nicolas Rapp and Matthew Heimer, "The Shrinking Middle Class: By the

scholar of the middle class C. Wright Mills by the 1950s, when he complained that theories regarding "white collar people" fostered the falsity that "there are no classes in the United States" and the co-conspiring notion that "psychology is the essence of classes."[25]

However, the United States is *not* a middle-class nation, in its present, recent past, or, in any compelling and coherent way, in its longer history. We have already seen something of how poorly middle-class people—or at least people in the center of the social structure—have fared since 1970. The squeeze they have experienced in an austere, neo-liberal world is emphasized by comparing the situation in the United States with other nations. Broad national comparisons placed in a graph by *Fortune* illustrated stark inequality in the United States, which looked more like Putin's Russia than France or the United Kingdom. The magazine bolded a telling headline to accompany the graph: "In Awkward Global Company."[26]

CNN Money illustrated the fate of the US working class in 2014 with another graph that offered a tidy math lesson on the difference between two kinds of averages. The

Numbers," *Fortune*, December 20, 2018, http://fortune.com/longform/shrinking-middle-class-math/.

25 Mills, *White Collar*, 294.

26 Rapp and Heimer, "The Shrinking Middle Class: By the Numbers," unpaginated.

left side of the graph arranged nations by their average wealth in the form of a mean—all the wealth divided by all the households. The $301,000 average showed the great private wealth in the United States, which per capita trailed only the relatively small nations of Switzerland, Australia, and Norway. On the right side, median wealth—50 percent have less and 50 percent more—determined the ranking of nations. Here the average wealth in the United States plummeted to $45,000 and the world ranking fell to a pedestrian nineteenth, trailing large economies such as France, Italy, the United Kingdom, and Japan (all in the top five) as well as Canada, Spain, Germany, and the Netherlands. When measured so as to account for great wealth at the top, the United States fared well. When measured from the middle, not so much. The article featuring the graph carried the apt title "America's Middle Class: Poorer than You Think." Meanwhile, in another investigation of the topic, the *New York Times* ran a piece under the headline "The American Middle Class Is No Longer the World's Richest." Looking at data on raises in the United States and "other advanced countries" over the last three decades, reporters found the United States suffering by comparison.[27]

27 Tami Luhby, "America's Middle Class: Poorer than You Think," *CNN Money*, August 5, 2014, https://money.cnn.com/2014/06/11/news/economy/middle-class-wealth/index.html. The data came from *Credit Suisse Global Wealth Databook*; see also David Leonhardt and Kevin Quealy, "The

We so live with praise songs regarding the middle class that it is possible to believe that the impassioned incoherence of the 2012 campaign was timelessly commonsensical and "American." History is valuable in puncturing such balloons. When Meyerson wrote of the 2016 election as possibly the "first" contest not centering on the middle class, the practice was in fact not even twenty-five years old. The specific electoral homilies regarding the middle class—as opposed to "forgotten Americans" or "silent majorities"—are relatively recent inventions in presidential politics. When Republican wunderkind Kevin Phillips wrote *The Emerging Republican Majority* in 1969, he produced what is in retrospect a kind of prequel to Stanley Greenberg's *Middle Class Dreams*, but coming from the right. Phillips urged the assembling of aggrieved ordinary Americans, as Republicans united behind a disdain for elites and a desire to move away from social justice. But he used the idea and language of a "middle class" hardly at all, organizing matters instead around opportunities for the right created by regional issues.[28]

The term middle class had worked its magic and malevolence in conservative causes on a smaller scale

American Middle Class Is No Longer the World's Richest," *New York Times*, April 22, 2014, https://www.nytimes.com/2014/04/23/upshot/the-american-middle-class-is-no-longer-the-worlds-richest.html.

28 Kevin Phillips, *The Emerging Republican Majority* (Princeton University Press, 2015, originally 1969).

prior to Clinton's 1992 campaign. It had served to organize opposition to integrated housing and schools in the 1960s, as Kevin Kruse's work on Atlanta shows, and to mobilize anti-tax revolts in California in the late 1970s. Pat Caddell, who was a strategist for both Jimmy Carter and Bill Clinton, had experimented with the effectiveness of the term "forgotten middle class." The Republican New Yorker Alphonse D'Amato made the same phrase a centerpiece of his 1980 Senate campaign, claiming his mom as his inspiration.[29] "Middle class" had at times seemed the property of white segregationist Democrats and at others of Republicans on the right, but overwhelmingly on the local and state level, not nationally. In the 1970s, rightward-moving Democratic adviser Ben Wattenberg reckoned about three-quarters of those in the United States were middle class.[30] Democrats who embraced middle-class dreams from the 1990s forward had reason to think that they were disarming reac-

---

29 Nicolas Lemann, "Survival of the Loudest," *New York Times*, July 12, 1992, https://www.nytimes.com/1992/07/12/opinion/survival-of-the-loudest.html; D'Amato, "The Forgotten Middle Class," *Long Island Herald*, October 15, 2010, http://www.liherald.com/baldwin/baldwin/stories/The-forgotten-middle-class,28169?content_source=&category_id=&search_filter=&event_mode=&event_ts_from=&list_type=most_commented&order_by=&order_sort=&content_class=&sub_type=&town_id=.

30 Kevin Kruse, *White Flight: Atlanta and the Making of Modern Conservatism* (Princeton: Princeton University Press, 2005), 14-15, 51-4, 68, and 263; Robert O. Self, *American Babylon: Race and the Struggle for Postwar Oakland* (Princeton University Press, 2003), 1-17, 120-25, and 256-327. On Wattenberg, see Lawrence R. Samuel, *The American Middle Class: A Cultural History* (New York: Routledge, 2014), 74.

tionary strategies. However, the "middle class" terrain on which they increasingly chose to fight remained one in which the right had more savvy and practiced arguments. Clinton and Greenberg's use of the term in 1992 was something of an experiment, and Obama's success with it in 2008 and 2012 still carried a heady air of discovery.

A 2013 study by the Center on Applied Research at Georgetown University comparing language used by the last ten presidents in public statements and official communications involving social class underlined this point. Obama mentioned "middle class" in just over half such statements, taking the leading position in its use. Bill Clinton, who came in second, used it only half as much. Obama occupied last place in references to the "poor" and to "poverty," mentioning them in only 26 percent of his statements, about half the figure for the next lowest, George H.W. Bush. In contrast, Lyndon Johnson referred to poverty in 84 percent of such communications and used middle class just 1 percent of the time. No president from late 1963 until early 1981 used middle class in more than 3 percent of their communications regarding class. Things changed.[31] And things stayed changed. In the heat of the 2016 campaign, Binyamin Appelbaum wrote in the *New York Times* under the headline

---

31 Dave Boyer, "Obama Gets Poor Ranking on Mentions of 'Poverty'; More Abundance for 'Middle Class,'" *Washington Times*, July 8, 2013, http://www.washingtontimes.com/news/2013/jul/8/obama-gets-poor-ranking-on-mentions-of-poverty/?page=all.

"The Millions of Americans Donald Trump and Hillary Clinton Barely Mention." After the colon, readers learned the identity of the taboo group: "The Poor." Amidst all the ink spilled connecting Clinton's defeat to the "white working class," almost no curiosity surfaced regarding how much the dearth of specific discussion of the poor, across color lines, suppressed voter turnout and shaped electoral outcomes. Nor is there recognition that it was specifically the rise of the middle class in political boilerplate that coincided with elbowing the poor out of public discussion.[32]

Misplaced paeans to the U.S. middle class as distinctive, timeless, and globally pace-setting chronically feature three emblematic quotations. For ballast within the western tradition, and disregarding questions of translation and political economy, Aristotle frequently speaks: "A city ought to be composed, as far as possible, of equals and similars; and these are generally the middle classes. Wherefore the city which is composed of middle-class citizens is necessarily best constituted in respect of the elements of which we say the fabric of the state naturally consists." Aristotle fangirl and anti-Communist novelist Ayn Rand comes next. "A nation's productive—and moral, and intellectual—top is its middle class," she writes. "It is a

32 Binyamin Appelbaum, "The Millions of Americans Donald Trump and Hillary Clinton Barely Mention: The Poor," *New York Times*, August 11, 2016, https://www.nytimes.com/2016/08/12/us/politics/trump-clinton-poverty.html

country's motor and lifeblood, which feeds the rest . . . the upper classes are merely a nation's past; the middle class is its future."[33] Walt Whitman's 1858 endorsement, itself perhaps gesturing toward the praise of the "middle station" in Daniel Defoe's *Robinson Crusoe*, affirmed that "The most valuable class in any community is the middle class." Bohemian, brilliant, and fully in the American grain, Whitman is invoked in order to establish a long national lineage for middle-class virtue. In fact, at the time he wrote, "middle class" was sufficiently unfamiliar as an expression in U.S. print culture that Whitman had to immediately offer a definition: "the men of moderate means living at a rate of a thousand dollars a year or thereabouts."[34]

Through most of US history, well beyond and before Whitman, "middle class" was scarcely available as an identity to those in the United States. Ngrams—graphs generated by searches of the huge numbers of words in

33   *"Politics* by Aristotle—Book Four," *Classical Wisdom Weekly* (undated) at https://classicalwisdom.com/greek_books/politics-by-aristotle-book-iv/4/; Ayn Rand, The Dead End," *Ayn Rand Newsletter*, 1 (1971): http://aynrandlexicon.com/lexicon/middle_class.html.

34   Walt Whitman, *I Sit and I Look Out: Editorials from the* Brooklyn Daily Times *by Walt Whitman*, Emory Holloway and Vernolian Schwarz, eds. (New York: Columbia University Press, 1932), 132; Stuart Blumin, *The Emergence of the Middle Class: Social Experience in the American City, 1760-1900* (Cambridge: Cambridge University Press, 1989), 1 and 245. For Crusoe, see Daniel Defoe, *The Life and Adventures of Robinson Crusoe* (London: Macmillan and Company, 1868, originally 1719), 3; B.C. Forbes, "Which Class Is Happiest?" *Forbes Quotes,* https://www.forbes.com/quotes/851/pillages *Crusoe*.

digitized databases to gain a sense of use of words and phrases over time—tell us that "middle class" hardly appeared at all in the US press until 1840, when it finally reached just one usage in every ten million words. Many of the nineteenth-century US print usages described the middle class abroad, especially in Europe, where the term had far greater currency. Usage climbed to twice 1840 levels only in 1880 and doubled again—to a rate of once in 2.5 million words—in 1920. In 1911, *International Socialist Review (ISR)*, the best US-based English-language journal of its kind, featured a long, belabored article titled "Which Class Is Your Class?" It did not even mention the middle class. Steep increases in the term's usage occurred with the crisis of capitalism in the Great Depression, when "middle class" appeared once every 1.4 million scanned words and it rose again in the period of the Cold War, when usage of the term was part of anti-Communist arguments emphasizing the standard of life and absence of class conflict in the United States. It reached its peak in the 1960s, skyrocketing to as much as an appearance every in 800,000 words. As the Cold War declined, so too did writing about the "middle class," returning to 1930s levels, though it would find a new life in specifically electoral rhetoric after Greenberg's interventions.[35]

---

35 Robert Wheeler, "Which Class Is Your Class?" *International Socialist Review*, 12 (July, 1911): 25-28; Jürgen Kocka, *White Collar Workers in America*

FIGURE ONE: NGRAM ON USE OF THE TERM "MIDDLE CLASS"

Further evidence of the late arrival of "middle class" in US discourse comes from the 1920s classic work of community sociology, *Middletown,* by Robert S. Lynd and Helen Merrell Lynd. The Lynds studied Muncie, Indiana, a middle-sized and Middle American city in what remains the best sociological account of a white community yet produced in this country. They used "middle class" just four times in a 550-page book, and only once substantively. Though noting use by other writers, the Lynds rejected without much apology the terms lower, middle, and upper class, favoring instead a simple dyad: working class and business class. Taking a view of the upper class as more or less the 1 percent, they doubted that more than ten Muncie families would belong in it.[36] By the mid-1930s,

1890-1940: A Social-Political History in International Perspective, Manra Kealey, trans. (London and Beverly Hills: SAGE Publications, 1980), 7-9.

36 Lynd and Lynd, *Middletown: A Study in Modern American Culture* (New York: Harcourt, Brace & World, 1956, originally 1929), 22, n.3, 23, and n.3 and 346.

however, when they returned to Muncie during the Depression, their *Middletown in Transition* reflected the uptick in awareness of a middle class that the Ngram shows us. They wrote then with hesitant acceptance of the idea that, though data remained "tenuous," a trend toward the "separating out of a middle class" had begun.[37]

Works recalled today as classic renderings of the role and life of the middle class actually got by without the phrase. Werner Sombart's argument in his early twentieth-century book *Why Is There No Socialism in the United States?* is remembered as hinging on the presence of a well-fed middle class, but we encounter that term primarily in front- and back-matter to modern editions rather than in the text itself. Sinclair Lewis's 1922 satire of the troubled realtor George Babbitt, whom we would now regard as the very embarrassing embodiment of middle-class man and of middlebrow culture, got along without use of the phrase middle class. However, when the Nobel Prize for Literature went to Lewis in 1930, the presentation speech found *Babbitt* to be the story of "the ideal of an American popular hero of the middle class."[38]

---

37 Lynd and Lynd, *Middletown in Transition: A Study in Cultural Conflicts* (New York: Harcourt, Brace and Company, 1937), 457-58 and 446-60, passim.

38 Werner Sombart, *Why Is There No Socialism in the United States?* (London: Macmillan, 1976, originally 1906); Sinclair Lewis, *Babbitt* (New York: Harcourt, Brace, and Company, 1922); Erik Axel Karfeldt, "Presentation Speech," December 10, 1930, http://www.nobelprize.org/nobel_prizes/literature/laureates/1930/press.html.

None of this means that "middle class" cannot be applied retrospectively. "Racism," usually considered by scholars to have come into common usage in reaction to systems of oppression under Nazi rule, has, for example, surely been usefully applied to social realities unfolding centuries before the term itself gained currency.[39] Similarly, the careful work on the nineteenth-century middle class by Stuart Blumin, Mary Ryan, Jeanne Boydston, Sven Beckert, Richard Sennett, Gwendolyn Wright, and others shows how new urban layers of businessmen, tradespeople, professionals, and eventually corporate-connected employees in sales, office work, accountancy, and management came together in families, churches, neighborhoods (eventually suburbs), colleges, ice cream parlors, reform politics, and elsewhere. These disparate figures forged linked identities through lived experiences and shared values and even through conflicts as the self-employed and white-collar corporate employees struggled to coexist in families. However, they only rarely knew themselves as middle class and did not produce anything like a middle-class nation.[40] As my old teacher Robert Wiebe wrote,

39 George Fredrickson, *Racism: A Short History* (Princeton: Princeton University Press, 2002), 5; Christopher Vials, *Haunted by Hitler: Liberals, the Left, and the Fight against Fascism in the United States* (Amherst: University of Massachusetts Press, 2014), 70-1.

40 Stuart Blumin, *The Emergence of the Middle Class: Social Experience in the American City, 1760-1900* (Cambridge: Cambridge University Press, 1989); Mary Ryan, *Cradle of the Middle Class: The Family in Oneida County, New*

the pre-1920s middle class "was a class only by courtesy of the historian's afterthought."[41]

Making the US Middle Class

By the 1930s, there was modestly growing good press for the idea of the United States as a middle-class nation. A boost for the idea came from editors and media owners with a self-interest in seeing matters that way in the age of mass industrial unionism. The Lynds had noticed as much by the time *Middletown in Transition* appeared in 1937. In it, they quoted at length from a 1936 editorial from a local newspaper, "The Middle Class Rules America." The editorial declared the United States immune from the

York, 1790-1865 (Cambridge, UK: Cambridge University Press, 1983); Paul E. Johnson, *A Shopkeeper's Millennium: Society and Revivals in Rochester, New York, 1815-1837* (New York: FSG Adult, 2004, originally 1990); Richard Sennett, *Families against the City: Middle Class Homes of Industrial Chicago, 1872-1890* (Cambridge, MA: Harvard University Press, 1984); Jeanne Boydston, *Home and Work: Housework, Wages, and the Ideology of Labor in the Early Republic* (Oxford and New York: Oxford University Press, 1990); Sven Beckert, "Propertied of a Different Kind: Bourgeoisie and Lower Middle Classes in the Nineteenth Century United States" in Burton Bledstein and Robert D. Johnston, eds. *The Middling Sorts: Explorations in the History of the American Middle Class* (New York: Routledge, 1993), 285-95; Gwendolyn Wright, *Moralism and the Model Home: Domestic Architecture and Cultural Conflict in Chicago, 1873-1913* (Chicago: University of Chicago Press, 1980). More globally, see Arno Mayer, "The Lower Middle Class as Historical Problem," *Journal of Modern History*, 47 (September, 1975).

41 Werner Sombart, *Why Is There No Socialism in the United States?* (London: Macmillan, 1976); Robert Wiebe, *The Search for Order, 1877-1920* (New York: Hill and Wang, 1967), 112.

"ferocity of the revolution in Spain" because it had never been "feudal." The United States always invested "sovereign authority [in] a great middle class," however much individuals were very rich and very poor. Although the rise of the Congress of Industrial Organizations dominated the news, the "class baiters" could never win in the middle-class nation of the United States.[42]

In February 1940, the then-stylish business magazine *Fortune* produced a breakthrough for the idea of a middle-class nation in popular media. The magazine expanded its regular "*Fortune* Survey" feature into a fat special issue developing a "self-portrait" titled "People of the U.S.A." The very first subheading affirmed a foundational fact: "The U.S. Is Middle Class." Those it identified as the "people," that collective noun so dear to the left at the time, roughly equaled the middle class. A spectacular statistic, if not fact, anchored the argument: 79.2 percent of respondents identified as members of the middle class even as the decade of the Great Depression and mass industrial unionism ended. With recovery still far from complete, supposedly only a quarter of factory workers described themselves as "laboring" or "working" class. Most of those Americans responding as middle class specified "middle middle" if they offered a further adjective. Less than 3 percent

42 Lynd and Lynd, *Middletown in Transition*, 446.

opted for "upper" or "upper-middle" class. As *Fortune* put it, there were "singularly few people," even executives, who were "willing to tag themselves as anything more than plain 'middle class.'" The most breathless article in the special issue especially admired the nation's "30,000 Managers: Earning $15,000 to $200,000 Plus, They Drive the Economic System and Coddle 56,000 Capitalists." Those in this group identified themselves as regular middle-class folks too. The "Great American Salesman," seen as a swashbuckling "artist bounding in and out of the halls of business," concurred. Though there had been precedents for holding that the middle class was larger than the working class, *Fortune*'s assertion that a startling four-fifths of a nation barely off the skids claimed to be middle class has meant its survey is still cited even today.[43]

The *Fortune* survey also raised questions that continue to trouble discussions of the middle class. The framing of the volume neatly illustrates that the ideal of a middle-class United States was not only embraced by many individuals but also loved by powerful elites. The ideology of a middle-class United States was and is central to the dream work of those elites and some ordinary residents. The special issue frankly strove to recapture the élan with

---

43 Editors, "The People of the U.S.A.: A Self-Portrait," *Fortune*, 21, February, 1940, 14, 20 and passim; Lewis Corey, *The Crisis of the Middle Class* (New York: Covici and Friede, 1935), 259 and 273.

which *Fortune* had been founded at the heady tail end of
the booming 1920s. It exulted that the nation remained
impervious to the formation of "any self-conscious proletariat such as a Marxist would wish for." Pollsters themselves sometimes expressed similar views. The researchers, who seem to have been even more committed to the
idea of a middle-class nation than the survey's respondents, vigorously massaged data to shore up the case.
Actually, only 47 percent of respondents to the survey had
initially said that they were middle class—impressive but
no majority. Researchers then went back to all those not
offering upper, lower, or middle class as an answer—27.5
percent originally gave responses putting them in a "Don't
Know" category—and asked which of those three choices
they would opt for if pressed.[44] The data therefore reflected
freely chosen self-descriptions in the first instance and
answers to guiding questions requiring an upper/middle/
lower rubric in the second. On the other hand, *Fortune*'s
editors at times seemed to relish a good provocation. Just
two years after the "Portrait" special issue, they featured a

---

44 Ibid, 14-20; Marina Moskowitz, "The Elephant in the Room: Culture,
    Cohesion, and Context in the American Middle Class," in Kevin Cahill
    and Lene Johannessen, eds. *Considering Class: Essays on the Discourse of
    the American Dream* (Berlin: LIT Verlag, 2007), 13; George Horace Gallup
    and Saul Forbes Rae, *The Pulse of Democracy The Public Opinion Poll and
    How It Works* (New York: Simon and Schuster, 1940), 169-71; on the *Fortune*
    Survey and construction of samples, see Unsigned, "Research Projects and
    Methods in Educational Sociology," *Journal of Educational Sociology*, 14
    (December, 1940): 250-53.

poll showing that one American in four favored socialism, with another 35 percent reporting having "an open mind" on the issue.[45]

The *Fortune* volume also engaged the ways in which academic researchers used "the middle class" as a term by claiming that class can be a matter of self-identification. Sociologist Robert S. Lynd both deployed the magazine's survey figures and derided self-identification as merely "subjective self-rating." The *Fortune* researchers could appeal to the large and enthusiastic 1935 study of the middle class by liberal writer Alfred Bingham, which held that "if the bulk of the people, in a modern capitalist country like the United States [think] of themselves as being middle class," they have established a social fact.[46] *Fortune*'s special issue reflected the knowledge that people who were objectively positioned differently in the economy chose to invent themselves as middle class. Thus, the survey remarked bemusedly on the propensity of "the prosperous" to nevertheless identify with the middle class and lingered over the fact that over 70 percent of the "poor" claimed middle-class status. In a rare nod to racial division, the researchers found that "the Negro" self-identified as

45 Christopher Vials, ed. *American Literature in Transition, 1940-1950* (Cambridge: Cambridge University Press, 2018), 5.

46 For Lynd and Bingham, see Moskowitz, "The Elephant in the Room," 13-14; see also David Ramsey, "Middle Class Attitudes," *New Masses* (April 7, 1936), 39, and chapters 4 and 5 of this book.

middle class less than half as often as whites, but also chose upper class far more often.[47] Such a breakdown suggests a fascinating further problem with self-reporting regarding class. Respondents doubtless drew on direct experience to position themselves—not within the nation but within communities segregated by race and class. To report being in the middle or at the top of the hierarchy in a ghetto or in a coal-mining town did not necessarily imply any attempt to compare oneself to the US population as a whole. Thus, the very workers who organized the Congress of Industrial Organizations in auto, steel, and rubber might have been tempted to portray themselves to *Fortune* pollsters as having risen to the middle of their communities.

In the terminology of the late French theorist Louis Althusser, *Fortune* successfully "hailed" those polled as being middle class, inviting them to—again Althusser— "interpellate" into the US class structure in a certain way, not unreasonable given their circumstances. Especially during World War II, and then during the Cold War, each featuring both political repression and celebration of the United States, the call got a certain response. There is little room for doubt that the WWII and postwar economic boom was concentrated in the relatively unscathed United States. This made for relatively high identification with the

47 Editors, "The People of the U.S.A.," 20.

middle class, if workers were approached in a certain way. Sixty years ago, the British Marxist Andrew Grant cited a Gallup poll in his country showing self-identification as middle class outpaced working class by 49 percent to 46 percent. Grant lamented that popularity of the middle-class label but added that in the United States, middle-class identification had reached 88 percent. The Institute for Public Opinion likewise found a whopping 88 percent of those polled in the United States claiming middle-class status, bracketed by an equally small sliver of uppers and lowers.[48]

Even so, the results remained uneven and highly dependent on the wording of the questions. In 1949, for example, a study by Richard Centers reported self-identification as working class outdistancing mid-dle class, 51 percent to 43 percent. Eight years after that, an extremely open-ended study by John Haer of the Rand Corporation found that in both Tallahassee (where only whites were surveyed) and in Minneapolis, middle-class responses outpaced working class ones handily. But in neither case was "middle" the majority response, and in Minneapolis it did not reach one-third. The "don't know" figures were astronomical and, when correlated with

---

48 Andrew Grant, *Socialism and the Middle Classes* (New York: International Publishers, 1959, originally 1957), 7; Gallup and Rae, *The Pulse of Democracy*, 169.

other data, identified those confused or reticent as also
poor. Other responses underlined a total failure in inter-
pellation as respondents self-identified as members of the
"white class," the "friendly class," or the "religious class."[49]

The Costly Marriage of the Middle-Class Nation and American Exceptionalism

There are understandable tendencies to regard today's
political chatter about the middle class as mere boilerplate, or as describing a vessel into which liberal and even
socialist ideas may be poured as easily as reactionary
ones. Instead, such rhetoric, now more firmly tied than
ever to the "American Exceptionalist" view of the United
States as a blessed and exemplary place, stunts political
imagination and possibility. To lots of us both American
exceptionalism and the idea of a middle-class nation ring
hollow. But they remain the twin pillars of political commonsense for those thinking electorally or at least tun-
ing into Fox News, MSNBC, or CNN. The history of how
slowly the middle-class nation and the idea of American
exceptionalism came to be joined in politics, social

49 Althusser, "Ideology and Ideological State Apparatuses" in his *Lenin and
    Philosophy and Other Essays* (New York: Monthly Review Press, 1971),
    available at https://www.marxists.org/reference/archive/althusser/1970/
    ideology.htm; John Haer, "An Empirical Study of Social Class Awareness,"
    Survey, 36 (December, 1957): 117-20; Richard Centers, *The Psychology of
    Social Classes* (Princeton: Princeton University Press, 1949), 77.

thought, and media, and then how fully they became merged, therefore deserves attention. Since the terms of that merger so privilege one tiny sliver of the middle classes—the entrepreneur—to stand in for the whole, the process carries even more importance.

If the Cold War nationalist efforts hailing almost everybody as middle class remained incomplete, they were nevertheless impressive and destructive. Joined, as we will see in the following chapter, by miseries even during good times that made for a sad but unifying middle-class experience, such hailing frequently found response. This was especially the case when the middle class being courted was placed by politicians and pundits within the context of a never-equaled nation, an "American exceptionalist" one. It seemed not so much capitalism, but the specific adoption of a US model of supposed free enterprise, capable of generating a giant middle class, that would best Communism. The middle class, nationalism, and the notion of a transcendent US model harmonized to identify the US middle class as the key to everything. For example, in the face of challenges from the New Left, Black Power, and above all the Vietnamese in 1968, the Bay Area philosopher and waterfront worker Eric Hoffer found fame as the voice of reason and order. For Hoffer, as for Ayn Rand, the middle class gave us Western Civilization, and the US example showed that such a class could become

"real" *Internationale*, rendering hopes of socialist solidarity hollow and ridiculous.[50] Politicians, as we have seen,
have increasingly championed such views. Labor unions
have also gravitated to a middle-class-forward approach,
attracted to it not only as a present strategy, but also as
something unions had supposedly supported "for generations." Kansas City activist intellectual Bill Onasch rightly
connects the post–World War II popularity of the idea of a
middle-class majority with "a hardening Cold War union
bureaucracy," but the end of the Cold War has not lessened
commitment to it.[51]

As with trade unionism, the period of steep decline
of the middle class domestically since 1970 nevertheless
coincided with the United States being put forward as
an exemplar of how to do things right in consolidating a
middle class. Fanfare greeted the doubling of the world's
middle class in twenty-five years—1.4 billion people
were said to dwell there in 2014. But the new global
middle class makes between $4 and $13 dollars per day,
leaving most far short of the poverty line in the United
States. Other optimists predicted that the US example

---

50 Eric Hoffer, "Sunday Thought," *San Francisco Examiner and Chronicle*,
    June 23, 1968; Hoffer, "The Middle Class Takes a Beating," *San Francisco
    Examiner*, September 24, 1968.

51 Preface to American Federation of Teachers president Randi Weingarten's
    "My Labor Day Mention" email to David Roediger (September 3, 2018);
    Onasch, "No Middle Ground," unpaginated.

and neoliberal policies could lead to a new dawn in which 90 percent of India would be middle class. More sober analysts suggest the actual figure is nearer to 2 percent. The labor journalist Paul Mason argues that the example of the United States and its "rich-world counterparts" does attract followers globally but leads "steadily to stratification and more service-oriented work."[52]

The idea that the United States occupies a special, leading, and exemplary place—the world's exceptional nation because of its middle class—has existed inchoately for a long while, but the connection between exceptionalism and the middle class has tightened over time. Patriots and European travelers saw the United States as especially promising for its particular freedoms, distribution of (formerly native) land, and absence of aristocratic and churchly restraints. Frederick Jackson Turner's writings on the frontier, like some of the work of Marx and Engels, posited that access to land set the United States apart from

---

52 A. Ricardo Lopez and Barbara Weinstein, eds. *The Making of the Middle Class: Toward a Transnational History* (Durham: Duke University Press, 2012), 7-9; Steve Knauss, "The Myth of the Global Middle Class," *Potemkin Review*, December, 2015, https://www.potemkinreview.org/the-myth-of-the-global-middle-class.html; cf. Rohan Venkataramakrishnan, "Almost Everyone in India Thinks They Are 'Middle Class' and Almost No One Actually Is," *Scroll.in*, September 21, 2015, https://scroll.in/article/740011/everyone-in-india-thinks-they-are-middle-class-and-almost-no-one-actually-is; Paul Mason, "Who Are the New Middle Classes around the World?" *The Guardian*, January 20, 2014, https://www.theguardian.com/commentisfree/2014/jan/20/new-middle-classes-world-poor.

class-ridden Europe, with Turner adding that the frontier itself made for democratic practices. However, for Marx, Engels, and Turner, this process had an end, as frontiers ran out and troubles lay ahead.[53]

The precise term "American exceptionalism" came much later and amidst rich irony. One recent account has it originating from Stalin, who in 1929 was searching for a name for a heresy within the world Communist movement he dominated. Jay Lovestone, a US labor leader, led a tendency inside the Communist Party, with his faction arguing in the late '20s that new strategies were necessary because US workers were not ready for revolution. Stalin branded this deviation as "American exceptionalism," and Lovestone, arguing his corner, did use the phrase "middle class" to describe elements to be targeted in party appeals.[54]

53 For Turner, see his *The Frontier in American History* (New York: Henry Holt, 1920) at http://xroads.virginia.edu/~HYPER/TURNER/; Engels, *The Condition of the Working Class in England* (n.p.: Panther Edition, 1969, originally in German in 1845 and in English, 1887), 6 at https://www.marxists.org/archive/marx/works/download/pdf/condition-working-class-england.pdf.

54 For some of the debate and language among US Communists, see Mark Liberman, "The Third Life of American Exceptionalism," *Language Log*, February 23, 2012, https://languagelog.ldc.upenn.edu/nll/?p=3798; for Stalin and Lovestone, see Terrence McCoy, "How Stalin Gave Us American Exceptionalism," *The Atlantic*, March 15, 2012, https://www.theatlantic.com/politics/archive/2012/03/how-joseph-stalin-invented-american-exceptionalism/254534/.

The most famous Cold War intellectual to take up what made the United States special, Louis Hartz, argued in 1955 in his incredibly ambitious volume, *The Liberal Tradition in America*, that lacking a feudal order against which to rebel, the United States could only generate limited traditions of revolt and even of social democracy. Hartz so fully embraced the idea that the United States was hardwired against socialist movements that he is often mistakenly remembered as a champion of the glories of American exceptionalism. He is better understood as a radical writing sadly and with deep awareness of Marxism. *Liberal Tradition*'s one use of "exceptionalism"—the term "American exceptionalism" does not appear—refers to the debates among Marxists in the 1930s. Hartz does use "middle class" centrally, though far less frequently than "bourgeois," as the goal is to discuss bourgeois revolutions and their ideas, more than class structures. Far from seeking to ground exceptional national glory in the middle class, Hartz stressed the limitations of both that class and the nation. "The Americans," he lamented, "though models to all the world in the middle-class way of life, lacked the passionate middle-class consciousness which saturated the liberal thought of Europe."[55]

---

55 Louis Hartz, *The Liberal Tradition in America* (New York: Harvest, 1991, originally 1955), 278, 51 and passim. On Hartz, see Rogers M. Smith, "Why No 'Liberalism' in the United States" unpublished paper, 2006, https://www.academia.edu/2806543/Why_No_Liberalism_in_the_United_States;

The "middle class nation" and "American exceptionalism" found each other late, and under specific circumstances. As the economic indices showing stagnating wages and soaring inequality have increasingly challenged both notions since 1970, the view that the United States is the product of their marriage has only gained political currency. Especially over the past quarter century, the reflexive response to middle-class decline has been to promise to defend the middle class and, through it, the nation.[56] When Burton Bledstein began his valuable 1976 history of the middle class with the words, "From the 1840s until the present, the idea of the middle class has been central to the history of American social attitudes," Cold War politics animated the over-reading involved in that assertion. The ersatz ubiquity that Bledstein assumed across space and time— one that led the historian Loren Baritz to liken the study of the middle class to "searching for air"—fed in particular on the American exceptionalist certainties of Bledstein's next sentence: "No other national identity has

on the *Fortune* Survey and construction of samples, see n.a., "Research Projects and Methods in Educational Sociology," 250-53.

56 Unsigned, "US Millennials Feel More Working Class than Any Other Generation," *The Guardian*, March 15, 2016), https://www.theguardian.com/world/2016/mar/15/us-millennials-feel-more-working-class-than-any-other-generation; Frank Newport, "Fewer Americans Identify as Middle Class in Recent Years," *GALLUP*, April 28, 2015, https://www.schwartzreport.net/fewer-americans-identify-as-middle-class-in-recent-years/.

been so essentially concerned with this one idea."[57] When Ronald Reagan established the potency of the direct invocation of "American exceptionalism" electorally in the 1980s and Bill Clinton the power of direct appeals to middle-class dreams in the '90s, the two came to prosper together among politicians and pundits.[58]

In 1996, the eminent centrist political scientist Seymour Martin Lipset revisited Hartz's ideas. Forty years down the road, American exceptionalism was front and center in his celebrated book, *American Exceptionalism: A Double-Edged Sword*. The middle class immediately made an entrance, as Lipset wrote of a nation "dominated by pure bourgeois, individualistic values" over the long haul. Although Lipset allowed that in some of the best-designed studies, more people in the United States identified as working class than middle class at the time, the emphasis on a nation exceptional because it was middle class ran through the volume. Hartz's gloom gave way in Lipset's

57 Bledstein, *The Culture of Professionalism: The Middle Class and the Development of Higher Education in America* (New York: W.W. Norton and Company, 1976), 1; Loren Baritz, *The Good Life: The Meaning of Success for the American Middle Class* (New York: Knopf, 1989), xi.

58 For a competent if politically uncongenial account of Reagan's long connections to American exceptionalism and allied notions, see Annelise Anderson, "Ronald Reagan and American Exceptionalism" in Terrence McCoy, *American Exceptionalism in a New Era* (Stanford: Hoover Institution Press, 2017), 143-49.

gleeful study.[59] Between 1980 and 2000, a recent study shows, there was "a lot of talk" about American exceptionalism—457 mentions in national publications. However, in the new century's first decade, this ballooned to 2,558 times. The first two years of the 2010s nearly doubled that of the entire prior decade. The most over-the-top example came in 2011 with the publication of conservative congressman and historian of sorts Newt Gingrich's *A Nation like No Other: Why American Exceptionalism Matters.*[60]

An early campaign profile for the relatively left-of-center 2020 presidential hopeful Elizabeth Warren appeared in a Salt Lake City publication under the headline, "Make the Middle Class Great Again." Her campaign must have smiled. As we have seen, commitment to saving the middle class animates campaigns across party lines and seems heartfelt at times. Obama, for example, faced no more elections when he said in 2014: "I believe in American exceptionalism with every fiber of my being." However, identification with the middle class wanes situationally. Beyond elections, the liabilities of pairing the "middle class nation" and American exceptionalist tropes are clear. In a 2017 Pew poll, a large majority of under-30s

---

59 Seymour Martin Lipset, *American Exceptionalism: A Double-Edged Sword* (New York: W.W. Norton and Company, 1996), 4, 252, and 51-59.

60 McCoy, "How Stalin Gave Us American Exceptionalism," unpaginated; Gingrich, *A Nation like No Other: Why American Exceptionalism Matters* (Washington, D.C.: Regnery Publishing, 2011).

believed that "there are other countries better than the US."[61] At such a relatively clear-sighted juncture, identifying American exceptionalism exclusively with the middle class risks disappearing the experiences of the poor, of victims of racial oppression, and of working-class people.

In still another way, the joining of the middle-class nation with the idea of American exceptionalism encourages fighting on terrain favorable to the Trumps of the world and to capital. Who is imagined and catered to when middle-class salvation gains a hearing? Since the middle class is such a hodgepodge of workers and owners involved in all sorts of different social relations, it can hardly surprise us that those writing about it consistently make one segment of it stand in for the imagined whole. To his credit, C. Wright Mills titled his major book on the subject *White Collar*, and referred in his subtitle to the *Middle Classes*, plural. Still, his work is taken as if it apprehends the whole of an actually existing middle class. British and German writers have similarly connected the middle class to a certain kind of employment (and dress),

---

61 Kelan Lyons, "Make the Middle Class Great Again," *Salt Lake City Weekly's Daily Feed*, April 18, 2019, https://www.cityweekly.net/BuzzBlog/archives/2019/04/18/make-the-middle-class-great-again; Jake Sullivan, "What Donald Trump and Dick Cheney Got Wrong about America," *The Atlantic*, January-February, 2019, https://www.theatlantic.com/magazine/archive/2019/01/yes-america-can-still-lead-the-world/576427/; Peter Beinart, "AOC's Generation Doesn't Presume America's Innocence," *The Atlantic*, June 21, 2019, https://www.theatlantic.com/ideas/archive/2019/06/aoc-isnt-interested-american-exceptionalism/592213/.

using either "white collar" or the very cool phrase "black-coated worker."[62] John and Barbara Ehrenreich shift back and forth between calling their subject the "professional-managerial class" and the "professional middle class." Her singly authored book on the subject, *Fear of Falling*, nevertheless uses a subtitle identifying the whole middle class as the book's subject. Immediately after that, the introduction bemoans how inadequate the very term middle class is.[63]

When we connect American exceptionalism to a middle-class nation, the small numbers of entrepreneurs in the United States acquire inflated importance. To suppose that the United States has "always" been middle class requires that huge numbers of farmers and a small number of independent businesspersons and professionals of the early United States be the founding fathers of the modern middle class. Their storied (and overstated) virtues of manly independence come to be writ large onto the modern United States, which has for a long time not resembled a society of independent proprietors at

---

62 Mills, *White Collar*; David Lockwood, *The Black-Coated Worker: A Study in Class Consciousness* (Fairlawn, NJ: Essential Books, 1958); Jürgen Kocka, *White Collar Workers in America 1890-1940: A Social-Political History in International Perspective*, Manra Kealey, trans. (London and Beverly Hills: SAGE Publications, 1980).

63 Ehrenreich and Ehrenreich, *Death of a Yuppie Dream*, 2-11; Barbara Ehrenreich, *Fear of Falling: The Inner Life of the Middle Class* (New York: Pantheon, 1989), 4-5.

all. As the historian Steve Fraser recently summarized this transformation, the (white, male) nation in 1820 was "80 percent self-employed and by 1940 80 percent worked for someone—or something—else."[64] Family farms (and their male heads of household), so important to the mythos of American exceptionalism, have long ranked among the least "American" things in the modern world. Less than one-half of 1 percent of the world's 500 million family farms are in the United States, which trails the European nations significantly and the Global South utterly in percentage of farmers.[65] Going behind such numbers, Mills wrote, "The nineteenth-century farmer and businessman were generally thought to be stalwart individuals—their own men." The white-collar man is "always somebody's man."[66] We would be tempted to add "or women," but it is not quite that easy, as the attendant ideology was and is masculine, though not always in a very self-assured way. The great dissenting US scholar G. William Domhoff,

64 Steve Fraser, *The Age of Acquiescence: The Life and Death of American Resistance to Organized Wealth and Power* (New York: Little, Brown and Company, 2015), 59.

65 For the World Bank data on this matter, see "Share of the Labor Force Employed in Agriculture, 2017 at https://ourworldindata.org/grapher/share-of-the-labor-force-employed-in-agriculture; see also Alex Callinicos, "The 'New Middle Class' and Socialist Politics,' *International Socialism*," 2 (Summer, 1983), esp. Table II at https://www.marxists.org/history/etol/writers/callinicos/1983/xx/newmc.html.

66 Mills, *White Collar*, xi-xii

for example, introduced Richard Parker's searing book on the new middle class a half century ago by describing its subject as "a class of property paper pushers and people manipulators who must go along to get along."[67] Interestingly, it was experience in this new middle class that sometimes sharpened dreams of being self-employed. In 1905, a poll of retail clerks found that half of them had imbibed enough of what the German historian Jürgen Kocka described as "businessman as model" ideology that they not only hoped but believed that they were transitioning to self-employment. After World War II, when unionized autoworkers were often seen as ascending to middle-class status, Eli Chinoy's celebrated study of them found widespread desires to instead own a business or farm.[68]

Today, just one American in sixteen is an entrepreneur, and since about half of small businesses fail within five years, ex-entrepreneur is a more robust category. But the cult worship surrounding this tiny group drives rhetoric and policy.[69] Again, the appeal is bipartisan, with

---

67 Domhoff introducing Richard Parker, *The Myth of the Middle Class: Notes on Affluence and Equality* (New York: Harper, 1972), x-xi.

68 Jürgen Kocka, *White Collar Workers in America*, 86; see also Ruth Milkman's intro in the second edition of Eli Chinoy, *Automobile Workers and the American Dream* (Urbana and Chicago: University of Illinois Press, 1992), xii-xvii.

69 For the figures, which show a significant decline even in the recent past, see http://www.bls.gov/cps/cpsaat11.htm and http://www.

liberal-seeming universities competing
which can most emphasize the entrepre...
vision statements. The peculiar recent US idea that be...
businessman or "delivering a payroll" qualifies a candidate
for political office finds its roots in the aggrandizement of
the entrepreneur. Not even the Trump presidency has yet
managed to discredit it. Where I live, in Kansas, the recent
past has delivered tax cuts that amount to business tax
exemptions specifically favoring entrepreneurs and established big businesses, bringing public education to the
brink of ruin. The highest-paid state employee, University
of Kansas basketball coach Bill Self, suddenly found the
bulk of his income untaxed, coming from allegedly entrepreneurial activity, not salaried coaching.[70] We deserve
bigger and better explanations for this obsession than
mis-leadership by demagogues. Michel Foucault's theo-
rizing of the "entrepreneurial self" among those far from
being self-employed offers clues. The desire to someday
become "independent," the importance of housing market

careerbuildercommunications.com/pdf/cb-emsi_SelfEmployment2014.
pdf; on failure rates see Chad Otar, "What Percentage of Small Businesses
Fail?" *Forbes*, October 25, 2018, https://www.forbes.com/sites/forbes-
financecouncil/2018/10/25/what-percentage-of-small-businesses-fail-
and-how-can-you-avoid-being-one-of-them/#5cf90be143b5.

70 Dan Margolies and Sam Zeff, "Thanks to Tax Cuts, Bill Self, Highest Paid
State Employee, Owes Little in Kansas Income Taxes," *KCUR 89.3*, May 16,
2016, https://www.cbpp.org/research/state-budget-and-tax/kansas-pro-
vides-compelling-evidence-of-failure-of-supply-side-tax-cuts.

decisions to personal wealth, and the self-management of retirement accounts, as well as the calibration of how and when to invest in one's own re-skilling, help shape such a self.[71] The political chorus regarding an exceptional middle-class nation, supposedly chock-full of entrepreneurs, remains with us, powerfully influencing how "saving the middle class" is heard and acted upon.

71 Andrew Dilts, "From 'Entrepreneur of the Self' to 'Care of the Self': Neo-liberal Governmentality and Foucault's Ethics," *Foucault Studies*, 12 (October 9, 2011): 130-46. On Kansas, see Michael Mazerov, "Kansas Provides Compelling Evidence of Failure of 'Supply Side' Tax Cuts," Center on Budget and Policy Priorities, January 22, 2018, https://www.cbpp.org/research/state-budget-and-tax/kansas-provides-compelling-evidence-of-failure-of-supply-side-tax-cuts.

Four

HOW THE LEFT HAS LIVED WITH THE PROBLEM OF THE MIDDLE CLASS

He succeeds with it; he fails with it; he dies with it. But why did he have it? Isn't it true that he had to have a false dream in our society?
—Fredric Wertham, psychologist, on the impoverished
middle-class dream of Willy Loman in Arthur Miller's
Death of a Salesman

Plenty of history runs through what follows in this chapter, so much so that we had best begin with what is at stake for our current moment in understanding that past. At its biggest convention to date, the Democratic Socialists of America (DSA) voted in August 2019 for Resolution 32, committing resources to its Labor Commission and to implement a "rank-and-file strategy." Suddenly having grown to 50,000 members, DSA promised to nurture "workers' sense of being part of something bigger—not just a union, but a working class—that is capable of fighting, winning, and ultimately ruling." Such stirring pledges and hopes have from time to time—but not recently—found expression in US history. In their heyday, the hope was attached to workers in heavy industry, to those on docks and in warehouses and mines, with images featuring male brawn and resolve, often as against the effete world of working and lounging without blue collars. Resolution 32 supports trying to send radicals to jobs in "strategic sectors" where they live. It gives a single example of such a sector, K–12 education. It mentions one publication as a model for others forthcoming, the pamphlet *Why Socialists Should Become Teachers.*[1]

That is, hopes for the longed-for rebirth of a working-class movement now cohere around an occupational group long considered middle class. Indeed, even Michael Zweig, the labor studies scholar most responsible for arguing over the last quarter-century that the working class still outnumbers the middle class in the United States, only very recently decided that teachers, along with nurses, had sunk into the working class. Setbacks in working conditions and pay, as well as losses of autonomy on the job, sent them down. There were further ironies. The DSA resolution called for the new initiative to use the

1   "Labor Strategy and the DSLC: Resolution #32 DSA," August, 2019, https://docs.google.com/document/d/1xulx3e-qz6qpJZ50oU61Lm3NnyfEaDzU-w7coBo69ZE0/edit; the chapter's epigraph is from C. Wright Mills, *White Collar: The American Middle Classes* (New York: Oxford University Press, 1956, originally 1951), xi.

"troublemakers" training program developed by activists around the publication *Labor Notes*. Some of those promoting the new DSA policy came from the valuable *Labor Notes* tradition, which began in part out of radicalized New Leftists, often college-educated and the children of professionals, moving to Detroit and elsewhere to be part of the struggles of industrial workers. To their credit, some of these activists themselves helped to write Resolution 32, with a new emphasis on leadership by teachers. They had by then long participated in and learned from the struggles of troublemaking teachers and nurses.[2]

Such a transformation had antecedents in a long process leading to a realization that teachers and nurses might not simply be in the working class, but leading it. For some time, writers on the left have connected teachers to the beginnings of new movements. In the wake of the Trump election in 2016, the most dramatic labor protests saw teachers in "red states"—that is, Republican-dominated ones—mount massive strikes and marches to confront austerity directed at themselves and at those whom they taught. The mobilizations in Oklahoma and West Virginia stood out especially in suggesting that teachers within and beyond conservative areas have

---

2 Michael Zweig, *The Working Class Majority: America's Best-Kept Secret* (Ithaca: ILR Press 2000), 26-7; cf. Zweig's 2012 edition with same publisher at 24-27 for the very halting inclusion of some teachers and nurses as working class; "Labor Strategy and the DSLC: Resolution #32 DSA."

begun a new workers' movement, conjoined with a new Democratic Party politics. "It started in West Virginia," we are told, sometimes with the added and more questionable proviso that the electoral campaigns of Bernie Sanders coalesced the movement of teacher activists there.[3]

When the reactionary governor Scott Walker of Wisconsin launched an attack on state workers, the poor, civil liberties, and the environment, an inspiring 2011 "Wisconsin Uprising" opposed him, occupying the State House in Madison. Lots of activists backed planning for a general strike, but some also wondered if the slogan "Re-organize Wisconsin" might have legs. That is, since anti-union forces were using Wisconsin as a laboratory for their worst ideas, might unions and the left not use the state to develop their best ones, by pouring in organizing resources and people while trying to make union-busting a strategy as costly as possible to Walker's corporate supporters? Although opponents tried to remind Walker that Wisconsin was a "union state," it had largely ceased to be one, particularly where private sector unionism was concerned. In choosing electoral strategies rather than a direct confrontation with that reality, organized labor reflected its own lack of resources, and a certainty that labor law

3   Eric Blanc, *Red State Revolt: The Teachers' Strike Wave and Working-Class Politics* (New York: Verso, 2019); cf. Michael Mochaidean, "Do All Organizing Roads Lead to Bernie?" Black Rose/Rosa Negra, February 28, 2019, http:blackrosefed.org/teacher-strikes-bernie-eric-blanc.

was not on its side. Lack of confidenc~
workers could do historic things also sha~

Worries about whether the labor movement co~
a time be centrally about teachers and other public employees went beyond wondering whether private-sector workers would support public employees. Given their position
at the point of attack and their militancy, any rebuilding
of the state's labor movement in Wisconsin would have
had to empower public employees to lead. Teachers in particular would have had to be in the forefront, including in
efforts to build momentum for private-sector unionism.
The electoral efforts that soon became the central strategy to defeat Walker achieved at best mixed results. When
I attended a post-mortem on the Wisconsin Uprising in
Madison in 2013, there were plenty of regrets to go around.
The clearest insights, though, regarded underestimating
the social power of public employees, too often considered as limited in their range of motion by professionalism and atomization. Tellingly mentioned, for example,
were workers who record deeds at the county level and the
teachers who, among everything else, provide childcare to
much of the labor force. [4]

4   Andy Kroll, "How the Wisconsin Uprising Got Hijacked," *Mother Jones*,
    June 11, 2012, https://www.motherjones.com/politics/2012/06/how-wis-
    consin-uprising-got-hijacked/; Michael Yates, ed. *Wisconsin Uprising:
    Labor Fights Back* (New York: Monthly Review Press, 2012).

During these hopeful moments "middle-class" occu-pations attract our attention as the working class's leading edge. However, they point to a set of problems, not to any easy solution. Certainly, real life is a great teacher, and the desire to draw firm lines between blue- and white-collar labor as if they had enduring and deep meaning is on the run. As recently as two decades ago, leading labor historian Nelson Lichtenstein wrote of a collar line that more resem-bled a chasm before conditions changed after World War II: "Unlike the blue-collar working class, public employees often sat behind a desk, public employees took a regular paid vacation, and kept their fingernails clean." Missing the large numbers of public workers doing blue-collar jobs (not to mention the numbers of private sector blue-collar workers with paid vacations and clean nails), Lichtenstein reflected a view that has some strong and even under-standable roots within the radical tradition of thinking about the middle class. Militancy among professionals and retail clerks, and, sadly, a sharp decline in blue-collar, pri-vate-sector organizing have, as Lichtenstein himself later shows, more than challenged such a view.[5]

But as important as it is to recognize that teachers, nurses, and millions of less adequately paid office and sales workers are key elements of the US working class,

5   Nelson Lichtenstein, *The State of the Union: A Century of American Labor* (Princeton: Princeton University Press, 2002), 181 and 180-84.

contradictions of everyday life won't let us rest there. What are we to do with a teacher, or nurse, or sanitation worker, or meatpacker from Green Bay who becomes a labor activist while professing to still (or also) be middle class? Must she pick? Should labor scholars decide for her? These questions are especially vexed because the working class is largely defined by a relation to capital and management, while the middle class includes a variety of such relationships and often turns significantly on personal choice.

The task of radicals turns only partly on showing how big and broad the working class is. Such corrections to the prevailing belief that the United States is an overwhelmingly middle-class society are helpful, but within limits. It is reassuring for those supporting labor to realize that, on some reckonings, a near majority in the United States sees itself as working class, and a whopping majority might reasonably be counted as members of such a class by social scientists. But even if Zweig's figures are correct—in my view, the "objectively" working-class population is far larger than two-thirds—the problem remains. At a minimum, one US resident in four labors in a working-class job but identifies at least situationally as middle class. Debunking can only move that figure so much.

This chapter discusses how recognizing the problem of the middle class, combined with appreciation of a fear of falling, creates a powerful socialist critique of middle-class conservatism, but also of white-collar conditions of work. The radical tradition has had sufficient problems with thinking about timing and tone as to leave itself open to charges that the left perpetually predicted a fall that never arrived and ignored white-collar workers. The socialist tradition was not so much wrong in its fear of a reactionary middle class, nor even in its hope that middle class forces would be recruited as they fell into dynamic working-class protests, as it was too optimistic about the staying power of the industrial labor movement. At times it failed to believe its own analyses regarding the working-class status of most white-collar and government employees strongly enough to imagine that the middle class could be disaggregated and won over patiently instead of in a pro-jected cataclysm. In that sense, the left shared with many pro-capitalist thinkers and mainstream sociologists the view that people in very different social relations never-theless occupied a middle-class position. To the extent that the electoral left and decimated labor movement appeal simplistically to the middle class today, they con-tinue what is least convincing in the socialist tradition, but without any sense that things will change in a cataclysmic transformation.

Socialism and the Middle Class: Marx's Marxism and the Weight of Classic Arguments

For upwards of four decades, I have written books thinking that almost no one who happened on them in a store would be interested in socialism. The changes of the recent past—polls now show that more young people in the United States have a positive view of an unspecified socialism than the capitalism they know too well—suddenly suggest an alignment of the market in books with my personal commitments. Well, one hopes.[6] In any case, a chapter on the problem of the middle class necessarily must address the story of socialism. The intimate connections of a socialism-proof American exceptionalism with ideologues busy inflating the size and trumpeting the virtues of the middle class ensure as much. The idea that the very presence of a middle class "disproves" Marxism remains ingrained and will have a further legion of publicists if socialism gains a substantial toehold in US politics. Much less familiar is the impressive tradition of radical thinking about the middle class by those wanting to transform society—and by those who oppose politics being transformed in a fascist direction. Sometimes counter-revolutionary and susceptible

---

6   Kathleen Elkins, "Most Young Americans Prefer Socialism to Capitalism, New Report Finds," *CNBC Make It*, August 14, 2018, https://www.cnbc.com/2018/08/14/fewer-than-half-of-young-americans-are-positive-about-;capitalism.html.

to mobilization by the far right, the lower middle class particularly has generated urgent attention. At its best Marxist concern with the middle class positioned socialist scholarship to shape much of the earliest and the best of all thought about the middle class. Even "falling," the keyword that structures investigations of the middle class from sociology to journalism, emerged from socialist tradition and extended into mainstream writings.

Radical thinking about the middle class has long insisted that playing to an aggrieved middle class fights on terrain favorable to right-wing projects and endorses a cultural wasteland. The left feared empowering the shock troops of reaction. As recently as the Cold War, even liberals counted the middle class as the lonely crowd, the organization men, and the victims of the feminine mystique. Its members did not need saving, but rather a new way. It is the ease with which the left campaigns for middle-class salvation that is new and untenable. The idea of "saving the middle class" is of no use in clarifying when and how white collar and professional workers act as working class people, or in explaining materially why the term "middle class" also seems meaningful to so many in the United States.

Present at the creation of modern socialism was the problem of the middle class. The 1848 revolutions and the publication by Engels and Marx of *The Communist*

Manifesto that same year heralded a movement beginning to seek roots in the working class in part by critiquing the middle class. The *Manifesto* consciously tried to effect a break from the middle class, or perhaps to acknowledge a break already made in real life, in its very title. In the preface to the 1888 English language edition, Engels called the work the foundational text of socialist literature, from "Siberia to California." He added that when he and Marx wrote *The Communist Manifesto* they could not have used "socialist" in its title because socialism was then considered a middle-class movement, and "communist" signaled a working class one. The two authors had no doubt about opting for the latter term and never "repudiated" it. Nevertheless Engels also liked the fact that, by the 1880s, socialism was understood as a working-class project. The *Manifesto* roundly dismissed any revolutionary potential of the middle class: "The middle class—the small manufacturer, the shopkeeper, the artisan, the peasant—all these fight against the bourgeoisie, to save from extinction their existence as fractions of the middle class." Engels and Marx concluded, "They are therefore not revolutionary, but conservative," except and until the moment of their impending transfer into the proletariat.[7]

---

7   Engels, "Preface to the 1888 English Edition" of Marx and Engels, *Manifesto of the Communist Party* (originally February, 1848), https://www.marxists.org/archive/marx/works/download/pdf/Manifesto.pdf, 8.and the *Manifesto* itself, 20.

The middle class seemed to validate such views in the 1848 revolutions. Opposition from the lower middle class, in the view of the Communists, proved decisive in the turning back of freedom dreams. In reflecting on the 1848 revolutions, Marx rehearsed the range of the responses that would dominate his thought and that of many social-ist revolutionaries for a century to come. For Marx, the German middle class and "its professors, its capitalists, its aldermen, and its penmen" had, from 1846 onward, exhib-ited an "unexampled spectacle of irresolution, incapacity and cowardice."[8] He wrote of France, where class issues and workers' militancy particularly stood out in the 1848 revolts, as a place where "[n]o one had fought more fanati-cally in the June days for the salvation of property and the restoration of credit than the Parisian petty bourgeois . . . The shopkeeper had pulled himself together and marched against the barricades in order to restore the traffic which leads from the streets into the shop."[9] As the Hungarian revolutionary Béla Kun wrote seventy years after their defeat, the 1848 revolutions "revealed the political bank-ruptcy of the revolutionary section of the bourgeoisie. That revolution laid bare not only their weakness, but also

8   Karl Marx, *The Civil War in France* (originally 1871), https://www.marxists. org/archive/marx/works/download/pdf/civil_war_france.pdf.

9   Karl Marx, *The Class Struggles in France, 1848-1850* (originally 1850), repub-lished at https://www.marxists.org/archive/marx/works/download/pdf/ Class_Struggles_in_France.pdf, 32.

how dangerous they were to the work of the revolution." In France, he argued, the working class was "crushed" by "this very lower middle-class," not by the capitalist class.[10]

In *The Communist Manifesto*, Marx and Engels argued that capitalism itself propelled history toward a solution to the problem of the middle class. They put matters in the baldest terms possible. "The lower strata of the middle class," they began, before describing what was surely the huge majority of that group, would simply step off the stage of history: "The small tradespeople, shopkeepers, and retired tradesmen generally, the handicraftsmen and peasants—all these sink gradually into the proletariat." They would do so both because their "diminutive capital" would lose out to concentrations of industrial wealth and because new methods of production would render "specialized skill" obsolete. The bulk of the middle class would rise by falling into the working class. "The whole society more and more splits into . . . two great classes," Marx and Engels wrote even more famously, "directly opposed to one another: Bourgeoisie and Proletariat."[11]

This elegantly simple solution carried its own problems, ones that have plagued socialist approaches to the

---

10 Marx as quoted in Béla Kun, "Marx and the Middle Classes," originally in *Pravda*, May 4, 1918, translated and published at Marxists Internet Archive, https://www.marxists.org/archive/kun-bela/1918/05/04.htm, which also contains the quotation from Kun himself.

11 Marx and Engels, *Manifesto of the Communist Party*, unpaginated.

middle class since 1848 where questions of terminology, timing, and tone are concerned. The lines in the *Manifesto* regarding the middle class sinking are seldom missed by those who ridicule socialism as being in the prediction business and as dead wrong on the disappearance of the middle class. These charges usually focus on the "mistakes" of Marx and Marxists. The fact that industrial capitalism transformed the United States from a nation 80 percent self-employed to one 80 percent employed in the space of a century therefore bears emphasis in response. The fall of the old self-employed middle class, including farmers, that Marx predicted did in fact occur. His identifying of a trend with an absolute direction frayed generalizations around the edges, and a new waged or salaried middle class produced within modern capitalism made for increasing complications. Thus, there is plenty of socialist sloppiness and smugness to critique and substantial critique has in fact come from within the socialist tradition. At the same time, however, the middle class and the working class have been moving targets, meaning that we are dealing with complexities in the world as much as mistakes in analysis, and the socialist "mistake" of misunderstanding or somehow ignoring the middle class remains largely an invention.

For Marxists, the complexity of the problems associated with the middle class made a simple opposition between workers and capitalists compelling. The British social historian Edward P. Thompson wrote, in perhaps the most famous passage on class written in English since World War II, "The [class] relationship must always be embodied in real people and in a real context. Moreover, we cannot have two distinct classes, each with an independent being, and bring them *into* relationship with each other. We cannot have love without lovers, nor deference without squires and labourers." Thompson continued with an equally famous sentence on class consciousness: "And class happens when some men as a result of common experiences, inherited or shared, feel and articulate the identity of their interests as against other men whose interests [differ]."[12] What then of the middle class? Who is their lover, their squire, their other? The answer must be multiple. Those in the middle can look up or down for a supposed adversary, or they can look both ways, seeing themselves as perpetually ground between those above and below. In the great European revolutions, the middle class could at first join those grown rich in the market to oppose the aristocrats above. However, when the other above was the industrial millionaire and the other below was the working class and/or the racialized poor, political parties have often directed class anger downward or, as in the case of the Democrats using Stanley Greenberg's

---

12 E.P. Thompson, *The Making of the English Working Class* (New York: Pantheon Books, 1964), 9.

services, were more willing to hear grievances directed against those below than against those on top.

The other half of Marxist hopes for the middle class is far less visible from our vantage point. The *Manifesto* and Marx's writings on the 1848 revolutions did not just foresee the decline of the middle class, but also its mid-descent attraction to a rising working class movement. This too began almost from the moment of the 1848 revolutions, especially in France. There, Marx reasoned, because the working-class movement had so advanced and basic liberties were secured enough, the middle class would soon learn to follow the lead of working-class militants, not only out of economic desperation but also because they were impressed by the social power of labor. Glimmers of such radicalization did occur but the picture painted by Marx illustrated problems with tone, and eventually with substance. Marx described a key moment in the French class struggles in a way appropriate to melodrama but also farce. After the middle class sold out street protests to restore commerce in their stores, "the workers were crushed and the shopkeepers, drunk with victory, rushed back to their shops, they found the entrance barred by a savior of property ... who presented them with threatening notices: Overdue promissory note! Overdue house rent! Overdue bond!

Doomed shop! Doomed shopkeeper!"[13] As underlined by George Orwell's satire of the inability of the left to take middle-class people seriously, making appeals to the middle class on the basis of the desirability of that group's imminent fall is a tricky business. To apprehend a class in terms of its descent offers opportunities for compassion—think, for example, of the recent and humane work of Barbara Ehrenreich and of Katherine Newman, or of Willy Loman's fate in *Death of a Salesman*. But the words of Marxists and sometimes of Marx himself emphasizing an awaited tumble had to seem unfeeling to those in the middle classes striving so mightily to stay upright.[14]

As the *Communist Manifesto* had it, the "industrial middle class" suffered defeat at the hands of the "industrial millionaires, the leaders of the whole industrial armies, the modern bourgeois."[15] The damage done to the precise vocabularies of class by this dramatic rendering was profound, given the plasticity of the term "bourgeois," especially as it suffered translation. The old "industrial

13 Karl Marx, *The Class Struggles in France, 1848-1850*, 32 and passim.

14 Orwell, *The Road to Wigan Pier*, 153-264; Barbara Ehrenreich, *Fear of Falling: The Inner Life of the Middle Class* (New York: Pantheon, 1989); Arthur Miller, *Death of a Salesman* (New York: Viking Critical Library, 1967, originally 1949); Katherine Newman, *Falling from Grace: The Experience of Downward Mobility in the American Middle Class* (Berkeley: University of California Press, 1999).

15 Marx and Engels, *Manifesto of the Communist Party*, unpaginated.

middle class" of small producers, plummeting already or poised to plunge, and the ruling capitalist class both counted as "bourgeois," also rendered at times as "middle class." Both terms were pressed to do far too much work. Jürgen Kocka's beautifully researched *White Collar Workers in America* included important comparative dimensions drawing on German examples. Kocka developed a long early section on problems of transnational usage and argued that both the French *classes moyennes* and the German *Mittelstand* shifted over the time Marx wrote to exclude the more upwardly mobile bourgeoisie amidst sharpening awareness of class differences between workers and a bourgeois ruling class. Kocka rightly insisted on this context for the rise over time of an identification of a "lower-middle class" as a catch-all term combining "artisans, retailers, government clerks, office workers, members of the lesser professions," and others. In the United States, he held, weaker class politics ensured that the language remained looser.[16]

But nowhere was it very tight. In *The Condition of the Working Class in England*, Engels used "middle class" (the German was *mittelklasse*) to refer to the "English classes corresponding with the French bourgeoisie." Marx made

---

16   Jürgen Kocka, *White Collar Workers in America 1890-1940: A Social-Political History in International Perspective*, Manra Kealey, trans. (London and Beverly Hills: SAGE Publications, 1980), 7 and 6-13, passim.

some effort to use *petit bourgeoisie* to signal reference to the lower-middle class, but by no means consistently. The language and the ethos involved, along with the anti-revolutionary actions of some of the middle class, made it possible to identify that group with opposition to labor's emancipation, at least until the instant of their falling.[17] Among later revolutionaries seeking to keep power, especially in the early Soviet Union, middle-class elements could seem again the key to every difficulty, especially when they sought to restore systems of private credit. Thus Béla Kun rehearsed Marx's arguments on the dangerous but doomed lower-middle class in a pointed 1918 birthday tribute in *Pravda:* "The [Soviet] Revolution, when celebrating the centenary of Marx's birth, will not forget the sentence he passed on the lower-middle class."[18]

For Marxists, the difficulty with terminology and sometimes with politics has resided in the lumping together of people in various social positions under the singular heading "middle class." Engels observed that popular use of the term in England was in fact "middle

---

17   Engels, *The Condition of the Working Class in England* (n.p.: Panther Edition, 1969, originally in German in 1845 and in English, 1887), 32, wherein Engels also observes that the English usage was usually plural—that is, the "middle classes." Available at https://www.marxists.org/archive/marx/works/download/pdf/condition-working-class-england.pdf.

18   Kun, "Marx and the Middle Classes," unpaginated.

classes," a considerably more precise tag.[19] The *Manifesto* stuck to aggregating those sliders about to fall from the perch of self-employment. Meanwhile, a far larger "new middle class" emerged, at first in large measure around the need to sell and advertise products and to keep track of the circulation of capital. Salespeople, secretaries, and bookkeepers reached Marx's radar, but as subplot to the great drama of commodity production in industry. He wrote of them fleetingly in works less read, less translated, and sometimes unpublished. Whether such fragments amount, as the New Left Marxologist Martin Nicolaus argued, to a "theory of the middle class"—elsewhere Nicolaus says of the "new middle class"—is debatable, but it is certain that Marx did not disseminate such a theory to socialists generally. The hints Marx provided were tantalizing, as in the insistence that there would be a "constant increase" in "the middle classes" poised between labor and capital. Their rise, he thought, lagged behind that of the working class, but was structurally necessary to "serve" the broader interests of capitalist development, in part by consuming the surplus bounty produced in the factories by workers. Marx also predicted that falling and fear of falling would structure the existence of this growing and important group, as they did for the declining numbers

19   Engels, *The Condition of the Working Class in England*, 32.

in the old middle classes. He added that what we would now call white-collar wages would fall faster than those of "average labor" when office labor was divided into smaller tasks requiring less skill and when more widespread education increased competition for office jobs.[20]

Marx's later work also offered a meandering discussion of a distinction between productive and unproductive labor, with the middle class linked to the latter. "Productive" workers directly fabricated commodities, or carted and ferried them about. The "unproductive" elements served capital and capitalism generally. The latter category inchoately included office workers, service workers, accountants, and salespersons alongside a wonderful list of categories unearthed from various sources by Nicolaus: valets of the industrial millionaires, landlords, night watchmen, civil servants, lawyers, the Kaiser, the Pope, politicians generally, paupers, and "elegant paupers" such as churchmen, as well as criminals and landowners. Here was Marx very much learning new things from the new economy and challenging his own insistence on a Manichean split between bourgeoisie and proletariat. But he also was spinning out a more or less aimless distinction, one undermined over time by the fact that the work of night watchmen and of caregivers,

---

20 Martin Nicolaus, "Proletariat and Middle Class in Marx: Hegelian Choreography and the Capitalist Dialectic," *Studies on the Left*, 7 (1967): 41 ("theory") and 46 ("new middle class"), 45-46 ("constant increase") and 22-49.

of secretarial labor, of janitors and all variety of other contracted-out services is now often itself the commodity produced in new regimes of accumulation.[21] The idea of the
"unproductive" clerk or secretary or call-center worker—
increasingly the workers called middle class—could hardly
have equipped socialists to understand white-collar and
service labor as like that of other workers. Nor did it create
urgency to organize them.[22]

The Political Problem of the New Middle Class

From a Marxist point of view—one valuing analysis of
material relations over time—it would be shocking if
ideas developed by socialists 175 years ago applied easily
today. Back then, a huge majority of people in the United
States were self-employed or enslaved; today, an equally
large majority is waged or salaried. At its best, Marx's
Marxism gave later thinkers a method that led to studying
the changed economy and finding a new, enduring, and

21 For the wild reach of the category, see Nicolaus, "Proletariat and Middle
    Class in Marx," 42 and 49, n.45.

22 Andrew Grant, *Socialism and the Middle Classes* (New York: International
    Publishers, 1959, originally 1957), 65; Karl Marx, *Capital: A Critique of
    Political Economy, Volume III, The Process of Capitalist Production as a Whole*
    (Chicago: Charles H. Kerr & Company Co-operative, 1909), 354 and 350-56
    passim. On this one Marx-citing point I think Nicolaus errs: that is in hold-
    ing that Marx did not regard clerks as workers. Cf. Nicolaus, "Proletariat
    and Middle Class in Marx," 49, n. 40, though perhaps the point more
    worth insisting on is that Marx did not so carefully mount a "theory of the
    middle class" that he spoke of with consistency on this central matter.

growing strata of the middle class doing working-class jobs. However, his more famous works spoke mainly of the self-employed middle class, one existing on borrowed time, typically opposing human emancipation, and interesting mainly for its predicted disappearance. Poised to enter decisively into history by accepting proletarian leadership, its members also appeared as figures of fun—feckless, fawning, and culturally philistine until being forced into glory for reasons they could not comprehend.

A particular difficulty in the classic socialist tradition of thinking about the "middle class" lay in defining it in terms of its opposition to revolutions and organizing. The differences between those victimized by capital in factories and those suffering in offices seemed not only a matter of where and how people worked but also whether they would become active politically. In the case of industrial workers, Marxism had a long tradition of insisting that, even in periods of long quiescence, social relations established the presence of a working class, though one sometimes unable to speak its own name. The conservative blue-collar worker remained a worker, however misled. On the other hand, where white-collar workers were concerned, inaction and conservative political behavior led Marxists to regard them as middle class, or at least to not challenge the tendency of the larger society to regard them as middle class. In many ways, then, socialist theory and practice regarding the middle class "failed" not because they wholesaled extreme ideas, but because they insufficiently challenged commonplace ones. Despite all these difficulties, for most of the twentieth century, Marxists and those attracted to Marxism increasingly took the middle class seriously as a political problem and, especially in Germany and the United States, wrote the best work ever produced on the subject.

Sometimes the desire for close empirical study of economy and society and for compelling revolutionary meta-narratives clashed. The idea of a lasting "new working class" emerging from the continuing development of capitalism—hinted at by Marx's later works—began to be explicitly theorized in the late nineteenth and early twentieth century. The setting, Germany, was significant, as it was not only a center of working-class support for socialist politics, but also a place with great appetite for drawing status distinctions within the occupational structure. Salary in Germany came in monthly installments, as opposed to the weekly pay and subtraction for hours taken off in sales positions in the United States around 1900. The "new middle class" analysis emerged initially from outside the left, or from the most reformist provinces of Marxism. Both put forward the new class as proof that capitalism could create buffers that kept it from lapsing into a two-sided class war destined to be won by workers. The leading evolutionary socialist, Eduard Bernstein, not only held that white-collar workers were not being ground down toward proletarian status, but that the self-employed would actually increase as capitalist development continued. Not surprisingly, many socialists opposed such theories; in doing so they sometimes minimized what was new in the world.[23]

The intellectual and political trajectory of the German Marxist economist Emil Lederer teaches much regarding how reactions to the idea of a new middle class were bound to be influenced by history and by tensions within the socialist tradition. Lederer published a spirited and complex, but sympathetic, critique of the theory of the disappearing middle class in 1912, showing the increase in new strata relative to the self-employed old middle class and to the industrial working class. He identified various strands within a new middle class. While arguing that the most immiserated white-collar employees would soon resemble the proletariat and be open to alliances with it, he also predicted that they would not readily accept working-class leadership. However, in the wake of German defeat in the First World War, the failed German Revolution, and the achievement of a brief, fragile democracy, they seemed

23 Val Burris, "The Discovery of the New Middle Classes" in Arthur Vidich, ed. *The New Middle Classes: Life-Styles, Status Claims and Political Orientations* (Washington Square, NY: New York University Press, 1995), esp. 24-32. See also Vidich's introduction to the volume at 9-10. On monthly salaries, see Kocka, *White Collar Workers in America*, 85.

to do just that. Membership in white-collar trade unions quadrupled from 1917 to 1923, and salaried workers both went on strike and met with socialist and Communist blue-collar workers in revolutionary workers' councils. Returning to the "new middle class" in 1926, now with Jacob Marschak as co-author, Lederer devastatingly critiqued his old position, deciding that "all gainfully employed" workers could unite, if not necessarily in "a single organi- zation." He elaborated a host of reactionary implications of "new middle class" analysis, holding that it obscured the presence of a ready-for-radicalism "employee" sector. This mistake, according to Lederer and Marschak, encouraged an alliance with the old middle class in defense of prop- erty. The authors argued explicitly against analytical focus on a new middle class and for emphasis on the "white-col- lar proletariat." Full of close statistical work, this research became a model for US studies of the middle class, espe- cially after German texts were translated by the New Deal's Works Progress Administration and after Lederer himself, exiled as both Jewish and Marxist, helped to found the New School for Social Research in New York City.[24]

---

24 Burris, "The Discovery of the New Middle Classes," 29 ("single organization"); and in the same volume, Lederer and Marschak, "The New Middle
   Class," in Vidich, ed. *The New Middle Classes*, 56 and 55-86; n.a., "Emil
   Lederer, 1882-1939," *History of Economic Thought* website, https://www.
   hetwebsite.net/het/profiles/lederer.htm.

If an upsurge in militancy provided seeming clarity for Lederer and Marschak in 1926, the "rumblings of fascism were already being heard," as they wrote. Indeed, the gains in white-collar organizing gave way in Germany after 1923. By the time of Nazi terror in and after the 1930s, German radical intellectuals faced a need to understand the unprecedented. They produced the most important body of anti-fascist scholarship to date. Grouped around the celebrated Frankfurt School, these researchers undertook detailed survey research seeking to grasp empirically the structures of belief and personality leading to acceptance of authoritarian rule. Their efforts generated models of sociological research unsurpassed anywhere, excepting the studies that W.E.B. Du Bois and others produced at Atlanta University. Their command of Marxism and psychoanalysis together produced profound insights. However, this work did little to advance the kind of disaggregating of groups stitched together within the so-called new middle class. Some studies did tackle white-collar workers specifically, none more creatively than Siegfried Kracauer's brew of poetry and empiricism in *The Salaried Masses*. Kracauer certainly regarded his subjects as proletarianized and even more miserable than industrial workers. But he also found them unresponsive when approached by the left and susceptible to Nazi appeals.[25]

The identification of the lower-middle class as the social base of fascism spread widely. Leon Trotsky, the Red Army leader turned exiled revolutionary, offered an intriguing variation on this theme. Speaking about French politics, he described the petit bourgeoisie as "human dust," incapable of self-organization but ready to be swept up into fascism or, given proper leadership, someday into socialism. The middle class and its character structure become in this view the sources of fascism's "detachments," with the word resonating militarily and psychologically.[26] The French revolutionary Daniel Guerin's almost instant 1939 history, *Fascism and Big Business*, turned out to be as much about the middle class as about corporations.[27]

Even the adventuresome and apt appeals to psychology tended to analyze a tragic lower-middle-class fascist subject. Thus, according to Frankfurt School leader Erich

---

25 Siegfried Kracauer, *The Salaried Masses: Duty and Distraction in Weimar Germany* (London: Verso, 1998, originally 1930), 88-112. For "rumblings," see Vidich's introduction to Vidich, ed. *The New Middle Classes*, 2. See also John Abromeit, "Siegfried Kracauer and the Early Frankfurt School's Analysis of Fascism as Right-wing Populism" (unpublished paper in the possession of its author at Buffalo State University).

26 Trotsky, "Whither France?" November 9, 1934, https://www.marxists.org/archive/trotsky/1936/whitherfrance/ch00.htm.

27 Daniel Guerin, *Fascism and Big Business* (New York: Pathfinder, 1973, originally in French 1939), 53-84 and passim.

Fromm, "Nazism resurrected the lower-middle class psychologically while participating in the destruction of its old socioeconomic position."[28] The emphases on psychology and class developed by Fromm and others centered on *Arbeiter und Angestellten,* which could be translated as "blue and white collar workers" or, nodding more to the sense that white-collar workers were not quite workers, as "the working class and salaried employees." Such ambiguities reflected the problem of the placement of the "white-collar proletarian" vis-à-vis the working class and the lower-middle class. When repeated in exile in the United States in the 1940s, the studies conducted by the Frankfurt School found the US middle class to be less authoritarian and anti-Semitic than the working class. The opposite had been true in Germany, though Fromm found considerable overlap. Amidst such ambiguities authoritarian personalities were increasingly linked with mass society under capitalism, less than with specific classes.[29]

28 Erich Fromm, *Escape from Freedom* (New York: Rinehart, 1941), 221.

29 Fromm, *Escape from Freedom,* 212 and 123-239; Mark P. Worrell, *Dialectic of Solidarity: Labor, Antisemitism, and the Frankfurt School* (Chicago: Haymarket Books, 2008), esp. xi-16 and 249-50; most useful on the 1929 studies is John Abromeit, *Max Horkheimer and the Foundations of the Frankfurt School* (Cambridge, UK: Cambridge University Press, 2013), 211-26. On relations of white- and blue-collar workers in that time and place, see Hans Speier, *German White-Collar Workers and the Rise of Hitler* (New Haven: Yale University Press, 1986), esp. 55-68.

In the United States, the idea of premising analysis on the presence of a fractured "new middle class" came later than in Germany and was more distinctly the product of leftist intellectuals. First and foremost was the Italian immigrant Louis Fraina, who led the formation and unification of the Communist Party. Running afoul of the Communist International after a series of purported scandals, Fraina changed identities in the early '20s, working as a printer and then reinventing himself as a left-liberal business journalist under the name Lewis Corey. As labor organizing quickened in the 1930s, Corey tried, in the words of his biographer, to "write his way" back into the Communist movement. His most successful effort was the 1935 study *The Crisis of the Middle Class*. That fat, readable volume featured charts like those in Lederer and Marschak's work, and, later, Mills's *White Collar*, detailing the transition to an employed and largely proletarianized new middle class. Positively reviewed in the Communist press, *The Crisis of the Middle Class* sold briskly in party bookstores, along with a printed critique of the book. For Corey, the "split personality" of the middle class left it pulled toward the workers' movement but also saddled with "outworn ideas" compatible with "the monster of fascism." In its own way, Corey's work matched Marx's in its certainty that the middle class rose by falling and then by falling under the sway of working-class leadership. When

Robert S. Lynd and Helen M. Lynd published *Middletown in Transition* two years later, they premised their new openness to the idea of a middle class in Middletown squarely on their reading of Corey.[30]

In comparison to peers in Germany or France, writers like Corey in the United States experienced less of the presence of a socialist movement and less of the threat of fascism. Nevertheless, in a minor chord, class and political conflicts did shape understanding of the middle class. In no case was this clearer than that of C. Wright Mills's post–World War II writings. In the United States, white-collar unions had long been relatively tiny. In 1935 in the United States, about one white-collar worker in twenty was in a union. In Germany, before the Nazis came to power, that figure reached over four in ten salaried workers. However, by the time Mills wrote enthusiastically about the middle class, proletarianization, and radicalism in *New Men of Power* in 1948, some victories had accumulated. These included new initiatives among retail workers, the impressive beginnings of organizing among foremen, a general white-collar workers union within the Congress

---

30 Paul Buhle, *A Dreamer's Paradise Lost: Louis C. Fraina/Lewis Corey (1892-1953) and the Decline of Radicalism in the United States* (Atlantic Highlands, NJ: Humanities Press, 1995), esp. 128-38 ("write" on 134); Lynd and Lynd, *Middletown in Transition: A Study in Cultural Conflicts* (New York: Harcourt, Brace and Company, 1937), 457; Lewis Corey, *The Crisis of the Middle Class* (New York: Covici and Friede, 1935), 151, 171, 283, and 112-70 and 278-309 passim.

of Industrial Organizations, and the growth of the United Public Workers, the latter two with important left leadership. Indeed, as the Communist Party itself shed an emphasis on immediate revolution centered on blue-collar workers, it highlighted a rising interest in white-collar organizing in a lavish special issue of *New Masses* in 1936. Experience with white-collar layoffs had by then undermined the notion that salaried employees enjoyed far greater job security. In 1948, Mills's confidence rested on the power of the industrial union movement, fresh off a major strike wave, to attract white-collar workers as much as on the downward trajectory of the salaried employee. He tempered such confidence with an awareness of how much the Taft-Hartley amendments to national labor law could change everything. That body of anti-labor law did seriously hurt the general momentum of labor, the specific prospects of unionizing foremen, and the possibilities of left union leadership. In the language of socialist theorists, it was not that the proletarianization of the white-collar middle class slowed, but that the attractive force of industrial unionism was attacked and curbed.[31]

---

31 C. Wright Mills, *New Men of Power: America's Labor Leaders* (Urbana: University of Illinois Press, 2001, originally 1948), 24 and 274-80; Kocka, *White Collar Workers in America*, 223-250; Steven Rosswurm, ed. *The CIO's Left-Led Unions* (New Brunswick, NJ: Rutgers University Press, 1992), esp. 2-4 and 143-46. The special issue of *New Masses* appeared on April 7, 1936.

With *White Collar,* his brilliant full study of the middle classes, Mills became the intellectual known for distinguishing the old from the new within those strata. He drew on Corey (with a sad absence of citation), right down to the tables the two books featured.[32] Informed by German radical scholarship available in part from reading WPA translations, Mills pivoted every bit as fully as Lederer had twenty-five years earlier. *White Collar* took stock of the dire changes in the three years since his 1948 book. What his biographer calls the newer book's "thoroughly disillusioned radicalism" directed itself not only toward the middle class but also at the inability of the labor movement to inspire middle-class supporters. Mills privately wrote that *White Collar* aimed at "total damnation of everything in this setup."[33]

White Collar reproduced more or less the whole analysis offered by the socialist tradition, including its contradictions, but without its hope. Its sense of loss has continued to be one we share, as industrial working-class

---

32 Cf. Mills, *White Collar,* 63-4 with Corey, *The Crisis of the Middle Class,* 274.

33 Daniel Geary, *Radical Ambition: C. Wright Mills, the Left, and American Social Thought* (Berkeley: University of California Press, 2009), 113-14 and 125 ("disillusioned"); Mills privately on the "setup" is as quoted in Robert D. Johnston, *The Radical Middle Class: Populist Democracy and the Question of Capitalism* (Princeton: Princeton University Press, 2003), 4; Corey, *The Crisis of the Middle Class,* 275; Anna Roboton, "Most Americans Are Hourly Workers," *CBS News,* February 17, 2017, https://www.cbsnews.com/news/most-americans-are-hourly-workers/.

militancy ebbs and blue-collar jobs vanish. In 1935, Corey believed that an advanced capitalist society without a majority of blue-collar workers was impossible. "Salaried employees," he wrote, "have not displaced the wage workers, and they cannot." Technically, he remains correct—about 59 percent of US workers were paid in wages in 2017—but only because so many people in traditionally "middle-class" jobs such as sales are wage earners. The century of glorious, flawed efforts of socialist intellectuals and socialist militants to figure out how to see and nurture radicalism among salaried workers and others termed middle class undoubtedly had its failures. It featured loose terminology, superciliousness, abrupt shifts in theoretical moorings in light of short-term setbacks and hopes, and disillusion. But it was also through immersion in social struggles, in big ideas, and even in illusions regarding the historic mission of blue-collar workers, that socialists became the leading interpreters of the middle class. If new movements are now coalescing, it is this fierce urgency that they should inherit, not specific homilies that we can glean from a tradition that could only go so far.

Even during continuing downturns in class conflict, Marxist and ex-Marxist writers have followed up on Mills's work. Up to the present, they have continued and deepened earlier left narratives of falling—though now with little possibility of falling into something grand. Their work has thereby intersected with mainstream media interest in, and political obsessions with, the decline of the middle class. Barbara Ehrenreich's career, producing both serious materialist analysis of the professional-managerial class and popular journalism on its "fear of falling," stands out in this regard. Studies in the labor process established how thoroughly and easily scientific management moved from factories to offices, making management able to monitor productivity and even motions of office workers. Harry Braverman's classic *Labor and Monopoly Capital* offered the provocation that office work, rationalized, became manual labor.[34] The middle class thus fell as a whole, fell in segments, fell by occupational category, and, in the work of Ehrenreich, Newman, and countless journalists, fell, poignantly, as individuals.[35]

In the late 1960s, when the New Left group Students for a Democratic Society (SDS) attempted to organize a disparate "new working class," the sociologist Richard Sennett participated in meetings of "shoe salesmen, secretaries, and office clerks" and inquired into the experience

34 See also Harry Braverman, *Labor and Monopoly Capital* (New York: Monthly Review Press, 1998, originally 1974), 319, 239, and 296-318, passim; Evelyn Nakano Glenn and Roslyn Feldberg, "Proletarianizing Clerical Work: Technology and Organizational Control in the Office," in Andrew Zimbalist, ed. *Case Studies in the Labor Process* (New York: Monthly Review Press, 1979), 51-72.

35 Newman, *Falling from Grace*, esp. 143-73 and 202-28; Ehrenreich, *Fear of Falling*.

of those who had "passed into" such jobs after growing up in blue-collar households. Sennett and coauthor
Jonathan Cobb later described the ways in which wear-
ing suits to work on jobs that involved going downtown
could command prestige from family and friends in the
neighborhood. That success, they argued, existed alongside the fact that the jobs themselves were "exhausting
and unrelieved." Cobb and Sennett took this to mean that
SDS's formulation of a new working class described reality
better than the sociological emphases on a "new middle
class" or "new petty bourgeoisie." One famous if dubious
formulation of the latter that became popular around the
time they were writing implied that 70 percent of the US
labor force fell into the latter category, which somehow
expanded to include all white-collar workers.[36]

The most ambitious US Marxist research on the class
and collar line since Mills undoubtedly came from the late
sociologist Erik Olin Wright. Wright found a clever and
mostly useful way to refuse a choice between, on the one
hand, retaining shibboleths regarding the necessity of a
large industrial proletariat in a mature capitalist society,
and, on the other, the view that only a new middle class

---

36 Richard Sennett and Jonathan Cobb, *The Hidden Injuries of Class* (New
York: Knopf, 1972), 185; a summary of the debates is found, amidst sad-to-
reread attacks on feminism, based on the loosest of links with the "new
middle class," in Alex Callinicos, "The 'New Middle Class' and Socialist
Politics," *International Socialism*, 2 (Summer, 1983), https://www.marxists.
org/history/etol/writers/callinicos/1983/xx/newmc.html#n20.

mattered. Wright is sometimes oversimplified today as a thinker forcing our confrontation with the presence of a large, important middle class, one that hidebound fellow Marxists allegedly refuse to acknowledge. However, from his early interventions, Wright is more convincingly read as arguing against "new class" theorists and holding that a large working class remained. He added that even the middle class, which he regarded as about the same size as the working class, contained elements of working-class experience and consciousness as well as elements of capitalist logic and interest. Wright thus theorized a middle class defined by multiple "contradictory class locations," with, for example, small businessmen working in their own enterprise and middle managers controlling workers in firms but not empowered to make decisions about investment and production. In my view, Wright quite underrepresented the numbers employed in working-class jobs, especially teachers and nurses. Nevertheless, he wrested precious insights from the data that he produced, elaborating the idea that middle-class experience included elements of working-class experience.[37]

---

37 Erik Olin Wright, "Class Boundaries in Advanced Capitalist Societies," *New Left Review*, 98 (July-August, 1976), 26 and 3- 41; for oversimplifications of Wright, see Vivek Chibber, "Erik Olin Wright (1947-2019)," *Jacobin*, January 24, 2019, https://www.jacobinmag.com/2019/01/erik-olin-wright-obituary-class-marxism; see also Peter Meiskins, "Beyond the Boundary Question," *New Left Review*, 157 (May-June, 1986): https://newleftreview.org/issues/I157/articles/peter-meiksins-beyond-the-boundary-question.

No significant part of the socialist tradition, from its most dismissive to its most humanely sympathetic treatments of the middle class, was naïve enough to maintain that simply "saving" that class was either possible or desirable. The following chapter argues that we can go further in seeing the ways that middle-class and working-class consciousnesses overlapped when we realize, with the help of the Frankfurt School theorists, that middle-class life had its own gathering of miseries—indeed was and is constituted by them. If we see the middle class as a plight as well as a perch, we can understand something of why many workers see themselves simultaneously as middle class, as working class, and as living impossible lives.

Five

FALLING, MISERY, AND THE IMPOSSIBILITIES OF MIDDLE-CLASS LIFE

The wedding is the chief ceremony of the middle-class mythology, and it functions as the official entrée of the spouses to their middle-class status. This is the real meaning of saving up to get married. The young couple struggles to set up an image of comfortable life which they will be forced to live up to in the years that follow.

—Germaine Greer, feminist

In a recent specialized article that somehow manages to live up to its wonderful title, Columbia University epidemiologist Seth Prins and colleagues associate the middle class and sadness in a way that complicates yet again the idea that there's something here to be saved. The title of their contribution to the journal *Sociology of Health and Illness* asks and answers questions: "Anxious? Depressed? You Might Be Suffering from Capitalism." The researchers specifically design strategies to assess the incidence of depression and anxiety in middle managers, the heart of the "professional managerial class." They adopt the sociologist Erik Olin Wright's ideas regarding "contradictory class locations" within the middle class to describe a torn and torn-up group, sharing some of the authority and compensation upper management enjoys but little of the decision-making power held by their bosses. They suffer, the article argues, with contradictions that follow them off the job, much as Herbert Marcuse maintained that production in advanced capitalism generated not only "socially needed occupations, skills, and attitudes but also individual needs and aspirations."[1] The results appear to include higher rates of anxiety and depression. In taking us to questions of middle-class pain, Prins and his associates follow a path Mills also took in *White Collar*, where he wrote, "The misery of twentieth-century man is psychological even more than it is material, at least here in America." The article so struck a nerve that it received wide reposting and became the grist for many journalistic spinoffs.[2] To separate the material and psychological, or for that matter work and leisure, will not prove to be easy

1   Seth Prins, Lisa Bates, Katherine Keyes, and Charles Muntaner, "Anxious? Depressed? You Might Be Suffering from Capitalism: Contradictory Class Locations and the Prevalence of Depression and Anxiety in the United States," *Sociology of Health and Illness*, 37 (November 2015), https://www. ncbi.nlm.nih.gov/pmc/articles/PMC4609238/#R80; Herbert Marcuse, One-Dimensional Man (Boston: Beacon Press; 1991), xlv-xlvi. The epigraph is from Germaine Greer, *The Female Eunuch* (New York: Bantam Books, 1972), 213.

2   As quoted in Geary, *Radical Ambition*, 114.

in a system inflicting daily and prospective pain on many who could plausibly claim a position in the middle class. But surely Mills and Prins pointed us in the right direction with a focus on misery.

In *Cubed,* Nikil Saval's stylish recent study of the "secret history" of the office, we learn the transnational story of the cubicle, the tomb where a majority of office workers spend much of their lives. Ninety-three percent dislike it. Born as reform-minded design by a visionary 1960s architect, it was debased enough by the 1970s that its originator lamented its existence. Tied to cost savings, valued for its ease of dismantling during downsizings, and smaller as decades progressed, the cubicle illustrates how hard it is in thinking about the tragedy of the middle class to separate the fear of falling from the grind of daily misery. Saval captures well what many of us know from experience or from relatives. "The surest sign of trouble," he tells us, came when an employee "lost his office." We meet a Kodak worker who knew something had changed when consigned to a cubicle after commanding a large office with a secretary. It is equally harrowing to be doubled up in cubicles, as the next shoe to drop can be loss of a job altogether. The fears of falling into and out of a cubicle compound the miseries of actually working in one.[3]

The towering, if abject, figures within nineteenth- and twentieth-century literary portrayals of white-collar and sales work likewise point us to a combination of misery in the present and fears for the future. Both the title character in Herman Melville's dark nineteenth-century short story "Bartleby, The Scrivener" and Willy Loman in Arthur Miller's twentieth-century play *Death of a Salesman* fall tragically. But the white-collar workplace from which Bartleby falls into incarceration in The Tombs, and then into his own tomb, is itself a site of poverty and illness. All the adult workers suffer from what we would now call occupational diseases. Threats of layoffs and cut hours for workers already managing only the barest of lives accompany the employer's faux compassion. The child laborer in the office brings in the cheap Ginger Nut wafers for which he is nicknamed and which allow the labor force to subsist. The most plausible reading of the story finds Bartleby *choosing* to fall further from an already unbearable situation.[4]

3   Nikil Saval, *Cubed: A Secret History of the Workplace* (New York: Doubleday, 2014), 242 ("lost"), 210-20 and 242-44 passim; Dwight Garner, "The Office Space We Love to Hate," *New York Times*, April 24, 2014, https://www.nytimes.com/2014/04/25/books/nikil-savals-cubed-tells-the-history-of-the-modern-workplace.html.

4   Herman Melville, *Bartleby, the Scrivener* (Brooklyn: Melville House, 2004, originally 1853), 6-15 and 59-60.

Similarly, Loman's fall and death—a suicide after a series of failed attempts—come not at once but over a lifetime of misery—of having to smile while mortally fearing being laughed at, of uncertainty in a job where confidence is a necessity. He experiences first what the cultural historian Daniel Clark has called the "crisis of the clerk" and then the particular crisis of "the clerk who isn't young," losing appeal in a trade predicated on charisma.[5] In *White Collar*, when Mills constructed composite ideal types of workers in "The Great Salesroom," one was "The Charmer" who "focuse[d] less upon her stock of goods than upon herself." Charmers had, if they stayed on even as little as a decade, to think about a transition to the often disgruntled and nostalgic ranks of "The Old Timer" category. Loman followed a male version of that declining path.[6]

This chapter grapples with why countless Willy Lomans in working-class jobs have long seen themselves as middle class. It tries to regard their choices, however tragic, as more than the result of being bamboozled by elites. It argues that the middle class occupies a place of misery even before it falls. That misery is itself part of what binds together those disparate elements who consider themselves middle class, with more than a few blue-collar workers included.

---

5   Miller, *Death of a Salesman*, esp. 62-63, 73, and 108-09.

6   C. Wright Mills, *White Collar: The American Middle Classes* (New York: Oxford University Press, 1956, originally 1951), 175-76.

Common sense does not completely mislead us when we regard prosperity and home-ownership—and in Macomb County, owning a boat—as the keys to making wage workers feel middle class, but such traces of *embourgeoisement* only take us so far in accounting for a material basis of buying into the middle class. Miseries, shared at times by industrial workers with white-collar workers, salespeople, technicians, lower and middle management, and professionals—likewise matter. They include debt, alienated labor in which personalities as well as production are for sale, and cycles of overwork and over-consumption. The spread of these miseries to larger strata of the population was in many ways the story of how the modern United States generated a middle class that was distended by world standards but bound together by its very sadness. Such glum solidarity, even bitterness, makes the idea of "saving" the middle class from falling at best a partial fix for a larger emptiness. Because being middle class involves a set of unrealistic expectations—of improvement of living standards across generations, of putting kids through college without debt, of a dignified retirement, of balancing labor and leisure—life in the middle has come to seem not only less desirable, but more and more impossible.

When the Middle Falls

Much of the misery of the middle class fits well within narratives of sudden descent in material terms, but much also
involves psychic pain in good times as well as bad. Of course,
if we accept the Obama/Romney/[H.R.] Clinton/Trump
definition of the middle class as the bottom 96 percent of
US income earners, it includes the poorest of the poor and
all manner of misery. But even above those mired below the
poverty line, the reach of "truly" middle-class desperation
surfaces regularly in the news. The "middle-class homeless," we learn, include teachers, nurses, and chefs, camped
in their cars to survive the California areas providing work
but also featuring exorbitant housing costs. They are often
elderly and/or disabled people reeling from medical setbacks, but they are also working families unable to make
ends meet. Or they are the seemingly prosperous early retir-
ees from the early 2000s, bent on enjoying bouts of travel in
their RVs and then wiped out by the Great Recession. Many
of them now use those same RVs as their sole domiciles, following Amazon jobs and living on Walmart parking lots.[7]

---

7   Emily Crane, "California's Hidden Homeless," *Daily Mail*, December 26,
    2017, https://www.dailymail.co.uk/news/article-5212977/Californias-
    middle-class-homeless-living-parking-lots.html, and Donna Freydkin,
    "When Homelessness Reaches Middle-Class Families," *Today*, January
    18, 2018, https://www.today.com/news/when-homelessness-reach-
    es-middle-class-working-families-t121406; Mary Jordan and Kevin
    Sullivan, "'I'm Going to Work until I Die': More Older People Travel the
    Country in Search of Seasonal Jobs," *Washington Post*, September 30, 2017,

Others living in vehicles or couch-surfing are homeless PhDs, young and old, teaching as adjuncts in colleges and universities as what the journalist Jim Hightower calls "the highly educated working poor."[8]

Middle-class hunger affects those who have lost and those who have kept their homes. In fact, it can flow from scrimping to avoid eviction from homes and then finding that "you cannot eat a house," the structure borrowers have over-extended themselves to acquire. *National Geographic* writes of the "new face of hunger" as that of middle-class people managing to keep up appearances while being unable to eat adequately. The college student, perhaps best symbolizing the intersection of the aspirant and the solidly established middle class, hungers for more than knowledge. Very conservative estimates of food insecurity within higher education have it afflicting 11 percent of four-year college and 17 percent of community college students, almost exactly the same figures as those for college student housing insecurity, whether couch-surfing,

http://www.chicagotribune.com/business/ct-elderly-workers-20170929-story.html.

8   Jim Hightower, "The Highly Educated Working Poor: Adjunct Professors," *Nation of Change*, February 5, 2014, https://hightowerlowdown.org/pod-cast/the-highly-educated-working-poor-adjunct-professors/; Alastair Gee, "Facing Poverty, Academics Turn to Sex Work and Sleeping in Cars," *The Guardian*, September 28, 2017, https://www.theguardian.com/us-news/2017/sep/28/adjunct-professors-homeless-sex-work-academia-poverty.

car-living, or on the street. Other studies place the incidence of college-student food insecurity above 40 percent.[9]

Neal Gabler's recent reporting on the "secret shame" of the middle class in *The Atlantic* touched a nerve. Gabler showed from Federal Reserve Board data that about half the middle class—himself included, he confessed, even after solid and enduring success as a writer—cannot imagine raising $400 in the face of an emergency without selling off assets or borrowing.[10] After thirty-five years of politicians declaring the need to save the middle class, the middle class has precious little accessible savings. It is the miserable experience of having fallen, or never risen, as much as the fear of falling that defines middle-class life.

From Contradiction to Impossibility

According to the Commerce Department study done for the task force on the middle class led by then

9   Alexandria Heisel, "You Cannot Eat a House: The Hunger Secrets in the Middle Class," *Hunger+Health*, September 8, 2017, https://hungerand-health.feedingamerica.org/2017/09/cannot-eat-house-hunger-secrets-middle-class/; Tracie McMillan, "The New Face of Hunger," *National Geographic*; July 16, 2014, https://www.nationalgeographic.com/food-features/hunger/; Ashley A. Smith, "Discrepancies in Estimates on Food Insecurity," *Inside Higher Ed*, April 30, 2019, https://www.inside-highered.com/news/2019/04/30/new-research-finds-discrepancies-esti-mates-food-insecurity-among-college-students..

10   Neal Gabler, "The Secret Shame of Middle Class Americans," *The Atlantic*, May, 2016, https://www.theatlantic.com/magazine/archive/2016/05/my-secret-shame/476415/.

vice-president Joe Biden in 2010, being middle class has revolved around a series of basic goals: striving "to own a home," "to save for retirement," "to provide [their children] with a college education," to "protect their own and their children's health," to "have a car" for each adult, and to manage "a family vacation each year." These goals, an uncharacteristically tart *Brookings* report on the middle class recently observed, far exceed the capacity of a single parent with two kids making the median income of $25,000 per year.[11] However, it is not only having to forego this or that particular expectation or aspiration that has begun to erode identification with the middle class. Rather, it is an increasing sense that the whole project of middle-class life is impossible.

The difficulties typically come in pairs and as contradictions. The Irish writer Terry Eagleton captured the main such contradiction and the impossible psychic demands structuring it. "Capitalism needs a human being who has never yet existed," Eagleton wrote, "one who is prudently restrained in the office and wildly anarchic in the shopping mall." Mills had gestured at the same point

---

11   Richard V. Reeves, Katherine Guyot, and Eleanor Krause, "Defining the Middle Class: Cash, Credentials or Culture?" *Brookings*, May 18, 2018, https://www.brookings.edu/research/defining-the-middle-class-cash-credentials-or-culture/. See also *Allstate Newsroom*, "New Poll Shows Middle Class to Be More Anxious than Aspirational," *Allstate Newsroom*, April 25, 2013, https://www.allstatenewsroom.com/news/new-poll-middle-class-more-anxious-than-aspirational/.

half a century before, lamenting the accelerating treadmill that had so much of the middle class "selling little pieces of themselves" at work and then "trying to buy them back each night and weekend with the coin of 'fun.'"[12]

I thought of Eagleton's remark in a loud restaurant bar in Minneapolis recently, on seeing advertisements on the wall for Red Bull and vodka, sold under the name of Liquid Cocaine. The wall menu sat next to cardboard cutouts advertising various brands of beer, each image a monument to hedonism (and sexism), but each also urging moderation in drinking in far smaller type. The larger tableaux and the particular mixture of hyper-caffeination and hard liquor in Liquid Cocaine catch perfectly US society's double addiction to honing concentration, especially at work, and to forfeiting restraint, judgment, and even consciousness at other moments. The results are so familiar that we do not much linger over their strange combinations of asceticism and abandon—hearing multiple public figures claim to have tried pot but not inhaled, and being the nation that leads the world in the consumption of both porn and church, for example. When I raise the contradictions pointed out by Eagleton to audiences, both in and out of classrooms, they can fill in the blanks with symbols of the twinned

12   Terry Eagleton, *After Theory* (New York: Basic Books, 2003), 28; Mills, *White Collar,* 237.

needs for productivity and restraint on the one hand and for profligacy and immediate gratification on the other. These include the casino ads with phone numbers for gambling addiction counselors; the cycles of credit card debt followed by the taking on of a second or third job, and even addictions to work.[13]

A simpler way to see the impossibilities of middle-class life would put matters in terms of overwork on the one hand and debt on the other. Here, the neglected research of the historically minded economist Juliet Schor captures better than any other scholarship how worker/spenders who had "never existed" historically came to be the ideal and the problem. Indeed, when business news talks about "positive economic indicators," it cites increased "consumer confidence" and rising hours of labor and labor force participation—that is, overspending and overwork. Schor's books show the problems with the idea that these are considered measures of what make economies and personal lives work. Her first book on these subjects is called *The Overworked American*, the second *The Overspent American*. Together, the pair chart much of what we need to know on both subjects. Because they're covered in separate books, readers might easily imagine one group

13 For elaboration, see David Roediger, "Jaw Breakers, Spuds MacKenzie, and Fordism," and "Waiting to Inhale," both in Roediger, *History Against Misery* (Chicago: Charles H. Kerr, 2006), 3-5 and 6-8.

in the United States afflicted with the first problem and another group with the second—that the overworkers stayed out of debt via high income and that the indebted needed to knuckle down and get out of the hole they'd dug. However, Schor shows that middle- to upper-income families are much plagued by debt. The two books challenge the widely held view that getting and spending are separate spheres. Schor shows how alienated labor contributes to sad attempts at psychically compensatory spending, developing the idea of "work and spend" cycles.[14] The very richness of statistical evidence in the books made them seem dated rather too quickly, but the imbricated tragedies that they identify very much abide with us. Schor's more recent work in these areas, identifying the ecological consequences of overwork and overconsumption, make her ideas more relevant than ever.[15]

This mix of overwork, hyper-management, desperate searching for satisfaction in consumption, and consequent debt spreads so widely that the resulting combination of anxiety and alienation has sometimes been termed a condition of mass society and advanced capitalism as a whole.

---

14 Juliet Schor, *The Overworked American: The Unexpected Decline of Leisure* (New York: Basic Books, 1993) esp. 108 and 119 ("work and spend"). See also 31 and 157-59, and Schor, *The Overspent American: Upscaling, Downshifting and the New Consumer* (New York: Harper Perennial, 1998), esp. 19, 108, and 113-28.

15 Juliet Schor, "What's Driving Consumption?" *Boston Review*, 24, Summer 1999, 4-9.

However, it was the conventionally defined middle class—salaried and suburban—that experienced a modern malaise born of overspending and overwork first. When they were joined in their miseries by others paid by the hour, often neighbors and family members, all identified as middle class as much out of shared pain and a common sense of impossibility as from a sense of triumph.

The Traffic in Personalities

Success writer Dale Carnegie avoided both the Missouri farm life into which he was born and the new middle-class life of selling other people's products, a career that he tried out in his twenties. Instead, he sold his own line of courses and books designed to teach others how to speak publicly, be happy, and win. Changing his name to Carnegie, which he thought would bring to mind the steel magnate Andrew Carnegie, he owned educational ventures with hundreds of thousands of graduates, and he earned extravagant royalties from books. His writing career culminated with the 1936 publication of *How to Win Friends and Influence People.* Endlessly reprinted, it sold five million copies before his death in 1955. Carnegie's marketing prominently featured speaking in public, being happy, and gaining friends, but his biggest selling point was getting ahead at work. A salesman himself, Carnegie appealed to salespersons by promising to help them identify what worked.[16] Perhaps no US historical figure has more perfectly embodied the wisdom of Joe Strummer, front man of The Clash, who reminded us that "Selling is what selling sells."[17]

Carnegie's further genius was to know that the modern middle class, especially the employed new middle class, was on display at work, the marketability of their very personalities mattering to their bosses as well as to their customers. He tapped complacently into a truth that C. Wright Mills would deliver a generation later as an indictment. According to Mills, "Salesmanship seems a frenzied affair of flexibility and pep, the managerial demiurge, a cold machinery of calculation and planning." However, he added, "the conflict between them is only on the surface; in the new society, salesmanship is much too important to be left to pep alone or to the personal flair of the detached salesman."[18] Carnegie worked this intersection of sales and management cheerfully, prospecting also in the byways of the office worker, the bookkeeper, the professional for hire, and the small businessman. "Dealing with people is probably the biggest problem you face,"

16   Steven Watts, *Self-Help Messiah: Dale Carnegie and Success in Modern America* (New York: Other Press, 2013), esp. 189-91; n.a., "Dale Carnegie, Author, Is Dead," *New York Times*, November 2, 1955.

17   From "Car Jamming" on The Clash's album *Combat Rock* (1982).

18   Mills, *White Collar*, 176.

Carnegie wrote, "especially if you are a businessman. Yes, and that is true also if you are an accountant, an architect, or an engineer."[19] He promised, "People who smile tend to manage, teach, and sell more effectively," adding as a near afterthought that they also "raise happier children." The novelist Sinclair Lewis's bitter critique of Carnegie as an advocate of "yessing the boss" pinpointed both the content of Carnegie's guide to the pursuit of happiness and the place to pursue it.[20]

Foucault applied his pronouncements on the transformation of the modern subject into an "entrepreneur of himself" and indeed "his own producer" to the era of neoliberalism, but it had long and disturbing roots in how the salaried middle class (got) managed, dating back at least to Carnegie.[21] Crafted and marketed selves were what the buyer wanted. Management thought shining images reflected well on the general state of things in the firm. To learn the secrets of the workplace, Carnegie studied Hollywood actors—their smiles and images—which he identified with the successful marketing of sincerity. He emphasized that

19   Dale Carnegie, *How to Win Friends and Influence People* (New York: Simon and Schuster, 1937), 18.

20   Carnegie as quoted in Watts, *Self-Help Messiah*, 64; Sinclair Lewis, as quoted in Marshall Fishwick, *Great Awakenings: Popular Religion and Popular Culture* (New York: Routledge, 2011), 48.

21   Andrew Dilts, "From 'Entrepreneur of the Self' to 'Care of the Self': Neoliberal Governmentality and Foucault's Ethics," *Foucault Studies*, 12 (October, 2011): 131 and 130-46, passim.

all of us "are evaluated and classified by four things: by what we do, by how we look, by what we say, and how we say it." Fourfold too was the solution. Success required "tact, praise, modesty, and a little hypocrisy."[22] Feigning interest in others became a job skill long before it was a speed-dating one.

So did smiling, everywhere a concern of the success/new-middle-class complex. Carnegie, for example, reckoned the steel magnate Charles Schwab's smile was "worth a million dollars." Correspondents told Carnegie of the fortunes their smiles earned and guidebooks tutored customers on the use of mirrors to perfect smiles that were sincere, practiced, and winning.[23] *How to Win Friends and Influence People* was such a sensation that a book-length parody, Irving Tressler's *How to Lose Friends and Alienate People*, became a best seller in 1937. Tressler's hero hated all things about the mass-produced personalities influenced by Carnegie and overrunning the business world. Each said that the narrator looked half his age and had a surpassingly cool middle name. "All," he continued, "sit on the edge of their chairs breathless for my next word, and with a smile on their faces that looks as though it was painted

---

22 Carnegie, as quoted in Reinhard Bendix, *Work and Authority in Industry: Ideologies of Management in the Course of Industrialization* (New York: Harper Torchbooks, 1956), 303; for Hollywood, see Carnegie, *How to Win Friends and Influence People*, 101, 104, and 234.

23 Ingrid F. Smyer, *Relationship Within* (Bloomington, IN: Balboa Press, 2013), 66; Watts, *Self-Help Messiah*, 13, 189; Carnegie, *How to Win Friends and Influence People*, 101, 104, and 234.

there." They clearly needed to put in more hours with the mirror. The deftest parody came from the great Armenian American writer William Saroyan, whose short story "The Dale Carnegie Friend" complained that conversation could only begin after the Carnegie convert "smiled the way that was supposed to be sincere" and found his "voice that was intended to be winning." Saroyan's narrator reckoned that three Carnegie protégés showed up at every party he attended.[24] Appropriately enough, the most penetrating scholarly writing on Carnegie comes from the expert on the sociology and history of management, Reinhard Bendix. In Bendix's massive 1956 classic *Work and Authority in Industry*, Dale Carnegie rightly assumes more prominence than Andrew Carnegie. The former claimed to have perfected, according to Bendix, "personality salesmanship" in workplaces in which "[h]ow [the worker] looked or what he said . . . was of great importance for the salaried employee."[25]

Selling one's personality hardly came into being with the ascendance of the new middle class. It was a stratagem of sales work even when that work was un-bossed. Music critic Greil Marcus's recent introduction to a reissue of Constance Rourke's classic study of humor and the US

24 Irving D. Tressler, *How to Lose Friends and Alienate People: A Burlesque* (New York: Stackpole Sons, 1937), 34; William Saroyan, "The Dale Carnegie Friend," in his collection *The Trouble with Tigers* (New York: Harcourt, Brace and Company, 1938), 229-30.

25 Bendix, *Work and Authority in Industry*, 303 and 304.

national character captures well Rourke's description of the solitary, itinerant "Yankee peddler." Marcus writes that if that salesman "has a true face, not even the mirror ever sees it."[26] Melville's Bartleby, the most famous white-collar worker in American literature, copied documents by hand a century and a half ago under the watchful eye and the abruptly shifting judgments of the lawyer who employed him and who narrates his story. (The employee and lawyer would, by the inflated standards of the mid-twentieth century, both be middle class.) Bartleby's character, appearance, dress, and personality are judged according to whether they please both the lawyer who hired him and potential clients. All the personal judgments delivered by the narrator focus on the workers, not the horrific workplace itself. Even the vantages of observation shift in Melville's tale, as a screen supplementing "ground glass folding-doors" comes and goes according to when the narrator wants to see Bartleby and others and when he does not.[27] Over time, salespeople and clerical workers have hugely increased in numbers, and the bureaucratic minutiae of judgment have matured without losing their potential for arbitrary managerial opinion.

26 Greil Marcus, introducing Constance Rourke, *American Humor: A Study of the National Character* (New York: New York Review of Books, 2004, originally 1931), xiv.

27 Melville, "Bartleby, the Scrivener," 15-16; Thomas Augst, *A Clerk's Tale: Young Men and Moral Life in Nineteenth Century America* (Chicago: University of Chicago Press, 2003), esp. 13-4 and 215-31.

In the middle of the twentieth century, the practice of personality salesmanship expanded still further,
enthralling many workers doing manual labor at the same
time that they were beginning to be hailed as middle class.
Earlier in the century, as Bendix concluded, "How [the
manual laborer] looked or what he said had little importance." Frederick Winslow Taylor, as the leading theorist of
the management of manual labor at the time, cared about
whether a worker could move forty-seven tons of pig iron
in a day or not. He liked temperance and energy among
workers and loathed sociability during the working day.
But everything he encouraged was in the service of directly
increasing production. Experiments in management at
the Hawthorne Works Western Electric plant outside of
Chicago in the 1920s and '30s began a shift in management
strategies. These experiments produced some evidence
of what was later called the "Hawthorne Effect," in which
the mere observation by and interaction with a management researcher seemed to spark positive changes in a
worker's behavior. The first lesson drawn from the study
emphasized the personality of the manager—the bigger
the better.[28] Over time, especially after World War II, judgments regarding the personalities of all workers, regardless

---

28 Bendix, *Work and Authority in Industry*, 301-13; Edgar Cabanas and Eva
Illouz, *Manufacturing Happy Citizens: How the Science and Industry of
Happiness Control Our Lives* (Cambridge, UK: Polity Press, 2019), 86-89. See
also Braverman, *Labor and Monopoly Capital*, 60-1.

of their class—including their positivity, enthusiasm, and commitment to team building and rules—became systematized. New and growing companies like IBM and Polaroid led this trend, which later spread into heavy industry and even fast food. Whether in a customer-facing job or in the back, a McDonald's worker, for example, is judged as productive based on his or her personality in the face of the pressures of frantically paced work.[29]

As such changes took place, a line between what was called the middle class and the working class blurred in an overarching emphasis on liberal and bureaucratic modes of management. Elites clearly believe in these modes, which were introduced when retention of trained workers was a priority but survived when it was not. As late as 1965, the sociologist Richard Sennett calculates, a white-collar career included on average four or five job changes. Now, more than a dozen job changes are typical, but bureaucratized judgments on the personalities of those who will be leaving still seem as important to employers. As Edgar Cabanas and Eva Illouz's searing new study of the "science and industry of happiness" argues, for just about all the employed, "happiness is required to succeed." Management increasingly has come to see deficiencies in enthusiasm—that is, deficiencies in the performance

---

29 Richard Edwards, *Contested Terrain: The Transformation of the Workplace in the Twentieth Century* (New York: Basic Books, 1979), 134-43 and passim.

of enthusiasm—as disloyalty. But there is scant evidence that anyone believes the bureaucratic rubrics measuring "positivity at work" are less arbitrary than the whim of a foreman in an earlier industrial workplace. Nor of course does positivity supplant the speedups of production.[30]

Indeed, our bone-deep understanding of the civilized horror of modern workplaces ought to help us understand that the middle class has historically labored in systems placing their personalities as well as their labor power on the market. The generalizing of such a regime of control can hardly count as an advance. If it contributes to more workers seeing their jobs as middle class, they do so out of shared misery as much as from registering a rise in status. It is easy enough to critique the increasingly alienating and sped-up office as "factory-like," but offices, burger joints, and universities also feature soul-killing management strategies that bleed into factory management.[31]

The tremendous emphasis on bought and sold performances of personality so overlapped with the performance of gender that white-collar alienation in early

30 Richard Sennett, "Office Max," *New York Times,* June 13, 2014, https://www.nytimes.com/2014/06/15/books/review/cubed-by-nikil-saval.html; Cabanas and Illouz, *Manufacturing Happy Citizens,* 91 and 82-110 passim; William *Davies,* The Happiness Industry: How Government and Big Business Sold Us Well-Being (New York: Verso, 2015), 114-15 (on lack of enthusiasm) and 105-37 passim.

31 Harry Braverman, *Labor and Monopoly Capital,* 239 ("factory-like") and 203-47 passim.

twentieth-century fiction was best conveyed through the plight of women, often young. Secretarial work abruptly switched from the male preserve depicted in "Bartleby" to a majority female labor force after 1920. If a "woman's place was at the typewriter," men still overwhelmingly supervised. They at times sought sexualization of the office and at other times (or simultaneously) they wanted a second domestic sphere in which women served coffee and emotional support while also producing relentlessly. However, personality saleswoman-ship in such work-places also offered opportunities for women workers to exercise agency. Managerial desires proved subject to manipulation, with the office sometimes seeming an over-whelmingly feminine space culturally, although not in terms of power.[32] Such agency had limits. Mills planned an extensive treatment of what would now be called sexism and sexual harassment in *White Collar*, collecting upwards of a hundred interviews on those subjects. However, he ended up jettisoning the projected chapter titled "Sexual Exploitation in White-Collar Employment." He did say that in offices and sales, "younger women tend to be sub-ordinated to older men." When Evelyn Nakano Glenn and Roslyn Feldberg revisited the "proletarianization" of

---

32 Margery Davies, "Woman's Place Is at the Typewriter: The Feminization of the Clerical Labor Force," *Radical America*, 8, July-August, 1974, 7 and 1-28.

clerical work in 1979, they concluded that management used "sex as a basis for control."[33]

Department-store sales work provided even more dramatic examples of women creating solidarities and women's spaces amidst rivalry, harassment, and surveillance. Women workers there forged ties not only with each other but also with middle-class female customers in ways that could be used against management. Appealing to customers made self-presentation as both attractive and proper even more important.[34] Theodore Dreiser's *Sister Carrie* became the best window into what the historical sociologist Richard Sennett called the "tawdry respectability of native-born lower-middle-class Americans." Especially in the 1920s, the "white-collar girl" figured prominently in American literature. Christopher Morley's novel of the cosmetics industry, *Kitty Foyle*, perhaps most capitalized on the ways that appearances mattered as it described autonomy and glamour but also peril.[35] The

33 Geary, *Radical Ambition*, 128-29; Nakano Glenn and Feldberg, "Proletarianizing Clerical Work," 66 and 51-72 passim.

34 Susan Porter Benson, *Counter Cultures: Saleswomen, Managers, and Customers in American Department Stores* (Urbana: University of Illinois Press, 1986).

35 Mills, *White Collar*, xi and 198-204 ("white collar girls"); Richard Sennett, "Middle Class Families and Urban Violence: The Experience of a Chicago Community in the Nineteenth Century" in Stephan Thernstrom and Richard Sennett, eds. *Nineteenth Century Cities: Essays in the New Urban History* (New Haven: Yale University Press, 1969), 387 and 386-420 passim; Christopher Morley, *Kitty Foyle* (Philadelphia: J.B. Lippincott Company, 1939).

title character in Booth Tarkington's *Alice Adams* learned in youth that her "delicate and fine" hands were her best "possession;" they surpassed her "mind and character," it was implied. She set out therefore to live a "life of gestures" in part to draw attention to those hands, her passport to avoiding business college through marriage into greater wealth. The most apt portrayal of a male office worker in the same era, James T. Farrell's short, powerful "The Jazz Age Clerk," captures a lonely and sad desire to emulate one's betters in swagger and fashion while desperately hoping there's more to life than what the office has offered.[36]

Punishing Hours, Crushing Debts, and Impossible Lives

Were life lived at a certain deliberate speed, in good faith, and on an endlessly renewable planet, there could be ways to mediate the claims of the workplace and the mall. In a crude way, the hegemonic system often described as reigning for most of the twentieth century, "Fordism," pointed towards a temporary peace settlement. At least the original "Fordist bargain," offered to workers at his sped-up Highland Park factory just before World War I, laid out possibilities. The unfamiliar assembly line production

---

36 Booth Tarkington, *Alice Adams* (Bloomington: Indiana University Press, 2003, originally 1921), 15; James T. Farrell, *$1000 a Week and Other Stories* (New York: Vanguard Press, 1942), 135-43.

and its pace ran through workers quickly, causing massive problems with turnover. The bargain required workers to accept the attendant alienation in return for a greater ability to consume—the much-publicized "$5-dollar day." Less remembered is the fact that Ford's original plan also cut the working day by as much as 20 percent.[37] That reform was part of a general move to the eight-hour day in industry and offices between the Civil War and World War II—a dramatic advance from almost no leisure to what workers announced as "Eight Hours for Work. Eight Hours for Rest. Eight Hours for What We Will." Almost everything conspired to suggest that more was coming. The great mainstream economist John Maynard Keynes predicted a fifteen-hour working week, and lawmakers nearly made the thirty-hour week the law of the land in the Great Depression. The industrial unions that finally triumphed in the 1930s and 1940s seemed bent on winning more leisure. And then, just as quickly, a long historical trend reversed, in the United States especially, but also throughout the advanced capitalist world. The acceptance of what would have seemed in 1900 extraordinarily overtaxing labor survived, and real wage increases lasted for a while, but the part of the Fordist bargain directly

---

37 Stephen Meyer III, *The Five-Dollar Day: Labor Management and Social Control in the Ford Motor Company, 1908–1921* (Albany: State University of New York Press, 1981).

lessening overwork by continuing the cutting of hours passed from the scene.[38]

Several of us wrote about the stalling of progress in shortening the workweek and the virtual blackout of talk about such a move at about the time that Schor did, but her contribution stood out. Moving beyond description and lament, she identified for a popular audience several key ways that lives became impossible. The first is that the crisis of overwork reached beyond seeming a glitch in history's longer trend towards more leisure. It could no longer be argued that workers, feeling deprivations born of the depression and war, naturally preferred buying things to more time off for a while. She showed a continuing trend, not only toward flat lines charting the workweek but to increases in overwork, long after the 1950s had passed. In particular, she compared 1969 and 1987 figures in a way that forced consideration of gender and of particular ways that overwork reached into life off the job.[39]

38 David Roediger and Philip Foner, *Our Own Time: A History of American Labor and the Working Day* (London and New York: Verso Books, 1990), esp. 101-277; Christopher Hermann, "Neoliberalism and the End of Shorter Work Hours," *Socialist Project E-Bulletin*, 590 (January 25, 2012), http://socialistproject.ca/bullet/590.php; David Kestenbaum, "Keynes Predicted We Would Be Working 15-Hour Weeks: Why Was He So Wrong?" *NPR*, August 13, 2015, https://www.npr.org/2015/08/13/432122637/keynes-predicted-we-would-be-working-15-hour-weeks-why-was-he-so-wrong.

39 Schor, *Overworked American*, esp. 17-41; Roediger and Foner, *Our Own Time*, esp. 257-77.

Schor found that average males fully participating in the labor force worked 2,054 hours in 1969. The average crept up 98 hours by 1987, about two more per week. Women's annual paid working hours increased from 1,406 in 1969 to 1,711 in 1987, about six more each week. When Schor added the labor necessary to maintain households and raise children, a fascinating symmetry, not to be mistaken for equality, emerged. In 1969, women, working far less in marketed labor than men, labored on unpaid tasks of social reproduction about thirteen more hours per week. As women's paid hours jumped, they cut hours devoted to unpaid household labor by about three per week, and male housework rose by a little over an hour. Remarkably, in both years the total number of paid plus unpaid hours of labor was virtually identical for men and women, though women still did the lion's share of housework and therefore suffered comparatively in terms of income. The average number of unpaid hours—male and female together—likewise remained constant. What changed was the number of hours worked for pay. On average, more than three hours of free time per person disappeared each week into marketed work. Schor called the change, when measured over the course of a year, the "extra month of work."[40]

40 Schor, *Overworked American,* 17.

The speed-up of work became a source of tension within families. Strains on families and on gender roles occurred, as did large increases in divorces and single parenting. The very healthy conversation and contestation that the women's movement called for in raising questions about how household work was to be valued and apportioned took place under dire conditions of fatigue and stress, compounded by debt. There was, in Schor's terms, a "time squeeze at home." Overwork became not only an enemy of time to sleep but also, in an insight expanded by recent scholarship, to the calm necessary for rest.[41]

In several ways, overwork on and off the job impacted the middle class in particular. First, as salaried employees, a large share of middle-class workers were exempt from federal labor law provisions regulating overtime. Their overwork therefore sometimes has remained uncompensated, even unrecorded. Overwork has afflicted middle-class families disproportionately. "Middle income" men are somewhat overrepresented among those working fifty or more hours a week and professionals are dramatically overrepresented. Among women, the crisis of overwork has had ideological as well as practical dimensions. The Cold War middle-class ideal insistently preached the

---

41   Schor, *Overworked American*, 8, 11, 13, 17 ("squeeze), 36 and, on the household, 83-106; Jonathan Clary, *24/7: Late Capitalism and the Ends of Sleep* (London and New York: Verso, 2013), 58-59 and passim.

value of stay-at-home mothers running child-centered households, havens separated from the world of work and somehow emblematic of the superiority of free enterprise. In reality, however, middle-class and professional women became both relatively and absolutely unlikely to be stay-at-home married mothers. Already by 1977, just 35 percent of women in middle income families made that choice, while the proportion of women in low-income families who chose to stay home was 55 percent. Within a decade, things shifted further in the same direction, so that mothers in the middle-income and professional brackets were almost three times more likely to work outside the home as lower-income family mothers.[42]

The historian of gender and the Cold War, Elaine Tyler May, identified what was then particularly praised in personal life by US free enterprise as being "located in suburbia and epitomized by white middle-class nuclear families." Of course, those same families provided the tragic raw material for Betty Friedan's *The Feminine Mystique*, a searching examination of the effects of isolating women from the world of work and power and a critique adopted by much of the second-wave of US feminism. In making bold claims to employment, women

---

42 Joan Williams and Heather Boushey, "The Poor, the Professionals, and the Missing Middle," *Center for American Progress*, January 25, 2010, https://www.americanprogress.org/issues/economy/reports/2010/01/25/7194/the-three-faces-of-work-family-conflict/. Tables 2 and 3.

thus did more than break with an old and define a new middle-class way of life. They also forfeited connections with nationalist mythologies and moved toward alliances with very different groups of women similarly plagued by overwork.[43]

The ways in which suburban women entered the labor force guaranteed that overwork comingled with emancipation; squeezed for time, working women had unprecedented opportunities to change household arrangements and leave dangerous domestic arrangements. By the time Schor was writing, the militant phase of women's liberation had ended, and *The Overworked American* registered her fears that private solutions, available only to women with resources, would supplant public ones. Sadly, she was right, and we do live in a time of unpaid family leave and expensive childcare. Books like *Overwhelmed: Work, Love, and Play When No One Has the Time* and *Glass Ceilings* and *100-Hour Couples: What the Opt-Out Phenomenon Can Teach Us about Work and Family* give us a harrowing sense of the problems, but little in the way of policy solutions to overwork and the time squeeze at home.[44] Elizabeth Warren's co-written 2004

---

43 Elaine Tyler May, *Homeward Bound: American Families in the Cold War Era* (New York: Basic Books, 2008), 8, 9-11 and 155-66; Betty Friedan, *The Feminist Mystique* (New York: W.W. Norton, 2013, originally 1963).

44 Schor, *Overworked American*, 150-52; Brigid Schulte, *Overwhelmed: Work, Love, and Play When No One Has the Time* (New York: Farrar, Straus, and

combination of encouragement and policy prescription, *The Two-Income Trap: Why Middle-Class Mothers and Fathers Are Going Broke,* likewise suffers from solutions incommensurate with the gendered middle-class plight that it describes.[45]

From the vantage of the present, almost three decades after Schor's indictment of overwork in the '80s, the crisis she describes looks both familiar and, at times, like the good old days. Measurement of working hours is vexed by trends toward holding more than one job. Schor's brief discussion of "moonlighting" assumed adding a sideline to a full-time regular job. Since she researched and wrote, virtually every president has bragged of being a record-breaking job creator. Just as routinely, the opposition has countered by quoting workers who say, "We know; we have three of them." (The three jobs themselves may be in three contradictory class locations: managing the night shift at Arby's, keeping the books for the megachurch, and selling franchised sex toys at parties in the homes of friends.) The data make it hard to say with confidence whether the United States is absolutely the "most

Giroux, 2014); Karine Moe and Dianna Shandy, *Glass Ceilings and 100-Hour Couples: What the Opt-Out Phenomenon Can Teach Us about Work and Family* (Athens, GA: University of Georgia Press, 2010), esp. 35-44.

45 Elizabeth Warren and Amelia Warren Tyagi, *The Two-Income Trap: Why Middle-Class Mothers and Fathers Are Going Broke* (New York: Basic Books, 2004).

overworked developed nation," as even career advice websites sometimes claim.[46] It surely ranks near the top in overwork, in lack of public policy protections against it, and in hostility toward vacationing.

Mills described a perpetual middle-class struggle to fashion a "holiday" personality, one set against the alienation at work. But contemporary figures showing a fifth of US workers laboring sixty or more hours a week, and twice that many workers at fifty or more, indicate they have given up on the struggle to construct a coequal "holiday" self, and instead embrace a "workaholic" addiction—or hardheaded bow to necessity—centering life on the job. The trends in overwork suggest what an uphill battle the struggle for free time has become. From 1980 until 2015, a Pew Charitable Trust study reports, the average working year increased by 173 hours—another month of extra work per year.[47] The gender differences continue to apply, with slightly more paid working time for men and about

---

46 Schor, *Overworked American*, 31; G.E. Miller, "The US Is the Most Overworked Developed Nation in the World?" *20 Something Finance*, January 2, 2018, https://20somethingfinance.com/american-hours-worked-productivity-vacation/.

47 Mills, *White Collar*, 237 and 258; Maurie Backman, "Here's How Many Hours the American Works," *Motley Fool*, December 17, 2017, https://www.fool.com/careers/2017/12/17/heres-how-many-hours-the-average-american-works-pe.aspx; Williams and Boushey, "The Poor, the Professionals, and the Missing Middle," unpaginated; on workaholism, see Barbara Killinger, *Workaholics: The Respectable Addicts* (Buffalo: Firefly Books, 1997).

six more hours per week of household labor of employed women compared to employed men. This continuing gap has remained so stubborn as to attract attention from the business press—as a drain on productivity![48]

Impossibly Indebted

Where debt is concerned, the story is much the same. This is true in terms of the extent of the misery involved, its tendency to worsen, and its specific impact on how the middle class lives, worries, and defines itself. Thirty years ago, Schor wondered in *The Overspent American* "Why We Want What We Don't Need?" Her answer hinged on the "work and spend" cycle, beginning with alienated overwork and spiraling into compensatory consumption, followed by the need for longer hours and still more work. She pinpointed four sad, exhilarating moments on the spending side—"seeing, wanting, borrowing, buying."[49] The self- and family-destructiveness of staggering on an ever steeper and accelerating treadmill sounds one-note, but the remorseless logic of hurtful choices also emerges clearly. Completing one half of the "work and spend" cycle requires

---

48 American Time Use Survey, "Charts by Topic: Household Activities," *Bureau of Labor Statistics*, undated but 2015 data, https://www.bls.gov/tus/charts/household.htm; Bloomberg, "The Economic Reason Why Men Should Do More Housework," *Fortune*, August 1, 2017, https://fortune.com/2017/08/01/women-men-housework-gender-divide-equality/.

49 Schor, *Overspent American*, title page and 68-76.

balancing our psychological and fiscal checkbooks through frantic activity on the other. Falling into that cycle ought not to imply irrationality, except at the level of the system itself. That system, Eagleton tells us, needs such divided selves. Good economic citizenship requires debt, figured as "consumer confidence," as well as overwork. The opioid and meth crises, to take up two illegal addictions among a host of legal ones, seem the epitome of wildly selfish pleasures. But the connection of the former to dragging oneself to work when injured, and the latter to initially heroic efforts by working parents to have it all, could not be more stark. One recent investigation identified meth's allure as the supposed "perfect drug for the suburban woman." Similarly, porn addiction invades workplaces, with specific connections to choosing not to work, so much so that we now read of "procrasturbation" as a drain on productivity or a seizing of pleasure amidst stress.[50]

Schor began with the acknowledgment that the overspent on whom she concentrated come overwhelmingly from what she calls the middle class. At about

---

50 N.a., "Opioids in the Workplace," Centers for Disease Control and Prevention/National Institute for Occupational Safety and Health, undated but with 2017 data, https://www.cdc.gov/niosh/topics/opioids/data.html; Miriam Boeri, *Women on Ice: Methamphetamine Use among Suburban Women* (New Brunswick: Rutgers University Press, 2013), 1 ("perfect drug"), and 3-53; Chelsea Summers, "'Procrasturbation' Is the Last Refuge of the Over-Burdened, Under-Pleasured Worker," *VICE*, May 26, 2015, https://www.vice.com/en_us/article/nn9vgb/procrasturbation-is-the-last-refuge-of-the-over-burdened-under-pleasured-worker.

the same time, Elizabeth Warren, then a legal scholar researching bankruptcy, reached just the same conclusion. She titled a coauthored book about "Americans in debt," *The Fragile Middle Class*. It described the victims of bankruptcy—whose numbers had increased by 400 percent from 1979 to 1997—as either "solidly middle class" or "once middle class." The record debts of the 1990s that Schor described came not mainly from the poor but especially from the layer making between $50,000 and $100,000 a year—the solidly upper-middle class of that decade. They consumed, she argued, less often with eyes on the Joneses, and more often on keeping going as individuals with impossible jobs and schedules. However, status anxiety still lurked, not insignificantly because looks and auras of success remained central to the marketing of personality on the job itself. Competing demands for stimulation, emotional compensation, relaxation, and family happiness secured by money rather than time meant that even very highly compensated workers suffered both from debt and from the sense that they could not buy what they needed. Between 1987 and 1996, survey responses to the question of how much income it took to live a good life rose from an average of $50,000 to $90,000. In 1995, 30 percent of those making between $25,000 and $35,000 annually reckoned that they could not afford the things that they "really need;" but so did about two-fifths of those earning between $75,000 and $100,000, and well over a quarter of those making over the latter figure. Mounting debt and a continuing sense of deprivation stood as middle-class facts of life even during good times and among the prosperous.[51]

Schor argued that from the late 1980s to the late '90s, the cycle of working and spending intensified. But the dynamics that she describes as middle-class miseries had a significant history and have in the decades since proven that they are not waning. The self-employed and those saving to be so in the nineteenth century rarely borrowed for personal and family pleasures—plantation owners being a spectacular exception. As Marx described the dominant ethos of his time: "Self-renunciation . . . is its principal thesis. The less you eat, drink and buy books; the less you go to the theatre, the dance hall, the public house; the less you think, love, theorize, sing, paint, fence, etc., the more you *save*—the *greater* becomes your treasure which neither moths nor rust will devour—your capital."[52] One

51 Schor, *Overspent American*, 7, 15, and 108 for the figures on "needs" and dissatisfactions and 6-16 passim. Cf. Juliet Schor, "What's Driving Consumption?" *Boston Review*, 24, Summer 1999, 4-9 for broaching of the ecological implications of the fact that 35 percent aspired to quickly be in top 6 percent income bracket and 84 percent in top 18 percent, with only 15 percent satisfied to live a "comfortable life." For Warren, see Teresa A. Sullivan, Elizabeth Warren, and Jay Lawrence Westbrook, *The Fragile Middle Class: Americans in Debt* (New Haven: Yale University Press, 2000), 3, 6, and passim.

52 Karl Marx, *Economic and Philosophical Manuscripts of 1844*, https://www.marxists.org/archive/marx/works/1844/manuscripts/needs.htm.

historian of debt in the United States has observed that
the "Victorian money management ethic" left room for
"productive" debt as not in conflict with Puritan homilies
regarding thrift and restraint.[53] Among those considered
middle class, personal fulfillment and family ambition
connected far more with renunciation than overspending.
Sizing up of "character"—so important to business and
family reputation—followed from this choice.[54]

Another historian of US borrowing periodizes the age
when "personal debt was really business debt" between
2000 B.C. and 1920. Changes during the two decades
before and after 1920 shaped the history of debt. The
intensifications of labor associated with scientific management and Fordism had by 1920 solidified, altering the first
step of the work and spend cycle dramatically, in offices
as well as factories. Indeed, some white-collar workplaces
had by then glimpsed the limits of the management of
time and motion and moved toward efforts to manage
personalities systematically.[55] The sharp post–World War I

53 Lendol Calder, *Financing the American Dream: A Cultural History of
    Consumer Credit* (Princeton, N.J.: Princeton University Press, 1999), 56
    ("ethic") and 45-75.

54 Louis Hyman, *Borrow: The American Way of Debt* (New York: Vintage
    Books, 2012), 17 ("B.C.") and 18-40. On character, see Calder, *Financing the
    American Dream*, 157-203.

55 Jerome Bjelopera, *City of Clerks: Office and Sales Workers in Philadelphia,
    1870-1929* (Urbana: University of Illinois Press, 2005), 27 and 40; Sharon
    Hartman Strom, *Beyond the Typewriter: Gender, Class, and the Origins of*

depression provided a reminder of Marx's little-developed point that having layers of the population who consumed the surplus bounty of industrial production but did not directly produce it had its uses in addressing downturns in the economy. The uneven but tremendous growth of the economy in the 1920s fueled the switch from regarding personal debt as suspect to casting it positively in terms of confidence. To the extent that national economies in the industrialized world had entered what the late historian Martin Sklar called a "disaccumulating" period, with more emphasis on spending surpluses and less on scrimping to save capital, indebted consumption could challenge the hold of the renunciating Victorian ideal.[56] The middle-class debtor appeared right on time as an exemplar of the new order and a cog in it. In 1910, installment debt, largely for household and family matters, stood at half a billion dollars. In 1930, it reached about seven billion.[57]

The '20s forged a connection of debt and social position that would grow stronger in the next decade, when those successfully struggling to regain a credit line during the Depression were often called middle class. In 1920,

Modern American Office Work, 1900-1930 (Urbana: University of Illinois Press, 1992), 35-47, 70, 72-3, and 236-51.

56 Martin Sklar, "On the Proletarian Revolution and the End of Political-Economic Society," *Radical America*, May-June, 1969, 1-41.

57 Calder, *Financing the American Dream*, 201.

the credit theorist and advocate William Post suggested how the middle class could cohere as an indebted class by redefining rather than renouncing respectability. Post's *Character, the Basic Rock Foundation of the Four Big C's in the Extension of Credit*, registered the possibility of the "deserving indebted," able to borrow because of their virtues. In terms of ideology, rising levels of debt did not endorse profligacy. Credit-buying for large household items, and of course mortgages for houses themselves, could suggest discipline—the focused commitment to sacrifice for a limited number of satisfying things rather than the frittering away of paychecks.[58] For some households, the extras bought on credit were appliances making housework easier, and the small but growing number of working wives in the '20s sometimes sacrificed for just those purchases. A growing share of "middle income" families were also ones with multiple earners.[59]

The '20s and '30s made debt a defining factor in who identified as middle class and how. The great Cold War expansion of (talk about) the middle class coincided with a wave of borrowing—it seems small only in retrospect— addressing demands pent up during depression and war

---

58 Hyman, *Borrow*, 57-58 and 261 (on character and on Post); Calder, *Financing the American Dream*, 58-68, 20-09 and passim.

59 Winifred Wandersee, *Women's Work and Family Values, 1920-1940* (Cambridge: Harvard University Press, 1981), 59-60 and 70-76.

and real shortages of housing. The golden age of the middle-class suburban family starred, according to the acerbic liberal scholar David Riesman, "the debtor class." Already in 1958, the hot-selling economist and social critic John Kenneth Galbraith was asking, "Can the bill collector or the bankruptcy lawyer really be the central figure in the good society?"[60] Credit provided enjoyment mixed with anxiety. Before his demise, Willy Loman lamented, "Once in my life I would like to own something outright before it was broken." For the strongly unionized autoworkers in Detroit in the '50s, not only high wages but also high debt and high anxiety made it plausible to call their lives middle class. As Daniel Clark's important new account of the travails of autoworkers shows, fluctuations in demand and model changes made employment in auto plants episodic and second jobs often necessary. Home foreclosures and evictions threatened regularly.[61]

60 Riesman, as quoted in Calder, *Financing the American Dream*, 11; John Kenneth Galbraith, *The Affluent Society* (Boston: Houghton Mifflin, 1998, originally 1958), 14.

61 Daniel J. Clark, *Disruption in Detroit: Autoworkers and the Elusive Postwar Boom* (Urbana: University of Illinois Press, 2018), 38, 81, 86, 150, 167-78, and 209.

The patterns and meanings of debt change over time, but the crisis that Schor described can hardly be said to have eased; in 1995, non-mortgage debt in the United States stood at about $1.2 trillion. At the end of the second quarter of 2019, the figure approached $4.5 trillion. Mortgage debt was at a record high, registering gains for the twentieth straight quarter. Total household debt and credit set records too, touching on the $14 trillion mark; Schor totaled such debt at about $5.5 trillion as late as 1997.[62] Credit card debt, meanwhile, approached its Great Recession peak by the middle of 2019, standing at $868 billion, roughly doubling its 1999 amount.[63] The skyrocketing category of student debt was just short of $1.5 trillion, over a fifth of it not serviced for three months or more. The figures dwarf those

62 Schor, *Overspent American*, 72; Federal Reserve Bank of New York, "Total Household Debt Climbs for Twentieth Straight Quarter as Mortgage Debt and Originations Rise," August 13, 2019, https://www.newyorkfed.org/newsevents/news/research/2019/20190813; Center for Microecomic Data, "Household Debt and Credit Report, Q2 2019" *Federal Reserve Bank of New York*, https://www.newyorkfed.org/microeconomics/hhdc.html.

63 Alex Morrow, "Americans Haven't Had This Much Credit Card Debt since the since the Eve of the Fiscal Crisis," *Business Insider*, December 16, 2016, https://www.businessinsider.com/american-credit-card-debt-nearing-all-time-highs-2016-12; Federal Reserve Bank of New York, "Total Household Debt Climbs for Twentieth Straight Quarter," unpaginated; Board of Governors of the Federal Reserve System, "Total Consumer Credit Outstanding," Federal Reserve Bank of New York, August 13, 2019, https://www.newyorkfed.org/newsevents/news/research/2019/20190813.

in the alarmed account provided by Elizabeth Warren in her 2004 call to arms against such debt.[64]

According to a 2015 Inequality.org study based on figures from the *Credit Suisse Global Wealth Databook*, nearly 50 million of the 243 million adults then in the United States ranked in the poorest one-tenth of the world's population. (This social fact pairs with figures showing that US adults are even more overrepresented in the top 10 percent of world wealth, underlining again how little the United States is a nation dominated by its middle class). Much more than a nation amassing great wealth while tolerating dire poverty is at play here. The lower 50 million includes some who have no property and no jobs. They are conjured into the middle class by politicians who portray them as presumptively aspirant members with poverty-level incomes. Others qualify for a place at the world's bottom based on steep debt. To get down there to the bottom requires credentials and credit in order to overextend so massively. They stave off loss of the already re-mortgaged house with the credit cards until they can't. They have both fallen and

64 Alexandre Tanzi, "US Student Loan Delinquencies Hit Record," *Bloomberg Businessweek*, February 22, 2019, https://www.bloomberg.com/news/articles/2019-02-22/u-s-student-loan-delinquencies-hit-record; Benjamin Landy, "Graph: Why Student Loan Delinquency Is Still So High," *The Century Foundation*, August 27, 2013, https://tcf.org/content/commentary/graph-why-student-loan-delinquency-is-still-so-high/; Elizabeth Warren and Amelia Warren Tyagi, *The Two-Income Trap: Why Middle-Class Mothers and Fathers Are Going Broke* (New York: Basic Books, 2004), 40-46.

fear falling. They deserve far more than restoration of an earlier era in which they also were not saved.[65]

The numbers illuminate and obscure. Those state actors who measure, report, and analyze trends do so mainly with a view to assessing the health and prospects of the US economy, mostly in terms of its potential for growth. Even very high levels of personal and national debt seem compatible with such growth except, as happened in the recent Great Recession, when they aren't. Individuals and families—both those going under and those staying afloat—cannot be quite so cheery. They know they can scarcely work more to square things. They often must give up parts of middle-class dreams, declaring them impossibilities—foregoing paying for the college education of children, travel for vacation, and a dignified retirement. One result is that debt and overwork become even more central to the definition of middle class as what is positive recedes.

The personal here is also political. Maurizio Lazzarato's recent *The Making of Indebted Man* makes this point well. While hoping that common indebtedness can unite the many, Lazzarato argues that the processing of the miseries and impossibilities of chronic debt can lead as easily to a politics of hopelessness as to a politics of resistance. From

---

65 Paul Buchheit, "The New American Exceptionalism," Inequality.org, October 22, 2015, https://inequality.org/research/2015-wealth-data/.

"learning how to live with debt" in K–12 curricula onward, what he calls the "debt economy" in the United States teaches worry, guilt, and supplication. The latter is true vis-à-vis the state (especially in the unforgiving brutalities of student loan debt collection), and with regard to private lenders and their contracted-out collection bureaucracies. The scandalous, litigious debt-collection aggression of the University of Virginia's hospital system against those whom they have treated exemplifies how hard it can be to untangle the public and private. Neoliberal regimes of debt, Lazzarato argues, so debase the very word "confidence" as to connect it to an inability to act, and in particular to act collectively. The notion that this is an "entrepreneurial" society arises not so much because productive property is widely shared, nor even because there are small armies of people day-trading stocks and dreaming of owning a carwash franchise. Far more widespread are the management of one's own debt and attempts to make overwork address it.[66]

---

66 Maurizio Lazzarato, *The Making of Indebted Man* (Los Angeles: Semiotexte, 2011), 20, 37, 65-83 ("confidence"), 112 ("learning" and "debt economy"), 113-14 and passim; Jay Hancock and Elizabeth Lucas, "'UVA Has Ruined Us': Health System Sues Thousands of Patients, Seizing Paychecks and Putting Liens on Their Homes," *Washington Post*, September 9, 2019, https://www.washingtonpost.com/health/uva-has-ruined-us-health-system-sues-thousands-of-patients-seizing-paychecks-and-putting-liens-on-homes/2019/09/09/5eb23306-c807-11e9-be05-f76ac4ec618c_story.html.

Starting in the 1950s, the psychological research on young people performed by Walter Mischel achieved great stature within the imaginations of the most thoroughly hegemonized parts of the upper-middle class and within the educational establishment in the United States. In his well-known "marshmallow test," Mischel offered his preschool subjects a choice between having a relatively small marshmallow now or delaying gratification until later, when, he promised, a bigger one would be on offer. The "high delayers," allegedly possessed of more self-control and emotional maturity, were said to be bound for success, and the "low delayers" for troubles. The celebration of one interpretation of his data means to show how easy it is to succeed within the current contradictions of capitalism by adopting middle-class values and virtues. It shows instead the difficulty of doing so, from youth onward. The cultural historian Michael Staub has recently addressed these matters in a marvelous book, demonstrating how racial and class assumptions helped popularize the marshmallow test. We might wonder if the high delayers have learned judgment, trust, and the virtues of accumulation or have divined at a scarily early age how to present, in the presence of authority, a disciplined self rather than a shopping mall, holiday self. We might also wonder how it is possible to impart consistent messages in childrearing when parents are expected to produce both the shopping mall (now increasingly home shopping) "anarchist" and the prudent office worker. Perhaps the perfect response to the impossible position of the middle class would be to refuse the small marshmallow and then to put a dozen large ones on a maxed-out credit card. Also apposite would be ordering online—yes, they really exist—the hopefully ironic "DON'T EAT THE MARSHMALLOW" coffee mug.[67]

67 Michael Staub, *The Mismeasure of Minds: Debating Race and Intelligence between Brown and The Bell Curve* (Chapel Hill: University of North Carolina Press, 2018); Staub, "Controlling Ourselves: Emotional Intelligence, the Marshmallow Test, and the Inheritance of Race," *American Studies*, 55:1 (2016): 60 (for the mug) and 59-80; see also Jessica McCrory Calarco, "Why Rich Kids Are So Good at the Marshmallow Test," *The Atlantic*, June 1, 2018, https://www.theatlantic.com/family/archive/2018/06/marshmallow-test/561779/.

Afterword

THE NEWEST RAGE? LISTENING TO THE WHITE WORKING CLASS JOINS SAVING THE MIDDLE CLASS

One of the many disturbing consequences of the Trump/Brexit tragedy has been the sudden widespread reference to the White Working Class in popular and academic debate . . . The focus of much deliberation has become the question of how politicians can better attend to the interests of working-class whites. For many of those who grew up with a working-class consciousness this is beyond chilling.

—Lisa Tilley, geographer

Recent political debate in the United States, especially in the wake of the 2016 presidential election, features a preoccupation with what is wrong with and what is wrong for the "white working class." This group is sometimes blamed for the problems in US politics; at other times, the problem is defined as the ignoring of the white working class by Democratic Party elites. Hillary Clinton, for example, came in for fierce criticism when she seemed to, though she didn't exactly, throw white working-class Trump supporters into a "basket of deplorables" as racists, sexists, homophobes, Islamophobes, and more.[1] In 2008, she had cast herself on the other side of anti-elitism when she excoriated Barack Obama for his overheard remarks charging whites in declining industrial cities with "clinging" to their guns, Bibles, opposition to immigration, and—less remembered—hatred of trade agreements.[2] In a broader sense, the hue and cry holding white workers responsible for Trump similarly critiques a large, politically diverse group of working people with a broad brush. We will return to the merits of such indictments, but there is a prior and better question to be raised. What are the uses of "white working class" as a category, one now being put forward in large measure by center-right Democrats?

The burst of attention to the white working class, combined with a less full-throated emphasis on the

1   Katie Reilly, "Read Hillary Clinton's 'Basket of Deplorables' Remarks about Donald Trump Supporters," *Time*, September 10, 2016, https://time. com/4486502/hillary-clinton-basket-of-deplorables-transcript/.   The remark applied to "half" of Trump supporters and did not specify which ones by class. The Trump campaign's response, aware that her speech came at an LGBT for Hillary gala, branded the comment as an attack on "ordinary Americans." The chapter's epigraph is from Lisa Tilley, "The Making of the 'White Working Class': Where Fascist Resurgence Meets Leftist White Anxiety," *Wildcat Dispatches*, November 28, 2016, http:// wildcatdispatches.org/2016/11/28/lisa-tilley-the-making-of-the-white-working-class-where-fascist-resurgence-meets-leftist-white-anxiety.

2   Ed Pilkington, "Obama Angers Midwest Voters with Guns and Religion Remark," *The Guardian*, April 14, 2008, https://www.theguardian.com/ world/2008/apr/14/barackobama.uselections2008.

middle class as the target demographic in electioneering, suggested for a moment a sea change in the vocabulary of US politics. Thus, any conclusion to a study of the history of saving the middle class must weigh the newfound visibility of the term "white working class" and the loud calls to pay attention to it. The foregoing analysis of the use of the term "middle class" should enable us to get beyond seeing the two terms simply as competitors. From Stanley Greenberg's 1980s writings on, talk of "middle-class dreams" have packaged strategies based upon, though only strategically mentioning, claims around knowledge of white workers. Indeed, Greenberg reappears below as central to the more explicit introduction of "white" into recent political debates. This afterword argues that at least in the short and medium term, "middle class" will remain the favored rhetorical term of Democratic strategists and, white nationalism notwithstanding, among Republican strategists as well. However, open appeals to white voters are more fully on the table than they have been in sixty years, again in a bipartisan way.

Since the 1970s my writing has tried to make working-class histories, interests, and struggles more known, especially to readers who are themselves working people. For about the last thirty years, another focus has emerged—naming "whiteness" as an identity that has contributed to the weakness of labor in the United

States. As whites, the latter argument goes, some workers have managed to access benefits that are usually meager but nevertheless unavailable to workers who are not white. They therefore have stood above, and sometimes imagined themselves as deserving to stand still further above, non-white workers. As Greenberg fatalistically and unproductively recorded in his early research on white residents of Macomb County, being white sometimes constituted proof that one was middle class. At other times white workers called themselves working class, but without feeling the need to say "white." They either knew that the adjective was assumed when the noun was worker, or they thought that class identity united labor in a way that made superfluous specific consideration of race. Now that class and white identity have come together in the voguish term "white working class," I feel every bit of the chill that Lisa Tilley's epigraph identifies.

The "white working class" explanations for Trump's victory spread in part via the brief splash made in 2017 by the popular writing of the legal scholar Joan Williams, who argued extravagantly that condescending elites forced white workers into Trump's arms. This afterword questions the accuracy of the notion that it was specifically the white workers, as opposed to whites in general, who provided the requisite votes electing Trump. It introduces a bit of proportion regarding the extent of the popular appeal and staying power of white working-class analysis. Taking off dramatically from a base so low as to be almost non-existent, usage of "white working class" has now already returned to earth, proving too divisive in this moment to be useful to strategists beyond a few Rust Belt and formerly coal-mining areas. Even so, the very fact that elite Democratic strategists appealed for a time directly to "white" interests made a bad situation worse and will likely remain somewhere in the policy arsenal of both Democrats and Republicans, especially when immigration is up for debate. To say as much is not to hanker for a return to the good old days of middle-class appeals, which cleared a path to where we have descended.

The White Working Class as Nonstarter and Political Project

As noted in chapter 3, usage of "middle class" was infrequent until the Great Depression, and it increased during the Cold War. "Middle class" peaked in the mid-'70s and has remained more or less constant since the early '80s. Its was a latecomer to US life and later still to US elections. Even so, it has a history and recently an important pattern of use in politics. "White working class" has scarcely existed at all in the lexicon of the United States.

So infrequent is the use of "white working class" that new axes are needed to gain any purchase on patterns of

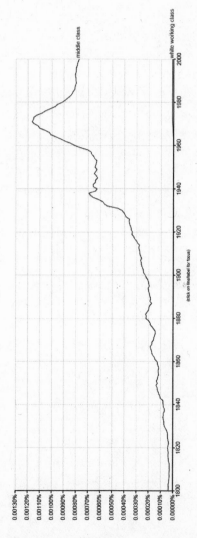

FIGURE TWO: NGRAMS PLOTTING "MIDDLE CLASS" VERSUS "WHITE WORKING CLASS"

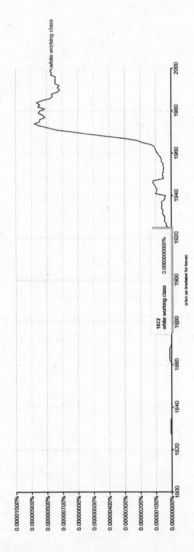

FIGURE THREE: NGRAM OF "WHITE WORKING CLASS" WITH NEW AXES

its usage in comparison to "middle class." Otherwise the former term simply hugs the bottom line of the graph.

The rising usage of "white working class," albeit only to still-low new levels, coincided with the triumphs of the civil rights movement and backlash against it. Usage peaked during the triumph of Reaganism, which coincided with the awful zenith of the career of California fascist and former Klansman Tom Metzger. Organizing around what he imagined to be the concerns of the white working class, Metzger professed to be inspired by the militancy of the Industrial Workers of the World, minus that union's inter-racialism. In 1980, Metzger won over 46,000 votes as the Democratic candidate for Congress in a San Diego-area district. He received a further 76,000 votes in a California US Senate primary in 1982 before presiding over the creation of the murderous White Aryan Resistance organization. Indeed, prior to its current vogue, I cannot recall ever seeing "white working class" in print in a sustained way apart from stories about Metzger.[3]

The lack of use of "white working class," especially as compared to "middle class," reflected two significant handicaps facing the fortunes of the former. The first was the Cold War, which made it hard to sustain any use of

3 On Metzger's career, see Steven Atkins, *Encyclopedia of Right-Wing Extremism in Modern America* (Santa Barbara: ABC-CLIO, 2011), 55-58; and Chip Berlet, "What Is the Third Position?" *Public Research Associates*, December 19, 2016, https://www.politicalresearch.org/2016/12/19/what-third-position.

"working class," whatever the adjective added. The term suggested Marxism, militancy, and ties to a world labor movement. Eventually, even union leaders opted for "middle class" because it mainstreamed labor's cause, seemed to make alliances with Cold War liberal groups easier, and opposed the language still used by oppositional left and pro-democracy groups in the unions. So potent was the censorship and self-censorship regarding the language of class that, thirty years later, there is still sufficient frisson at seeing "working class" in print that writers in the leading socialist publication *Jacobin* sometimes lean on Greenberg's recent "white working class" arguments as if he represented a class struggle tendency inside the Democratic Party.[4]

If "working class" was a hard sell, so too was "white." As Michael Omi and Howard Winant have argued, the moral grandeur of the civil rights movement made open appeals to white interests and white supremacy—so regular a feature of earlier US politics—harder to utter in its wake. If the new order seemed to require color blindness, with the center-right of the Democratic Party its champion, open

4   See, for example, Josh Mound, "What Democrats Must Do," *Jacobin*, September 30, 2017, https://jacobinmag.com/2017/09/democratic-party-2016-election-working-class.

appeals to "white" interests carried liabilities that "middle class" did not.[5]

However, a number of Democratic Party strategists kept the term "white working class" alive as a way to couch political appeals. As chapter 2 showed, Greenberg promised to teach Democratic politicians how to appeal to white workers before, and during, his shift to naming his research subjects as "middle class." Others stuck more consistently to "white working class" at about the time that Greenberg's star rose, but without insisting that they were proposing an alternative to talking about saving the middle class. The most intelligent contribution was an early meditation on what would later be widely called "dog whistle politics," initiatives that made racial appeals to whites without using the word "race." Mary and Thomas Edsall, who raised the issue in *The Atlantic* in 1991, repeatedly invoked the "white working class" in discussing such appeals but sometimes added "and lower-middle class." Their major book, *Chain Reaction: The Impact of Race, Rights, and Taxes on American Politics*, published the following year, used "white working class" as a collective noun just once, generally preferring

---

5   Aaron Brenner, Robert Brenner, and Cal Winslow, eds. *Rebel Rank and File: Labor Militancy and Revolt from Below during the Long 1970s* (New York: Verso, 2010); Michael Omi and Howard Winant, *Racial Formation in the United States* (New York: Routledge, 2015), 109-32 and 185-270.

(lower) middle class.[6] "Middle-class" and "white working-class" appeals were thus put forward by the same strategists and commentators, but with "middle class" holding
more attractions and carrying less baggage. Moreover, the
two terms performed similar functions in defining a group
key in all elections to establishing political horizons that
constrained what could be demanded in terms of racial
justice. The limits set by an austerity-minded, neoliberal
ruling class tended to receive little emphasis.

A knot of books, articles, and authors has continued
to make the white working class the key to selling politics
catering to timidity regarding racial justice and preferring
center-right Democratic candidates. They have argued for
the white working class's centrality because of its size and
its tendency to swing from one party to another. Often they
have implied the same first-person-to-be-brave-enough-
to-tell-hard-truths self-image that had characterized
Greenberg's *Middle Class Dreams* but now with a new—or
newly named—"white" class at the center. With the possible exception of mystery writers, no other group of authors
more lavishly blurbs each other's work.

6   Thomas Byrne Edsall and Mary Edsall, "Race," *The Atlantic*, May, 1991,
    https://www.theatlantic.com/past/docs/politics/race/edsall.htm;   Edsall
    and Edsall, *Chain Reaction: The Impact of Race, rights, and Taxes on American
    Politics* (New York: W.W. Norton, 1992). On Greenberg, see his *Middle Class
    Dreams: The New American Majority* (New York: Times Books, 1996, orig-
    inally 1995), 12 and 92 for the book's two uses of "white working-class,"
    both adjectival and chapter 2 above.

Appearing in conjunction with the 2000 presidential election was Ruy Teixeira and Joel Rogers's *America's Forgotten Majority: Why the White Working Class Still Matters,* a book in which self-declared left authors emphasized that a *white* working class, not "the working class," counted as the nation's forgotten majority.[7] During and after the Obama years, fears that the Democrats were abandoning white workers grew as it became clear that white workers were fast becoming a forgotten *minority,* their ranks dwindling. As Thomas Edsall, who frequently breaks out of the limitations of the "white working class" paradigm that he helped to create, wrote of the 2012 vote, much of the press wrote so insistently on the "white working class" that they pushed both voters of color and the racial views of whites in other classes to the margins.[8]

---

7   Ruy Teixeira and Joel Townsley Rogers, *America's Forgotten Majority Why the White Working Class Still Matters.* Cf. Andrew Levison, *The White Working Class Today: Who They Are, How They Think and What Progressives Can Do to Regain Their Support* (n.p.: Democratic Strategist Press, 2013). A CBS News report recently put working-class whites at about 40 percent of the US population. See Aimee Picchi, "America's White Working Class Is the Smallest It Has Ever Been," *CBS News,* September 26, 2019, https:// www.cbsnews.com/news/americas-white-working-class-is-the-small-est-its-ever-been/; John Hudak, "A Reality Check on 2016's Economically Marginalized," *Brookings,* November 16, 2016, https://www.brookings.edu/blog/fixgov/2016/11/16/economic-marginalization-reality-check/.

8   Thomas B. Edsall, "The Persistence of Racial Resentment," *New York Times,* reposted at *Portside,* February 10, 2013, https://portside.org/2013-02-10/persistence-racial-resentment; cf Edsall, "How Democrats Can Compete for the White Working Class," *New York Times,* March 11, 2014.

In the run-up to the 2014 Congressional elections, Andrew Levison defined the Democrats' greatest challenge as the "white working-class problem." For Teixiera, 2012 was the election in which the "white working class" would "decide Obama's fate."[9] By 2014, Greenberg himself would publish "Why the White Working Class Matters." He was then active in the White Working Class Roundtable, which met often and produced streams of articles under the auspices of the Democratic Strategist group. The second of the group's major roundtables centered on responses to Greenberg's paper, "The Battle for the White Working Class Is Just Beginning."[10] What Susan Glasser has called the "Democratic Civil War" heated up during the 2016 election, with the critics of Hillary Clinton's perceived orientation to women and minorities—those critics included Greenberg and those around him, Joe Biden, and on some

9 Andrew Levison, "Democrats Have a White Working Class Problem—and Not Just in the South," *The New Republic*, August 6, 2014, https://newrepublic.com/article/118960/democrats-white-working-class-problem-isnt-just-south; Teixiera, "The White Working Class: The Group that Will Likely Decide Obama's Fate," *The New Republic*, June 20, 2011, https://newrepublic.com/article/90241/obama-election-2012-working-class-kerry.

10 Stanley Greenberg, "Why the White Working Class Matters," *Washington Monthly*, June-July-August, 2014, https://washingtonmonthly.com/magazine/junejulyaug-2014/why-the-white-working-class-matters/; *The American Prospect* and the White Working Class Roundtable, *Democrats and the White Working Class* (Lexington, KY.: Democratic Strategist Press, 2017), frontmatter; The Democratic Strategist and *Washington Monthly*, *The Second Roundtable on the White Working Class*, https://thedemocraticstrategist.org/the-white-working-class-roundtables/.

accounts Bill Clinton—taking up the white working class banner.[11]

While it is true that a Clinton victory in 2016 would have disarmed many of the "nasty" post-election conflicts that Glasser has described, the achievements of the "white working class" thinkers in the Democratic Party before Trump were significant and divisive. They insisted on invoking both the middle class and the white working class to counter the identity politics wing that they saw as dominant in the Democratic Party. One of their leading lights captured the group's confusion on defining class when he cast the target audience as those with "working-class and small business values."[12] Lacking any clear program to address the pressing needs of working people, they seldom allowed that the main roadblock to doing so was not identity politics but limits set by what change was permissible to capital. Nor had they made a popular breakthrough. Happily, no large group of people has signed up for the white working class label, however much they have identified as whites and as workers. In trying to convey a sense of "white

---

11 Susan Glasser, "The Democratic Civil War Is Getting Nasty Even If No One Is Paying Attention," *The New Yorker*, November 1, 2017, https://www. newyorker.com/news/news-desk/the-democratic-civil-war-is-getting-nasty-even-if-no-one-is-paying-attention.

12 Levison, "Winning (Some) Middle-of-the-Road Working-Class Whites" in *The American Prospect* and the White Working Class Roundtable, *Democrats and the White Working Class*, 132-33 ("small business").

working class" to readers, Katherine Connor Martin, head of US dictionaries for *The Oxford English Dictionary*, has recently observed that "Overwhelmingly when people are using the phrase 'white working class' it seems to be in the context of electoral politics," tracing that usage from the 1960s forward.[13] The Trump victory seemed to offer the chance for Democrats advocating for a white working-class strategy—again, they simultaneously invoked the middle class—to break through to greater influence.

Blood Soup and All-Nighters

If the legal scholar Joan C. Williams was not the first person to begin writing in response to Donald Trump's 2016 election victory, she was at least tied for first. In introducing the eventual book stemming from that earliest effort, Williams describes herself as working late into the night responding to a disaster. Since networks did not call the election until 2:35 A.M. Eastern time, she may have had a fair start on an all-nighter already, depending on where she watched the returns. A bloggish article, properly rageful and admirably breezy, poured out. The website of *Harvard*

---

13   Connor Martin as quoted in Sam Harnett, "What We Talk about when We Talk about the 'White Working Class,'" (San Francisco) *KQED News: The California Report*, November 7, 2017, https://www.kqed.org/news/11620388/what-we-talk-about-when-we-talk-about-the-white-working-class.

Business Review—get ready for several ironies—published the piece as "What So Many People Don't Get About the U.S. Working Class" two days after the election.[14] Hits and retweets encouraged a book, published by the journal's press a mere six months later.[15] The book, praised by Joe Biden, sold well enough to hover on the edges of best-seller lists and was widely reviewed.[16]

Williams's book proved to be a not very serious one—the election year repackaging of it will include a foreword by television's *Shark Tank* entrepreneur and Dallas Mavericks owner Mark Cuban—but it remains potently symptomatic of where we are, have been, and ought not go. Nowhere does this fact stand out more than in the book's slipperiness regarding the languages of race and class. Williams wanted to follow Stanley Greenberg's 1990s model of calling her aggrieved subjects the "middle class," in her case kicking the "clueless" professional-managerial elite out of that group in favor of genuine sons and daughters of toil, minus the poor. Her publisher

14 Joan C. Williams, "What So Many People Don't Get about the US Working Class," *Harvard Business Review*, November 10, 2016, https://hbr.org/2016/11/what-so-many-people-dont-get-about-the-u-s-working-class.

15 Joan C. Williams, *White Working Class: Overcoming Class Cluelessness in America* (Cambridge: Harvard Business Review Press, 2017).

16 Biden's endorsement is found on the book's Amazon webpage at https://www.amazon.com/White-Working-Class-Overcoming-Cluelessness/dp/1633693783.

convinced Williams to substitute "working class" for "middle class."[17]

Arriving at class categories by asking the people marketing your book what's best turns out to create confusion. The book version of Williams's research occasionally still uses "middle class," and it offers definitions of "working class" as essentially middle income. The result is a "class" defined by an annual income of $41,005 to $131,962 (median: $75,144), and by holding values alternately seen as understandable or wonderful. (Teachers, professors, and indeed much of the professional-managerial class fall very largely in that income range, but they disappear as members of the working class and instead stand in as its enemies.) Williams has moments of appearing to want to talk about the whole working class, but her book is rightly titled *White Working Class*. So much does her work lean on the racially identified collective noun that Williams resorted to using the acronym WWC in the initial article as a space saver. In the book, as one reviewer puts it, "The 'white' modifier mostly disappears after the

---

17 Williams, *White Working Class*, 9-10; for fuller critiques of the book see David Roediger, "Who's Afraid of the White Working Class," *Los Angeles Review of Books*, May 17, 2017, https://lareviewofbooks.org/article/whos-afraid-of-the-white-working-class-on-joan-c-williamss-white-working-class-overcoming-class-cluelessness-in-america/.

title page," but the whiteness of her subject remains clear throughout.[18]

The practices of designedly mixing up middle class and white working class are, as we have seen, longstanding. Williams perhaps does a favor to debates on these matters with the outsized "WHITE" on her book's cover. But the potential costs are great, and the incoherence of her categories concerning both race and class is striking. At one point, Williams hopes that restaurant owners will oppose Trump's border policies in order for them to better secure immigrant labor. The restaurant owners are considered working class, and their immigrant employees are somehow not.[19]

Both the original short article and the book begin with a "native informant," Williams's father-in-law, credentialed as working class because he "grew up eating blood soup." Hostile to unions, which he considers "a bunch of jokers who take your money," and, she speculates, ashamed of his diet as a child, the father-in-law counted as "a man before his time." He was a "blue collar white man," Republican voter, and *Wall Street Journal* reader from the 1950s forward. Fair enough—there were such workers. But

18 Anthony Perrin, "The Invention of the 'White Working Class,'" *Public Books,* January 30, 2018, https://www.publicbooks.org/the-invention-of-the-white-working-class/.

19 Williams, *White Working Class,* 115.

the jobs held by the father-in-law do not sound very blue collar. He might better be described instead as a serially failing entrepreneur who moonlighted in self-employment. Even his waged or salaried job, as an inspector in a factory making museum-quality hygrometers, hardly fits the extravagance of the claims made for him as a precocious proletarian outlier. In half-endorsing his views on unions, Williams finds that "starting in the 1970s, many blue collar whites followed his example," a particularly unfeeling summary of what happened to the organizations representing working people and the vast amount of coercion and disinvestment that made it happen.[20]

Dismissive of unions, *White Working Class* offers scant hints regarding what programmatic reforms can increase the power and organization of working people or what would force elites to be better listeners. It addresses inequality, but of a sort based on supposed disparities in "paying attention," not wealth. It asserts an "identity politics" that plumps for, as the sociologist Anthony Perrin has put it, white workers to receive "*recognition* not redistribution." At one low point, Williams offers the non sequitur, "Progressives have lavished attention on the poor for over a century," urging what might be called "attention

---

20 Williams, *White Working Class*, 1 ("soup"), 3 ("jokers" and "followed").

reparations" for the "white working class," which again is defined so as to exclude the white working poor.[21]

If the shortcuts and errors of *White Working Class* were found nowhere else, a critique such as this one would be interesting mainly to those radicals who want to keep class categories as clear as possible and to labor historians, with me guilty on both counts. However, it is the extent to which she participated in, and even led, the recent and sudden burst of loose talk about the "white working class" that makes Williams's book command interest despite its inadequacies.

Indeed, as Williams's article appeared and then her book, the possibility that mainstream political parties would appeal openly to the white working class seemed suddenly to be real. In no small measure, this reflected the work done by those around Greenberg and the White Working Class Roundtable, and Trump's own desire to portray himself as a champion of the blue-collar worker. The pace of change was dizzying. The day after the election, based on quite unreliable exit polls, the *New York Times'* front page piloted the idea that the election was "a decisive demonstration of power by a largely overlooked coalition of mostly blue-collar white and working-class voters." The broad and insistent consensus around this

---

21 Williams, *White Working Class*, 13; Perrin, "The Invention of the 'White Working Class,'" unpaginated, for "*recognition*," emphasis original.

interpretation included liberals more than ready to see white workers as uniquely backward, Democratic strategists sharing Williams's view that elites were to blame, and Republicans giddy at capturing a new constituency. Bernie Sanders, who has mostly admirably avoided "white working class" rhetoric, nevertheless tweeted in the aftermath of the election, "I come from the white working class."[22]

Biden's election post-mortem emphasized the need for his party to "show enough respect" for the white working class and expressed a conviction that racism did not play any significant role in the election results. Google Trends, which measures internet searches for specific terms, showed a seven-fold increase in searches for "white working class" after the election over a typical month before the election.[23] A spate of celebrated books, including J.D. Vance's *Hillbilly Elegy*, Nancy Isenberg's *White Trash*, and Arlie Russell Hochschild's *Strangers in Their Own Land*, appeared either just before or shortly after the 2016 vote,

---

22 Nicholas Carnes and Noam Lupu, "It's Time to Bust the Myth: Most Trump Voters Were Not Working Class," *Washington Post*, June 5, 2017, https://www.washingtonpost.com/news/monkey-cage/wp/2017/06/05/its-time-to-bust-the-myth-most-trump-voters-were-not-working-class/ includes the *Times* quote and much more. For Sanders' November 14, 2016, tweet, see https://twitter.com/berniesanders/status/798192678785716224?lang=en. See also Perrin, "Invention," unpaginated.

23 John T. Bennett, "Biden: Democrats Must Show 'Respect' for Working-Class Whites," *Roll Call*, December 8, 2016, https://www.rollcall.com/politics/democrats-must-show-respect-working-class-whites. The Google Trends search was done on September 29, 2019.

gaining notoriety in that context. Most were of course begun long before Trump's triumphs, showing again how the ground had been seeded for the swelling of interest in the white working class before he was taken seriously.[24] Further contributing to the rise of such discourse were splashy and weighty studies of the health crisis, and particularly of drug addiction in white working-class communities.[25]

The use of "white working class" took off after Trump's election partly because it coincided with similar turns toward that phrase in what the political writer Pankaj Mishra has called the "white Anglosphere."[26] The British vote to leave the European Union in the Brexit referendum came not five months before Trump's victory. Amidst some complicated cross-currents, the "leave" forces contained a fair share of far-right nationalists who objected to the movement of migrants to England and became the

24 For review essays on this literature see Perrin, "The Invention of the 'White Working Class,'" unpaginated and Mark Bergfeld's astute "The Perils of 'the White Working Class': Analysing the New Discussion on Class," *Global Labour Journal* (January, 2019), https://mulpress.mcmaster.ca/globallabour/article/view/3868.

25 Anne Case and Angus Deaton, "Mortality and Morbidity in the 21st Century," *Brookings Papers on Economic Activity*, Spring, 2017, https://www.brookings.edu/wp-content/uploads/2017/08/casetextsp17bpea.pdf; cf. Jonathan M. Metzl, *Dying of Whiteness: How the Politics of Racial Resentment Is Killing America's Heartland* (New York: Basic Books, 2019).

26 Pankaj Mishra, "The Religion of Whiteness Becomes a Suicide Cult," *New York Times*, August 30, 2018.

movement's public face. In Britain, there was a far sturdier tradition of using "working class" by socialists and in popular culture. The writings of Tilley, Richard Seymour, and Robbie Shilliam offer some of the most illuminating reflections on appeals to the white working class. That the term echoes across the Anglosphere and beyond, in places where the electoral demographics of race so differ, underlines Seymour's point that white working class analysis functions less to "leave anyone informed" as to political realities and more as a "cover story" that enables neoliberalism to at once bemoan racism and undertake new racist initiatives of its own.[27]

Redeployments: The White Working Class, the Middle Class, and Thinking Beyond the Electoral Strategies on Offer

Reacting to the peak of rhetorical attention to the white working class after Trump's election, Anthony Perrin wrote: "The white working class was made, not found;

---

27 Tilley, "The Making of the 'White Working Class,'" unpaginated; Richard Seymour, "What's the Matter with the 'White Working Class'?" *Salvage*, February 2, 2017, http://salvage.zone/online-exclusive/whats-the-matter-with-the-white-working-class/; Robbie Shilliam, *Race and the Undeserving Poor* (Newcastle-on-Tyne: Agenda Publishing, 2018), 135-64 and, from an empirical standpoint though not analytically, Justin Gest, *The New Minority: White Working Class Politics in an Age of Immigration and Inequality* (Oxford and New York: Oxford University Press, 2016). More broadly still, see Bergfeld, "The Perils of 'the White Working Class,'" unpaginated.

deployed, not discovered."[28] Moreover,
elites well before that election. To take aboaɪ..
insight requires that we regard ersatz languages of elections and class as malleable in the short run as well as the
long. Indeed, the furor surrounding the role of the working class seems to have already subsided. A return to "saving the middle class" discourse that the bulk of this book
has described is well under way, though much of the political work done by the deployment of "white working class"
survives.

The initial inflated claims that white workers uniquely
contributed to Trump's election themselves proved unsus-
tainable. Within days of the election, even before better
data than exit polls came in, such a view suffered sharp
challenges. The lack of substantial movement of such
workers toward Trump in relation to their votes for Mitt
Romney in the 2012 election cast doubt on assertions that
the new president had a special bond with white blue-collar workers.[29] As more sophisticated data emerged, other
social facts came to seem more compelling than the association of white workers with Trump. One concerned the
enormous non-voting of the working poor and even the

28 Perrin, "The Invention of the 'White Working Class," unpaginated.

29 Hudak, "A Reality Check on 2016's Economically Marginalized," unpagi-
    nated; Thomas Edsall, "The 2016 Exit Polls Led Us to Misinterpret the 2016
    Election," *New York Times*, March 29, 2018.

middle reaches of the working class. Those making less than $30,000 per year furnished 56 percent of the nation's non-voters and just 28 percent of its voters, with those making between $30,000 and $75,000 less dramatically but still significantly underrepresented in the ranks of voters.[30]

Instant analyses, and political polling more generally, make having a high school diploma or less a convenient proxy for working-class membership, even though 22 percent of the white electorate has a high income and no college degree. They are, as Edsall writes, "rock-ribbed Republicans" who are counted as working-class conservatives but are often not actually working class. Conversely, one white voter in seven possesses a college degree but earns a low income. They are the "most loyal white Democratic constituency." Often poor, they count as "middle class."[31] Most importantly, among whites, Trump won not one particular income category but all income categories. The voting patterns of white workers were far more like those of whites in other class positions than like those of other groups of workers. Astonishingly, with his endorsement of sexual violence as a perk of being rich

---

30 N.a., "An Examination of the 2016 election, Based on Validated Voters," *Pew Research Center*, August 8, 2018, https://www.people-press.org/2018/08/09/an-examination-of-the-2016-electorate-based-on-validated-voters/

31 Thomas B. Edsall, "We Aren't Seeing White Support for Trump for What It Is," *New York Times*, August 28, 2019.

and male ringing in voters' ears, he carried white wom-
en's votes. To displace this broad white consensus onto the
white worker misses much.[32]

The bubble of attention around the white working
class ended about as quickly as it began, although the
term lurks in the playbooks of white nationalists in the
Republican Party as well as in those to the center-right of
the Democrats. Within a year of the 2016 election, Google
Trends registered the same levels of (dis)interest in the
term as during the decade before. Stanley Greenberg was
writing briefly that his party did not "have a 'white working-class problem'" but a "working-class problem." In 2017,
he briefly argued for a strategy that would attack a system
that only worked "for the rich, big corporations and cultural elites," but not "for average Americans."[33] Biden, the

32 Carnes and Lupu, "It's Time to Bust the Myth," unpaginated;
    Aamna Mohdin, "American Women Voted Overwhelmingly for
    Clinton, Except the White Ones," *Quora* , November 8, 2016, https://
    qz.com/833003/election-2016-all-women-voted-overwhelming-
    ly-for-clinton-except-the-white-ones/. Even the statistics on white
    health and morbidity came in for revision in, for example, Malcolm
    Harris, "The Death of the White Working Class Has Been Grossly
    Exaggerated," *Pacific Standard*, June 14, 2017, https://psmag.com/news/
    the-death-of-the-white-working-class-has-been-greatly-exaggerated.

33 Ronald Brownstein, "The Democratic Debate over Winning Back Trump's
    Base," *The Atlantic*, May 2, 2019, https://www.theatlantic.com/politics/
    archive/2019/05/joe-bidens-bid-white-working-class-vote/588613/;
    Stanley Greenberg, "The Democrats' 'Working Class Problem,'" *The
    American Prospect*, June 1, 2017, https://prospect.org/labor/democrats-work-
    ing-class-problem/; cf. Stanley Greenberg, *R.I.P. G.O.P.: How the New America
    Is Dooming the Republicans* (New York: Thomas Dunne Books, 2019).

presidential candidate most situated in the center-right Democratic tradition and the language of class it has proposed and enforced, vaulted early in the 2020 election cycle to leading contender status based on hopes that the white working-class base of the party would support him against Trump. He also liked to say that everybody called him "Middle Class Joe," though reporters found that almost no one did.[34]

It is of course good to listen to all workers, white or not. That is part of the job of ethnographers, reporters, politicians, union leaders, and even pollsters. However, to hail some workers as a "white working class" and to promise them respect and a sympathetic ear only on that specific basis courts disasters.[35] If such discourse has collapsed in the short run, we should delight in that fact, as the accent will always fall on "white" and the mumbling on "working class" when the term is used. Indeed, before, during, and after the phrase's burst of popularity in 2017, the use of "white working class" far exceeded that of a Black working class in the United States. Nor have appeals simply to the working class as a whole increased. Greenberg's new book,

---

34 Arthur Delaney, "Who Calls Joe Biden 'Middle Class Joe'?" *HuffPost*, March 7, 2019, https://www.huffpost.com/entry/joe-biden-middle-class_n_5c8032 d8e4b06ff26ba55799; Ben Schreckinger, "Biden, Inc.," *Politico*, August 2, 2019.

35 Doyle McManus, "Democrats' Hunt for the White Working-Class Male Voter," *Los Angeles Times*, April 18, 2015, https://www.latimes.com/nation/ la-oe-0419-mcmanus-whites-20150419-column.html.

which appeared when this one was entering production, dangerously refers to the European immigrant working class of a century ago as the "real working class."[36]

Deployments of the labels "white working class" and "blue-collar middle class" may represent honest efforts to win an election, and they may contain the broken bits of grander hopes, even the odd remembrances of that one inspirational working-class studies course taken in college. There is perhaps no need for harshness regarding how people use these discourses on election day. But in thinking about larger possibilities and local social movements, we do need to contest the ways in which such labels enforce constraints and spread illusions. In making the white voter in Macomb County—shouted out to according to his or her worst impulses—the center of political life in America, we immobilize ourselves, especially as elections loom so large in how we consider political action. In their hardened forms, appeals to the (white) middle class and the white working class function as pedagogy, not sociology. They teach us what it is impossible to demand and, in doing so, account not for the opinions of white workers, but of the white workers who are most reactionary. Polling recently commissioned by the AFL-CIO counts about 40

36 Malaika Jabali, "Joe Biden Is Not a Blue-Collar Candidate," *Jacobin*, May 2, 2019, https://www.jacobinmag.com/2019/05/joe-biden-presidential-primary-working-class; Greenberg, *R.I.P. G.O.P.*, 199 and 200-04.

percent of the white non-college-educated electorate as Democratic or as leaning in that direction. Eighty percent of these white working-class Democrats approve of Black Lives Matter, and 82 percent want no border wall.[37] Here is a demographic of white workers that is truly "forgotten."

The emphasis on "winning back" the white working class—they've been at best episodically voting Democratic for forty or fifty years—exposes all of us to what Eric Levitz has termed the "tyranny of the unwoke white swing voter," especially where immigration is concerned. Hochschild's sadly under-criticized "cutting in line" analogy is in danger of becoming all that anyone remembers from her often perceptive *Strangers in Their Own Land*. She offers it as an image shared by her white-working class informants, whose dashed hopes for the American Dream seem stymied by line-jumping migrants rather than the chemical companies who dominate and scar the land where they live.[38] Hochschild herself constructed the "cutting in line" image by

37 Eric Levitz, "The Tyranny of the Unwoke White Swing Voter," *New York Intelligencer*, June 26, 2019, http://nymag.com/intelligencer/2019/06/the-tyranny-of-the-unwoke-white-swing-voter.html; Thomas B. Edsall, "There Are Really Two Distinct White Working Classes," *New York Times*, June 26, 2019.

38 Arlie Russell Hochschild, *Strangers in Their Own Land: Anger and Mourning on the American Right* (New York: New Press, 2018), esp. 135-45. Hochschild seems not to use "white working class" as a noun, and rarely as an adjective but the paperback edition's back cover makes the "white working class" the book's subject.

synthesizing many conversations and then gave it back to her informants, whom we are told liked it. For a researcher to report these perceptions is apt, but without also challenging such views, organizers are left unable to speak to and listen to white workers who are finding their ways to social and environmental justice and support for indigenous rights. Similarly, Greenberg's recent book predicting the end of the Republican Party as we know it says many of the proper things regarding how a new and diverse United States beckons. But it then issues a warning that all the positive momentum will stall if Democrats are—his view—foolish enough to "rescue" the Republicans by "passing landmark comprehensive immigration reform . . . that is viewed as . . . comparable to the passage of the civil rights laws of the 1960s."[39]

Arguing in *The Democratic Strategist* for "the diverse white working class" as the focus of the 2020 election campaigns, Ruy Teixeira has recently offered a longer list of policy proposals that progressives must take off the table to win the mythical white working-class constituency:

How to make these gains? Hint: not by decriminalizing the border, not through Medicare for All that abolishes private health care plans; not by providing

---

39   Greenberg, *R.I.P. G.O.P.*, 268 and 265-69 passim.

health coverage to undocumented immigrants and other similar—and similarly unpopular—ideas.[40]

This use of white working people, and at other moments of the (white) middle class, to preempt demands for justice and well-being cannot be turned on for election day and turned off after. We who believe in freedom have to dream better and fight harder than the discourses of saving the middle class or paying attention to the white working class allow. Social movements will have to look for their poetry, and their clarity, beyond the social analysis offered by electoral politics.

40 Ruy Teixeira, "The Diverse White Working Class," *The Democratic Strategist*, July 9, 2019, https://thedemocraticstrategist.org/2019/07/teixeira-the-diverse-white-working-class/.

INDEX

"1 percent," the, 90, 114, 135

activism
    and electoral politics, 11–12
    labor, 85, 126, 141–142, 145
    and middle class studies, 101
    and Stanley Greenberg, 53
affirmative action, 17, 25, 70, 75
AFL-CIO, 251
African National Congress (ANC),
    78–79, 81
alienation of labor, 23, 45, 182, 189,
    198, 202, 210
Alinsky, Saul, 43
alt-right movement, 14, 19
Althusser, Louis, 122
American exceptionalism, 21,
    124–125, 128–135, 147
American Studies, 34, 38, 52
anti-Semitism, 79, 167
anxiety, 23, 177–178, 189, 217
apartheid, 52–53, 78, 81
Appalachian people, 36, 43–44, 46
Appelbaum, Binyamin, 110
Aristotle, 111
austerity, 32, 71, 74, 141, 234
authoritarianism, 14, 104, 165, 167
auto industry, 58, 64, 122, 127

United Auto Workers (UAW), 19,
    64, 93

Banfield, Edward, 39–41
bankruptcy, 212
Barak, Ehud, 80
Baritz, Loren, 130
"Bartleby, The Scrivener" (Herman
    Melville), 180, 195, 199
Baudrillard, Jean, 9–10
Beckert, Sven, 116
Bendix, Reinhard, 194, 196
Bernstein, Eduard, 163
Biden, Joe, 86, 94, 186, 239, 244, 249
Bingham, Alfred, 121
Blacks in the US
    Black freedom struggle, 33
    Black Lives Matter, 83, 252
    Black voters, 20
    Black working class, 250
    and Hillary Clinton, 83
    and middle class
        designations, 104–105
    in South Africa, 53
    and Stanley Greenberg,
        31, 33–35, 41–43, 48, 53,
        63–64, 68–70, 83
    and unions, 64

Black Lives Matter, 83, 252
Black Panthers, 48
Black Power, 69, 125
Blair, Tony, 79
Bledstein, Burton, 130
blue-collar workers
    "blue-collar middle class," 251
    Donald Trump and, 243
    Joan Williams, on 241–242
    Marxism and, 161, 164, 170,
      172
    Stanley Greenberg on, 61,
      63, 65
Blumin, Stuart, 116
Bolivian election, 2002, 80
border, US-Mexico, 15, 104, 241,
    252–253
borrowing, 185, 210, 214, 216
bourgeoisie
    and *The Communist
      Manifesto*, 149–151, 155
    definitions of, 155–156
    petit, 157, 166, 174
    and revolutions, 117
    values of, 131
Boydston, Jeanne, 116
Braverman, Harry, 173
Brexit, 224, 245
Britain, 79, 123, 133, 152–153, 246
    Brexit, 224, 245
Brown v. Board of Education, 34
bureaucracy, 126, 195, 197–198, 221
Bush, George H.W., 68, 110
business
    and American
      exceptionalism, 134–137
    Dale Carnegie and, 191–192
    and Democratic party, 237
    fascism and, 166
    Herbert Hoover and, 29, 31
    and middle class conceptions,
      114, 116, 119, 175, 214

    Stanley Greenberg and, 37,
      75, 77

Cabanas, Edgar, 197
Caddell, Pat, 109
capitalism
    and American
      exceptionalism, 125
    and blue-collar workers, 172
    and Great Depression, 113
    and marshmallow test, 222
    and Marxism, 22, 150–152,
      156, 158–159, 162–163, 174
    and middle class conceptions,
      22, 121
    and misery, 177–178, 186,
      189, 202
    pro-capitalist thinkers, 146
    and socialism, 147
Carnegie, Dale, 190–194
Carville, James, 72, 76, 80–81, 88
Catholics, 39, 57, 61
center-right Democrats, 31, 33, 68,
    225, 232, 234, 249–250
centrists, 18, 32, 51, 76, 82, 131
    center-right Democrats,
      31, 33, 68, 225, 232, 234,
      249–250
Chavez, Hugo, 81
Chinoy, Eli, 136
civil rights
    civil rights movement, 31–32,
      35, 231, 253
    and US Right, 14, 142
Clark, Daniel, 181, 217
class
    class war, 90, 162
    new class theorists, 162, 175
    self-identification of,
      100–102, 121, 123
    See also blue-collar workers;
      class consciousness;

white-collar work; working class

class consciousness, 24, 45, 63, 99, 104, 153
    middle, 129, 276
    working, 175–176, 225
clerical workers, 195, 200
Clinton, Bill
    and American exceptionalism, 131
    and middle class as term, 109–110, 131
    and Stanley Greenberg, 19–20, 24, 32, 49, 54, 62, 72–75, 81
    and white working class, 237
Clinton, Hillary, 17, 84, 91–93, 111, 183, 114, 236–237
coal mining, 2, 122, 228
Cobb, Jonathan, 174
Colbert, Stephen, 85
Cold War
    and American exceptionalism, 125–126, 129–130
    and debt, 216
    and gender, 205–206
    and middle class as term, 20, 113, 122, 228, 231–232
college education
    cost of, 220
    and Democratic voters, 252
    and food insecurity, 184–185
    and income, 13, 104, 248
    and labor movement, 141
colonialism, 55, 59
color lines, 32, 34, 65, 111
commodity production, 158–160
Communism
    and American Exceptionalism, 125, 128
    anti-Communism, 111, 113

and *The Communist Manifesto*, 148–151, 155, 158
Communist Party, 49, 128, 168, 170
    and labor movement, 164, 168, 170
    and Stanley Greenberg, 35, 49–51
Communist Manifesto, The, 148–151, 155, 158
Congress, United States, 53, 68, 72, 76, 109, 231, 136
Congress of Industrial Organizations, 118, 122, 169, 251
conservatives
    in Britain, 79
    and Donald Trump, 141
    and Joan Williams, 24
    in Macomb County, Michigan, 19, 28, 55–56, 61–62
    and Marxism, 149, 161
    and middle class, 108, 132, 146
    and Stanley Greenberg, 38–39, 47, 55
    working-class, 248
consumption, 23, 98, 189, 210, 215
    consumer society, 9, 211
Corey, Lewis, 22, 169, 171–172
corporations
    corporate efficiency, 31
    and Donald Trump supporters, 18
    and fascism, 166
    nineteenth-century, 116
    and Scott Walker, 142
    and Stanley Greenberg, 75, 77–78, 249
    US in South Africa, 53
credit, 157, 188, 215–219
Cuban, Mark, 239
cubicles, 179–180

D'Amato, Alphonse, 109
Davidson, Carl, 11–12
Death of a Salesman (Arthur
    Miller), 139, 155, 180
debt
        and Donald Trump, 17, 93
        and middle-class, 23, 97, 182,
            188–189, 205, 210–221
        student, 97–98
Defoe, Daniel, 112
Delauro, Rosa, 50, 52, 72, 76–77
democracy, 129, 163, 222
Democratic Alliance (DA), 81
Democratic Party
        center-right, 31, 33, 68, 225,
            232, 234, 249–250
        Democratic Leadership
            Council (DLC), 67, 71
        and Democratic Socialists of
            America (DSA), 139–141
        and labor activism, 142
        and Mitt Romney, 87
        party politics of, 49, 142
        Reagan Democrats, 19, 54
        and saving middle class,
            rhetoric 8–9, 12, 17, 85,
            95, 109
        and Stanley Greenberg,
            19–20, 31–33, 38–39, 48–50,
            54–63, 67–71, 81–84
        and "working class whites,"
            23–24, 224–226, 228,
            231–238, 248–250, 252–253
Democratic Socialists of America
    (DSA), 139–141
depression, economic, 30, 215–216
        Great Depression, 113, 115,
            118, 202–203, 228
Detroit, Michigan, 19, 42–43,
        58–59, 63, 141, 217
Dobbs, Lou, 88
Dodd, Christopher, 52–53

Domhoff, G. William, 135
downward mobility, 18, 96, 153, 170
Dreiser, Theodore, 23, 200
Du Bois, W.E.B., 165
Dukakis, Michael, 68
Duke, David, 74

Eagleton, Terry, 186–187, 211
economy
        and 2016 election, 17, 93
        economic citizenship, 211
        and inequality, 220–221
        and Karl Marx, 154, 159–160,
            162, 215
        in Macomb County, Michigan,
            19–20, 27
        and middle class conceptions,
            90, 105, 121–122, 130, 188
        political, 43, 50, 111
        and Stanley Greenberg, 71
Edsall, Thomas, 233, 235, 248
education, 13, 105, 222
        higher, 184, 186, 220
        K–12, 34, 140
        post-high school, 37
        public, 137
Ehrenreich, Barbara, 22, 103, 134,
        155, 173
Ehrenreich, John, 103, 134
elections
        2012, 16, 86, 87, 90, 108, 110,
            235–236, 247
        2016, 16, 83–84, 91, 108, 141,
            224, 236–238, 244
        2020, 11, 94, 132, 250, 253
        and American
            exceptionalism, 132
        and appeals to middle class,
            86–87, 90–91, 95
        and Bill Clinton, 73
        endless cycles of, 9–15
        and Herbert Hoover, 30

national, 12, 91
and Ronald Reagan, 54–55
and Stanley Greenberg,
    19–20, 54–56, 59, 68, 73, 76,
    82–84
and white working class,
    224, 226–228, 234–239,
    243–247, 249–251
elites, 24, 96, 108, 119, 197, 227, 244
Emanuel, Rahm, 76–77
employment
    employers, 102, 104, 180, 197
    and immigration, 241
    and Marxism, 152, 161,
        163–164
    and middle-class conceptions,
        21, 116, 133, 146, 191, 197
    public employees, 143–144
    salaried, 22, 152, 164, 170,
        172, 194, 205
    self, 22, 116, 135–136, 137,
        152, 158, 160–161, 163, 213
    and women, 206, 210
Engels, Friedrich, 127–128,
    148–149, 151, 156–157
England, 153, 156–157, 245
entrepreneurship
    American exceptionalism
        and, 21, 125, 134, 136–138
    Donald Trump's failure at, 242
    and debt, 221
    Michel Foucault on, 192
    and Stanley Greenberg, 82
ethnographers, 24–25, 250
Europe
    and Brexit, 245
    class in, 113, 128–129, 153
    family farms in, 135
    immigrants from, 251

factories
    and Fordism, 201, 214

and middle class conceptions,
    118, 198
and Stanley Greenberg, 36, 47
Marxists on, 158, 161, 173
falling
    fear of, 25, 134, 146, 173,
        179–180, 185, 230
    Marxists on, 158, 172
    into middle class, 151
    of middle class, 23, 148, 168,
        182
family
    family farms, 135
    income, 66
    and middle class, 116,
        205–207, 210, 212–217
    Stanley Greenberg's, 33–37
    stigmatization of Black,
        41–42
    working families rhetoric,
        92–93, 97
    wealth, 104
farming, 134–136, 152
fascism
    anti, 147, 165
    Leon Trotsky on, 166
    Donald Trump and, 14
    of Tom Metzger, 231
    threat of, 169
Feldberg, Roslyn, 199
feminism, 61, 177, 206
Fletcher, Bill, Jr., 11–12
food insecurity, 184–185
Ford Foundation, 52
Fordism, 201, 214
foremen, organizing of, 169–170
Fortune magazine, 105–106,
    118–122
Foucault, Michel, 137, 192
Fraina, Louis, 168
France, 106–107, 150–151, 154,
    156, 166, 169

Frank, Waldo, 10
Frankfurt School, 22, 165–167, 176
Fraser, Steve, 135
free enterprise, 125, 206
free trade agreements, 20, 65, 81, 84
freedom, 254
    Black freedom struggle, 33, 39
    Karl Marx on, 150
    and US, 127
Friedan, Betty, 206
Fromm, Erich, 167
frontier, the, 127–128

Gabler, Neal, 185
Galbraith, John Kenneth, 217
gender
    and family strain, 65,
        205–206
    feminism, 61, 177, 206
    justice, 27
    manliness, 21, 134
    and overwork, 209
    roles, 205
    sexism, 187, 199, 225
    and white-collar alienation,
        198–199
    See also women
Germany, 22, 107, 133, 150, 156,
    162–166, 167–169, 171
Giamatti, A. Bartlett, 51
Gingrich, Newt, 132
Glasser, Susan, 136–137
Glenn, Evelyn Nakano, 199
Gramsci, Antonio, 51
Grant, Andrew, 123
Great Depression, 113, 115, 118,
    202, 228
Great Recession, 183, 218, 220
Greenberg, Stanley, 18–20, 24, 27,
    31–32
    and academia, 37, 47–49,
        51, 53

on African Americans, 31, 34,
    34, 41, 43
and conservative mentors,
    38–48
Democracy Corps, 76
Greenberg Quinlan Rosner
    (GQR), Research, Inc., 76, 80
and "hillbillies," 41, 44
and Macomb County studies,
    54–75
Middle Class Dreams (MCD)
    by, 20, 54, 57, 60–61, 68–71,
    108, 234
and middle class rhetoric,
    110, 113
in New Haven, Connecticut,
    57–50
Politics and Poverty by, 40–41,
    43–44, 74
as progressive, 48–50, 52
Race and State in Capitalist
    Development by, 50–52
rightward turn of, 75–88, 153
and South Africa, 50–54, 67
upbringing of, 32–37
and white working class
    rhetoric, 226–227, 232–234,
    236, 239, 243, 249–251, 253
Greer, Germaine, 177
Guerin, Daniel, 166

Haer, John, 123
Hamill, Pete, 55
happiness, 190, 192, 197, 212
Harrington, Michael, 48n26
Hartz, Louis, 129, 131
"Hawthorne Effect," 196
Hayden, Tom, 81
health care, 64, 73, 103, 253
hegemony, 15, 201, 222
Herrnstein, Richard, 41
Hightower, Jim, 184

Hillbilly Elegy (J.D. Vance), 43, 244
Hitchens, Christopher, 62
Hochschild, Arlie Russell, 25, 244, 252
Hoff Wilson, Joan, 28–30
Hoffer, Eric, 125
Hoover, Herbert, 27–34, 55, 84
Horton, Willie, ads about, 68
household labor, 204, 210, 216
housing market, 137, 183, 217
    home ownership, 182, 186, 217
    housing insecurity, 184
    racism in, 36, 109
How to Win Friends and Influence People (Dale Carnegie), 190, 193
hunger, 97, 184

identity politics, 31, 58, 70, 237, 242
ideology, 21, 58, 99, 119, 135, 147, 216
Ignatiev, Noel, 14
Illouz, Eva, 197
immigration
    and Donald Trump, 18, 225, 241
    European, 251
    and white working class, 24–25, 228, 241, 252–254
    undocumented immigrants, 12, 154
incarceration, 25, 83
income
    and debt, 189
    and Donald Trump, 248
    and gender, 204–206, 208
    and inequality, 219
    in Macomb County, Michigan, 58, 66
    median, 100, 186
    and middle class definitions, 89, 92, 98, 100, 183, 186, 212

    and white working class, 13, 240
Indigenous people, 59, 80, 253
industrial capitalism, 151–153, 158–159, 197–198, 215
    industrial middle class, 155
    industrial working class, 163, 165, 171, 174
industrial labor movement, 117–118, 122, 140–141, 146, 170, 202
Industrial Workers of the World, 231
inequality, 40, 92, 101, 106, 130, 219, 255
integration, 20, 25, 109
    and Stanley Greenberg, 34, 36, 56, 58, 63–64, 66
International Socialist Review (*ISR*), 113
Isenberg, Nancy, 244
Israel, 50, 79–80

Jackson, Jesse, 59, 69, 73–74
    and Rainbow Coalition, 59, 68, 73–74
Jacobin, 232
Jewish people, 34–36, 61, 164
Jillson, Cal, 86
Jim Crow, 35, 39
Johnson, Lyndon, 39, 110
Judis, John, 82–83
justice
    class, 8
    environmental, 253
    gender, 27, 61, 69
    injustice, 34
    racial, 8, 27, 32, 61, 74, 234
    social, 35, 108, 254

Kennedy, John F., 38
Kennedy, Robert F., 38–39, 60

Keynes, John Maynard, 202
Kitty Foyle (Christopher Morley), 200
Kocka, Jürgen, 136, 156
Kracauer, Siegfried, 165
Kruse, Kevin, 109
Ku Klux Klan, 231
Kun, Béla, 150, 157

labor
        in "Bartleby, the Scrivener," 180, 199
        child labor, 93
        and class, 103–105
        and gender, 204, 207
        and Herbert Hoover, 30
        household labor, 204, 210, 216
        immigrant, 241
        industrial labor movement, 117–118, 122, 140–141, 146, 170, 202
        Karl Marx on, 154, 157–160
        labor studies, 102, 140, 243
        and misery, 182, 188–189, 196, 198, 204–205, 209–210
        and scientific management, 173, 214
        and Stanley Greenberg, 31, 66
        and "white working class," 226–227
        See labor law; labor movements
labor law, 12, 64, 104, 142, 270, 205
        anti-labor law, 77, 170
labor movements
        and Democratic Socialists of America, 140–141
        and electoral politics, 12
        and Karl Marx, 22
        in Macomb County, 19
        manual, 105, 173, 196

middle class appeals of, 8–9, 85, 126
organizing strategies of, 141–146
and Stanley Greenberg, 32, 37, 49–50, 64–65, 71, 77
in twentieth century, 168, 170–171
and "White Working Class," 232
Labor Notes, 141
layoffs, 170, 180
Lazzarato, Maurizio, 220–221
Lederer, Emil, 22, 163–165, 168, 171
left, the
        and electoral politics, 11, 14
        and Herbert Hoover, 30
        and Marxism, 22, 162, 168, 170
        and middle class appeals, 15, 17, 21, 88, 101, 118
        and middle class critiques, 146, 148
        New Left, 125, 158, 173
        and organizing strategies, 141–142, 170
        and Stanley Greenberg, 38–39, 41–42, 48–49, 60–62, 71–72, 75, 78–81, 84
        and "white working class," 232, 235
leisure, 178, 182, 202–203
Lenin, Vladimir, 51
Levin, Melissa, 81
Levison, Andrew, 236
Levitz, Eric, 252
Lewis, Sinclair, 115, 192
liberal politics
        and American exceptionalism, 124, 129
        and Cold War, 129, 148, 232

and race, 58
and Robert Kennedy, 60
and Stanley Greenberg, 41,
    45–48, 61, 71–72, 75, 78, 84
and "white working class,"
    244
Lichtenstein, Nelson, 144
Lieberman, Joseph, 53, 68
Lind, Michael, 71
Lipset, Seymour Martin, 131
Lovestone, Jay, 128
Lynd, Helen Merrell, 114, 169
Lynd, Robert S., 114, 121, 169

Macomb County, Michigan, 19–20,
    37, 47–49, 54–69, 72–75, 82–84
    and white working class
        rhetoric, 65, 74, 227, 251
Mandela, Nelson, 78
management, 71, 189, 191–192,
    196–198, 200
    managers, 21–22, 104, 119,
        175, 177
    middle, 177, 177, 182
    scientific, 173, 214
    upper, 178
manual labor, 105, 173, 196
Marcus, Greil, 194–195
Marcuse, Herbert, 178
marketing, 190–192, 204, 212, 240
markets, 73, 153, 198
    housing, 137
    stock market crash, 30
Marschak, Jacob, 164–165, 168
marshmallow test, 222–223
Martin, Katherine Connor, 238
Marx, Karl, 147–152, 154–159, 162,
    168
    and American
        exceptionalism, 127–128
    on middle class, 22
    and misery, 213, 215

and Stanley Greenberg, 45, 50
See also Marxism
Marxism
    Academic, 47–48
    and American
        exceptionalism, 129
    and middle class, 22, 147–149,
        152, 154–155, 157, 160–165,
        174–175
    and Stanley Greenberg, 18,
        36–37, 45, 50–51, 61, 71
    and "white working class,"
        232
Mason, Paul, 127
May, Elaine Tyler, 206
McAlevey, Jane, 7
McCormick, Thomas, 78
McGovern, George, 19, 49, 56, 65, 73
Melville, Herman, 23, 180, 295
    "Bartleby, The Scrivener,"
        180, 195, 199
Metzger, Jack, 102
Metzger, Tom, 231
Mexico, 79
    Partido Revolucionario
        Institucional (PRI) in, 79
    US-Mexico border, 15, 104,
        241, 252–253
Meyerson, Harold, 71, 91–92, 108
middle class
    consciousness of, 129
    in France, 156
    in Germany, 156
    imagined as white, 9, 19, 105
    lower, 36, 55, 148, 150–151
    Middle Class Task Force, 86
    misery of, 177–179, 181–187,
        190–192, 198, 212, 216, 220
    new, 22, 136, 158, 163–165,
        168, 174, 191
    self-identification of,
        100–102, 121, 123

tax cuts for, 94
US as middle class nation, 20,
   105–106, 117–118, 124, 130,
   132–134
Middle Class Dreams (MCD)
   (Stanley Greenberg), 20, 54, 57,
   60–61, 68–71, 108, 234
Middletown (Helen and Robert
   Lynd), 114
Middletown in Transition (Helen
   and Robert Lynd), 115, 117, 169
militancy, 1, 3, 70–71, 143–144,
   165, 172
Miller, Arthur, 139, 180
Mills, C. Wright, 22, 99, 106, 133,
   135, 168–172, 189–179, 191, 209
Mischel, Walter, 222
Mishra, Pankaj, 245
Morales, Evo, 80
Morley, Christopher, 200
mortgages, 216, 218–219
Moynihan, Daniel Patrick, 41–42
Muncie, Indiana, 114–115

Nakano Glenn, Evelyn, 199
Nazis, 116, 165–167, 169
neoliberalism, 9, 55, 71, 106, 127,
   192, 221, 246
New Deal, 55, 164
New Left, 81, 125, 141, 158, 173
Newman, Katherine, 155, 173
Ngrams, 112, 114–115, 229–230
Nicolaus, Martin, 158–159
non-voters, 15, 247–248
North American Free Trade
   Agreement, 20, 65
nurses, 103, 140–141, 144–145,
   175, 183

Obama, Barack, 86–90, 94, 110,
   132, 225, 236
Occupy movement, 104

Office of Economic Opportunity
   (OEO), 40
office work, 1–2, 116, 173–179,
   199, 201
   and Karl Marx, 159
Omi, Michael, 232
Onasch, Bill, 85, 126
organizing
   Civil Rights, 35, 38
   and electoral politics, 11–12,
      13
   labor, 64–65, 122, 142,
      160–161, 168–170, 173, 242
   and middle class rhetoric, 109
   and Stanley Greenberg, 43,
      49–50, 73
   and "white working class"
      rhetoric, 231
Orwell, George, v, 155
Overspent American, The (Juliet
   Schor), 188, 210
overwork, 182, 188–190, 203, 205,
   207–211, 220–221
Overworked American, The (Juliet
   Schor), 188, 207

Parker, Richard, 136
Peck, Don, 90
Perrin, Anthony, 242, 246–247
personality
   and authoritarianism, 165,
      167
   and middle class, 168, 209
   selling of, 21, 23, 182, 191,
      193–199, 212
petty bourgeoisie, 150, 157, 166
Phillips, Kevin, 108
plutonomy, 91
policing, 40–41, 73
political economy, 43n21, 50–51,
   111
politics

and American
  exceptionalism, 124, 147
broader conceptions of, 15
Cold War, 130
and debt, 220
dog whistle, 233
electoral, 8–13, 15–16, 27, 47,
  142–143, 238, 254
identity, 31, 58, 70, 237, 242
and Marxism, 156–157, 162,
  166
and middle class pandering,
  91, 103
political news, 10
political parties, 3, 30, 78, 86,
  90, 153, 243
politicians, 13, 78, 126, 131,
  185, 219, 233
progressive, 20, 31–32, 72, 75
presidential, 16, 68, 108
and Stanley Greenberg,
  32–33, 40–47, 49–50,
  64–66, 74–75
and "white working class,"
  224, 226, 228, 232, 234
See also Democratic Party;
  Republican Party
Politics and Poverty (Stanley
  Greenberg), 40–41, 43–44, 74
polling, 27, 53, 66, 73–74, 76–77,
  81, 248
populism, 17, 71, 93
positivity, 197–198
Post, William, 216
poverty
  anti-poverty initiatives, 40,
    43
  Barack Obama and, 88, 110
  "culture of poverty"
    arguments, 46

and middle class definitions,
  88–89, 97, 100, 118, 121,
  212, 248
"middle class poor," 70
politicians' references to,
  110–111, 183
Politics and Poverty (Stanley
  Greenberg), 40–41, 43–44,
  74
poverty line, 126, 183
and race, 121, 133, 153
and Stanley Greenberg, 33,
  36, 38, 40–42, 46–47
and wealth inequality, 219
and "white working class"
  rhetoric, 239, 242, 247
Prins, Seth, 177–179
production, capitalist, 30, 151, 158,
  178, 198, 201, 215
productivity
  Ayn Rand on, 111
  Herbert Hoover and, 29
  Karl Marx on, 22, 159
  and misery, 188, 210–211
  and scientific management,
    173
  "unproductive" work, 22,
    159–160
professionals
  Karl Marx on, 22
  and middle class, 21, 103, 105,
    116, 134, 148
  militancy of, 144
  misery of, 182, 205–206
  professional managerial
    class, 134, 173, 178,
    239–240
Progressive Policy Institute, 72
progressive politics
  and Herbert Hoover, 27–32

and Stanley Greenberg, 18,
20, 38, 48–49, 54, 72, 75,
78–81
and "white working class"
rhetoric, 242, 253
proletariat
gender and, 199
Marx and Engels on, 149, 151,
159, 161
Marxists on, 163, 174
nurses and teachers as, 103
white-collar, 164, 167–168,
169–170
property ownership
and American
exceptionalism, 136
Marx on, 22, 150
racism and, 36
and wealth inequality, 219
prosperity, 100, 104, 182
psychoanalysis, 69, 165
psychology, 23, 41, 106, 166–167,
178, 222
public employees, 143–144
Putnam, Robert, 95

race
and American
exceptionalism, 133
Democrats and, 8, 32, 233,
235
and elections, 10, 15, 24
and Herbert Hoover, 29
interracial organization, 38,
70, 231, 233
and Joan Williams, 239
and marshmallow test, 222
and middle class conceptions,
104, 121–122, 153, 234
racial justice, 32, 61, 74, 234
and segregation, 122

and Stanley Greenberg,
35–38, 43–44, 50–52,
54–58, 60, 66–68, 70–74,
82–83
whiteness, 58, 226, 241
See also Black people; racism;
white working class
racism
Bill Clinton and, 17
and "blue-collar workers," 63
Donald Trump and, 13, 225
Joe Biden and, 244
in Macomb County, Michigan,
56, 60, 70
neoliberalism and, 246
in nineteenth century, 116
Stanley Greenberg and, 36
radicalism
and electoral politics, 10,
13, 18
and labor organizing,
140–141
and middle class, 21, 23, 96,
144–148, 154, 164–165,
169, 171–172
and Stanley Greenberg, 19,
31, 39, 44–46, 49–50, 72
and white working class
rhetoric, 243
Rainbow Coalition, 59, 68, 73–74
Rand, Ayn, 111, 125
Reagan, Ronald, 56, 62, 131, 231
Reagan Democrats, 19, 54
Reed, Adolph, Jr., 11
religion, 28, 34, 36, 124
Republican Party
end of, 253
and Herbert Hoover, 30
and labor organizing, 141
and Macomb County,
Michigan, 27, 54, 57, 68

and middle class appeals,
       86–87, 104, 108–109
and "Southern Strategy," 63
and "white working class," 13,
       226, 228, 244, 248–249
retirement, 138, 182, 186, 220
revolutionary politics, 14, 26
       counter-revolutionary
              politics, 147
       and labor organizing, 128
       and Marxism, 148–151,
              153–154, 157, 161–164,
              166–170
       Stanley Greenberg on, 47, 67
Riesman, David, 217
right-wing politics
       alt-right, 14, 19
       center-right Democrats,
              31, 33, 68, 225, 232, 234,
              249–250
       far right, 148, 245
       and Herbert Hoover, 30, 32
       and middle class, 3, 8, 18, 91,
              103, 108, 110
       rightward shift of Democratic
              Party, 53, 67–68, 75, 109
       and Stanley Greenberg, 32,
              77–78, 82
Rogers, Joel, 235
Rogin, Michael, 63
Romney, Mitt, 87–89, 92, 183, 247
Rotenstein, David, 36
Rourke, Constance, 194–195
Ryan, Mary, 116

salaried workers
       in Germany, 162, 164
       and historical shifts, 160
       as middle class, 22, 152, 190,
              192, 205

and personality
       salesmanship, 194
and US unionism, 170, 172
salespeople, 167, 169
       and gender, 199–200
       and labor organization, 145,
              173
       and misery, 180–182
       and Marxism, 158, 162
       and middle class, 21–22, 172
       and personality, 21, 23, 182,
              190–199, 212
Sanders, Bernie, 17, 84, 92–93, 95,
       142, 244
Saroyan, William, 194
Saval, Nikil, 179
Schor, Juliet, 188–189, 203–205,
       207–208, 210–213, 218
Schwab, Charles, 193
scientific management, 173, 214
secretaries, 158, 160, 179, 199
segregation, 34–35, 109, 122
self-employment, 22, 116, 135–138,
       152, 158, 160–161, 213
Self, Bill, 137
Sennett, Richard, 116, 173–174,
       197, 200
sexism, 187, 199, 225
       of Donald Trump, 13, 248
Seymour, Richard, 246
Shilliam, Robbie, 246
Sirabella, Vince, 49
Sister Souljah, 73–74, 83
Sklar, Martin, 215
Skocpol, Theda, 72
slavery, 16, 59, 160
social movements, 11, 38, 77, 104,
       205, 254
       civil rights, 31–32, 35, 231,
              253

and Marxism, 129, 140–141,
    149, 154, 169, 172
racist, 14, 19, 246
and Stanley Greenberg,
    49–50, 77
See also labor movement
socialism
    and Bernie Sanders, 17, 92
    and Democratic party, 95
    Democratic Socialists of
        America (DSA), 139–141
    and Marxism, 147–149,
        151–152, 160–164, 166
    and middle class, 146, 176
    and Stanley Greenberg, 29
    and US history, 113, 115, 121,
        126, 129, 169–172
    and white working class
        rhetoric, 232
solidarities, 126, 182, 200
Sombart, Werner, 115
South, United States, 31, 35–36,
    63, 73
South Africa, 43, 47–53, 60, 67, 72,
    78, 81
Soviet Union, 66, 157
Spain, 107, 118
Stalin, Joseph, 128
Staub, Michael, 222
Stephanopoulos, George, 32
Strangers in Their Own Land (Arlie
    Russell Hochschild), 25, 244,
    252
strikes, 3, 15, 49–50, 70, 141–142,
    164, 170
Strummer, Joe, 191
student debt, 97–98
Students for a Democratic Society
    (SDS), 173–174
suburbs
    and Bill Clinton, 17

and Macomb County,
    Michigan, 19, 31, 37, 57–58
and meth, 211
and middle class, 73, 190,
    206–207, 217
and Stanley Greenberg, 35,
    63, 73
Sweet, Mark, 89

taxes, 20, 58, 66, 202
    anti-tax revolts, 109
    tax cuts, 92–94, 137
Taylor, Frederick Winslow, 196
teachers
    as middle class, 3, 183, 240
    organizing by, 140–145
    and Stanley Greenberg, 19,
        41
    as working class, 103,
        140–145, 175, 183–184
Teixeira, Ruy, 235–236, 253
Thatcher, Margaret, 79
Thompson, Edward P., 153
Tilley, Lisa, 224, 227, 246
Torma, Julien, 97
trade agreements, 20, 65, 225
trade unions, 19, 55, 63–65, 70,
    126, 164
    in Britain, 79
    in South Africa, 50, 53
Tressler, Irving, 193
Trotsky, Leon, 166
Trump, Donald
    and American
        exceptionalism, 133
    and entrepreneurship, 137
    and labor organizing, 141
    in Macomb County, Michigan,
        84
    and middle class appeals,
        13–18, 92–94, 111, 133

racism of, 13, 225
and white working class
rhetoric, 23–24, 224–225,
227, 237–238, 245–249
Turner, Frederick Jackson, 127–128

unions, 1–3, 7
anti-union legislation, 17,
92, 142
in Britain, 79
in Macomb County, Michigan,
19–20, 55–56, 62–66, 70–72
mass industrial unionism,
117–118
and middle class appeals,
7–8, 128
and middle class definitions,
103, 117–118
organizing strategies of, 139,
141–143, 202
and Stanley Greenberg, 35,
50, 53, 71–72
United Auto Workers (UAW),
19, 56, 64
white-collar, 164, 169–170
and white working class
appeals, 231–232, 241–242,
245
United Auto Workers (UAW), 19,
56, 64
United Kingdom, 106–107
universities, 97, 137, 165, 184, 198
Stanley Greenberg and, 19,
28, 38
"unproductive" work, 22, 159–160

Vance, J.D., 43–44, 244
Venezuela, 80
Vietnam War, 29, 125
voting
Black voters, 20, 31
and electoral politics, 11–14, 16

in Macomb County, Michigan,
19–20, 54–56, 60, 62–64,
72–73, 84
and middle-class appeals,
89–91, 94, 101
non-voting, 15, 247–248
Stanley Greenberg on, 33,
67, 83
and white working class
rhetoric, 82, 111, 226–227,
231, 235, 241, 245–252

wage workers, 2, 103–104, 152,
160, 182, 242
Walker, Scott, 142–143
Wallace, George, 19, 56, 63
Warren, Elizabeth, 94, 132, 207,
212, 240
Wattenberg, Ben, 109
wealth, 138, 219, 242
median, 104, 107
and middle class, 91, 98, 100,
102, 103, 107
welfare, 17, 20, 25, 40
Wertham, Fredric, 139
West Virginia, labor movement in,
141–142
White Collar (C. Wright Mills), 99,
106, 133, 168, 171, 178, 181, 199
white-collar work, 1
in Germany, 134, 167
in Macomb County, Michigan,
64
and middle class, 105, 116,
135, 143–144, 146, 148,
159–165, 167–170
and misery, 180, 182, 195,
197–200, 214
white nationalist movement, 14,
74, 226, 232
white working class rhetoric, 8, 10,
12–13, 18, 20, 25, 224–254

and Donald Trump, 23–24
and Stanley Greenberg, 27,
  31–32, 44, 56, 59, 64–66,
  74–75, 82
White Working Class
  Roundtable, 236, 243
White Working Class (Joan
  Williams), 238–244
whiteness, 226, 241
  of Macomb County, Michigan,
    58
  "white middle class," 9, 19, 105
  white nationalist movement,
    14, 74, 226, 232
  white workers, emphases on,
    23–25, 28, 225–227, 233,
    235, 247–248, 251–253
  See also white working class
Whitman, Walt, 112
Wiebe, Robert, 116
Wilhelm, John, 50
Williams, Joan, 24, 227, 238–244
Wilson, James Q., 39–41
Winant, Howard, 232
Wisconsin, labor movement in,
  142–143
women
  and 2016 election, 236
  feminism, 61, 177, 206
  as "housewives," 62, 69
  in Macomb County, Michigan,
    64, 66, 69–70
  and overwork, 204–207, 210
  and personality selling,
    199–200
  sexism, 187, 199, 225
  Stanley Greenberg on, 42,
    69–70
  unpaid labor of, 204, 207
  and white-collar work, 135
  work

overwork, 182, 188–190, 203,
  205, 207–211, 220–221
"unproductive," 22, 159–160
workaholism, 209
See also labor; white-collar
  work; workers
workers, 2, 13, 15, 13, 225, 237, 242
  and 2016 election, 17–18
  clerical, 195, 200
  in Macomb County, Michigan,
    55–56, 58, 65
  Marxism and, 22, 150, 152,
    158–170, 172–174
  and middle class, 21, 118,
    123, 136
  and misery, 179–182,
    188–189, 195–203, 209
  organization of, 32, 128,
    139–145, 217
  racialized, 55
  wage, 2, 103–104, 152, 160,
    182, 242
  white workers, emphases on,
    23–25, 28, 225–227, 233,
    235, 247–248, 251–253
  "working families," defense
    of, 17, 92–83, 183
  See also blue-collar workers,
    labor; salaried workers;
    white-collar work, white
    working class rhetoric
working class
  and American
    exceptionalism, 131, 133
  electoral catering to, 12–13,
    16, 18
  the left and, 139–141, 144–
    146, 167–168, 173–176
  Marxism and, 22, 148–154,
    156, 158, 161–163

and middle class, 1, 7–8,
   100–103, 106, 114, 123, 197
movements of, 15, 142, 171
self-identification as, 97–98,
   145
Stanley Greenberg and, 36,
   55, 59–60, 64, 73
See also white working class
   rhetoric
World War I, 30, 163, 201, 214
World War II, 1, 57, 122, 126, 136,
   144, 153, 196, 202

Wright, Erik Olin, 22, 36, 174–175,
   178

Yale University, 30, 40, 48–49,
   51–52
      Local 34 at, 50, 52

Zionism, 80
Zweig, Michael, 101–103, 140, 145

DAVID R. ROEDIGER teaches American Studies at the University of Kansas. His books include *Seizing Freedom, The Wages of Whiteness, How Race Survived U.S. History, Towards the Abolition of Whiteness,* and *Working Toward Whiteness.* His book *The Production of Difference* (with Elizabeth Esch) recently won the International Labor History Association Book Prize. He is past president of the American Studies Association and of the Working-Class Studies Association. A long-time member of the Chicago Surrealist Group, his work grows out of engagement with social movements addressing inequality, from the United Farm Workers grape boycott to Black Lives Matter.